Pelican Book A1010
Microbes and Man

John Postgate is Professor of Microbiology at Sussex
University and assistant director of a unit for research
on nitrogen fixation. He was educated at Kingsbury County
School and Balliol College, Oxford, where he took a first
degree in chemistry before turning to chemical microbiology.
He then spent fifteen years in government research establish-
ments – studying mainly the sulphur bacteria and bacterial
death – with a visiting professorship at the University of
Illinois in 1962–3.

His family finds it amusing that he has become the third
Professor John Postgate: the first (his great-grandfather)
did medicine at Birmingham, the second (his grandfather)
did classics at Liverpool. His other grandfather was George
Lansbury, the Socialist leader, and his father is Raymond
Postgate, the historian and gourmet. Long ago John Postgate
led the Oxford University Dixieland Bandits (on cornet), and
he is known as a jazz writer. He and his wife, who read
English at St Hilda's College, Oxford, have three daughters.

Microbes and Man

John Postgate

Penguin Books

Penguin Books Ltd, Harmondsworth,
Middlesex, England
Penguin Books Inc., 7110 Ambassador Road
Baltimore, Maryland 21207, U.S.A.
Penguin Books Australia Ltd, Ringwood,
Victoria, Australia

First published 1969
Copyright © John Postgate, 1969

Made and printed in Great Britain by
C. Nicholls & Company Ltd
Set in Monotype Times

For H. J. Bunker

Contents

Acknowledgements

To Mrs Inga Wass, who not only converted my illiterate scrawl into immaculate typescript but actually read the contents and improved them as she did so; to my wife, who went through them with a grammatical and semantical toothcomb and who helped at every stage of this book's gestation; to my father, Raymond Postgate, who constructively amended Chapter 5; to Mr Gerald Leach, whose idea the book was.

JOHN POSTGATE
Kingston, Sussex, 1968.

CHAPTER 1

Men and Microbes

This is a book about germs, known to scientists as microbes (or to some, who cannot use a short word where a long one exists, as micro-organisms). These creatures, which are largely invisible, inhabit every place on earth where larger living creatures exist; they also inhabit many parts of the earth where no other kinds of organism can survive for long. Wherever, in fact, terrestrial life exists there will be microbes; conversely, the most extreme conditions that microbes can tolerate represent the limits within which life as we know it can exist.

The 'biosphere' is the name biologists give to the sort of 'skin' on the surface of this planet that is inhabitable by living organisms. Most land creatures occupy only the interface between the atmosphere and the land; birds extend their range for a few hundred feet into the atmosphere; burrowing invertebrates such as earthworms and nematodes may reach a few yards into the soil but rarely penetrate farther unless it has been recently disturbed by men. Fish cover a wider range, from just beneath the surface of the sea to those depths of greater than a mile inhabited by specialized, often luminous, creatures. Spores of fungi and bacteria are plentiful in the atmosphere to a height of about half a mile, blown there by winds from the lower air. Balloon exploration of the stratosphere as long ago as 1936 indicated that moulds and bacteria could be found at heights of several miles; recently the U.S.A.'s National Aeronautics and Space Administration has detected them, in decreasing numbers, at heights up to eighteen miles. They are pretty sparse at such levels, about one for every two thousand cubic feet, compared with 50 to 100 per cubic foot at two to six miles (the usual altitude of jet aircraft), and they are almost certainly in a dormant state. Marine microbes have been detected at the bottom of the deep Pacific trench, sometimes as deep as seven miles; they are certainly not dormant. Living microbes have also been obtained on land from cores of rock drilled (while prospecting for oil) at depths of as much as 1,200 feet. Thus we can say, disregarding the exploits of astronauts, that the biosphere has a maximum thickness of about twenty-five miles. Active living processes occur only within a compass of about seven miles, in the sea, on land and in the lower atmosphere, but the majority of living creatures live within a zone of a hundred feet or so. If this planet were scaled down to the size of an orange, the biosphere, at its extreme width, would occupy the thickness of the orange-coloured skin, excluding the pith.

In this tiny zone of our planet takes place the multitude of chemical and biological activities that we call life. The way in which living creatures interact with each other, depend on each other or compete with each other, has fascinated thinkers since the beginning of recorded history. Living things exist in a fine balance which is often taken for granted – for, from a practical point of view, things could not be otherwise. Yet it is a source of continual amazement to scientists because of its intricacy and delicacy. The balance of nature is obvious most often when it is disturbed, yet even here it can seem remarkable how quietly it re-adjusts itself to a new balance after a disturbance. The science of ecology – the study of the interaction of organisms with their environment – has grown up to deal with the minutiae of the balance of nature.

At the coarsest level, living creatures show a pattern of inter-dependence that goes something like this. Men and animals depend on plants for their existence (meat-eating animals do so at one remove, because they prey on herbivores, but basically they, too, could not exist without plants). Plants, in their turn, depend on sunlight, so the driving force that keeps life going on earth is the sun. So much every schoolchild knows. But there is a third class of organisms on which both plants and animals depend, and these are the microbes. I shall introduce these creatures more formally, as it were, in the next chapter, but I think it will be helpful to give here a sort of pre-view of what their importance in the terrestrial economy is; to show broadly how basic they are to the existence of higher organisms before going more deeply, in later chapters, into those aspects that most influence mankind.

Microbes, then, are those microscopic creatures that one calls germs, moulds, yeasts, algae, and so on: the bacteria, viruses, lower fungi and lower algae, to use their technical names. It will be instructive to give some idea of the abundance of microbes compared with other creatures.

In every gramme of fertile soil there exist about 100,000,000 living bacteria, of an average size of 1 or $2\mu^3$ (μ, a micron, is a thousandth of a millimetre; to use a familiar image, one thousand of them, laid end to end, would span the head of a pin). We can express this information in a form that is, to me, more impressive: there are 200 to 500 pounds of microbes to every acre of good agricultural soil. In world terms, this means that the total mass of microbial life on this planet is almost incalculably large – it has been estimated at twenty-five times the total mass of all animal life, both aquatic and terrestrial. (I do not know what the actual figures for the masses of the world's microbes and of the world's animals are. Probably no one does, because it is easier to estimate ratios than absolutes in a calculation like this: one can consider a few sample areas and, if they come out similar, one can fairly assume the result is generally true).

Microbes multiply very rapidly when food and warmth are available. One type of bacterium divides in two every eleven minutes; many can double in twenty to thirty minutes; the slowest double every two or three hours. This, of course, is a fantastic rate of multiplication compared with most organisms – one cell of the bacterium *Escherichia coli* could, if sufficient food were available, produce a mass of bacteria greater than the mass of the earth in three days. Consequently, since microbes constitute some ninety per cent of the living material of this planet, and can multiply almost as fast as they can get suitable food, it follows that they are responsible for most of the chemical changes that living things bring about on this planet.

Now I must digress a moment. At intervals in this book I shall have to bring in a certain amount of chemistry, because it is in chemical terms that we can best understand most of the economic activities of microbes. I shall keep the chemistry as simple as possible, but I shall assume the reader has at least some familiarity with chemical symbols: that he knows, for example, that N symbolizes a nitrogen atom or Na a sodium atom; that free nitrogen gas occurs as molecules consisting of two atoms, formulated as N_2; that the formula of methane is CH_4 and signifies that its molecule consists of one carbon and four hydrogen atoms; that when one writes methane so:

$$
\begin{array}{c}
\text{H} \\
| \\
\text{H} - \text{C} - \text{H} \\
| \\
\text{H}
\end{array}
$$

it signifies that the hydrogen atoms are independently linked to the central carbon atom in the molecule and that they are symmetrically arranged around it.

I shall make use of the organic chemist's shorthand of:

for six carbon atoms linked in a ring. Written out in full, the compound above (which is benzene) looks like this:

but chemists learned long ago that writing out all those 'C's and 'H's was generally a waste of time.

I shall also assume an awareness, at least in principle, that dissolved salts dissociate into ions. That sodium nitrate, potassium nitrate, and calcium nitrate, for example, all yield nitrate ions in water, so that when a plant uses 'nitrate' from a fertilizer, it is irrelevant whether it arrived as sodium, potassium or calcium nitrate. Thus, for many purposes, it is legitimate to talk of 'nitrate' (NO_3^-), 'sulphate' ($SO_4^=$) and so on even though it would be impossible to obtain a bottle of 'sulphate'.

Taking these principles for granted, I shall try to explain any more complex chemical concepts as we encounter them.

After that brief excursion into what the reader's 'homework' should have covered, let us return to the question of the importance of microbes in the world's chemistry. Our next thought on these matters is this: that nearly all the chemical changes that do take place on this planet are caused by living things. A few inanimate processes do occur: volcanoes bring about alterations in the neighbouring rocks and atmosphere; lightning causes oxides of nitrogen and ozone to appear; ultra-violet light from the sun does so as well, and also causes a layer of ozone to exist in the upper atmosphere that protects us from some of the more harmful UV-wavelengths. Rainstorms and erosion by the sea cause gradual chemical changes in rocks and minerals as they are exposed; radio-active minerals induce a certain amount of chemical change in the neighbouring rocks and keep the earth's interior hot. But at the earth's surface the purely chemical changes are trivial compared with those that took place in the infancy of this planet: the earth's own chemistry has settled down, as it were, to a pretty quiescent state. The most obvious chemical changes are brought about by plants, with animals as secondary agents, both on land and in the sea, and the energy needed to perform these chemical transformations comes from the sun. The biosphere, therefore, is a dynamic system of chemical changes, brought about by biological agents, at the expense of solar energy.

We shall see in Chapter 9 how the emergence of living things wrought dramatic changes, many millions of years ago, in the chemical composition of this planet's surface. The composition of the atmosphere, soil and rocks underwent gradual changes, often taking tens of millions of years, to yield the sort of biosphere we know today. No doubt that is still changing slowly, but as far as the last million or so years are concerned the average chemical composition of the biosphere has been constant. Another way of putting this point is that all gross chemical changes which occur on earth, brought about by any one kind of biological activity, are reversed by some other activity. If one considers the elements that undergo chemical transformation on this planet they are found to undergo cyclical changes: from biological (or organic) combination to non-biological (inorganic) combination and back again.

Consider the element nitrogen, nowadays plentiful as the gas that occupies four fifths of our atmosphere. It occurs as free nitrogen molecules and is normally pretty inert. It is harmless to living things; it neither burns nor supports combustion, and it is generally reluctant to enter into spontaneous chemical combination. Yet all living things consist of proteins: their muscles, nerves, bones, hair, and the enzymes that manufacture these and everything else, that provide energy for growth, movement and so on, all consist of protein molecules. And something like 10 to 15 per cent of every protein molecule is nitrogen. Not, obviously, N_2 molecules, but nitrogen atoms combined with others including carbon, hydrogen, oxygen, sulphur and so on. Compared with nitrogen molecules, protein molecules are huge and complicated, containing tens of thousands of atoms; this is why proteins can be so diverse in appearance and function. And since they constitute the major part of most living things, one can safely say that most living creatures consist of between 8 and 16 per cent of nitrogen. (The main exceptions are creatures that form thick chalky or siliceous shells; they seem to have low nitrogen contents, but even they have the usual chemical composition if one regards the shell as a non-living appendage and excludes its composition from one's calculations.)

Living things thus need nitrogen to grow. When they die, they rot and decompose, and the nitrogen becomes available for other living things. Rotting and decomposition are largely the result of the action of microbes on the organism and, of course, microbes die too, either naturally or by being consumed by protozoa, nematode worms, and so on. Gradually the nitrogen is assimilated by larger living things – plants, worms, birds, etc. – and so it becomes part of new creatures. (A process dramatically enshrined in that essentially macabre song *On Ilkley Moor b'aht hat:* 'Then shall ducks have eaten thee . . .'.) So a process of constant transformation of the state in which nitrogen atoms are combined takes place, which is known to biologists as 'The Nitrogen Cycle'. In this cycle certain microbes return nitrogen as N_2 to the atmosphere (the 'denitrifying' bacteria) and others bring it back to organic combination (the 'nitrogen-fixing' bacteria). One can write the nitrogen cycle schematically like this:

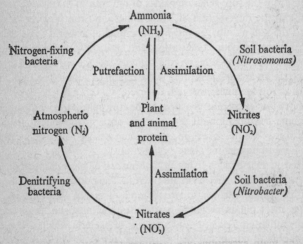

In this scheme nitrates in the soil are used by plants for growth, become plant and animal protein. Later these decompose through the action of microbes, releasing ammonia. Plants can re-cycle this, but they prefer nitrates, and two groups of soil bacteria convert ammonia back to nitrate by way of nitrite. Denitrifying bacteria, found in soil, compost heaps, and so on, can release the nitrogen of nitrates as free nitrogen molecules, and this loss of biological nitrogen to the atmosphere is compensated for by the

17

activities of the small group of nitrogen-fixing bacteria. Some of these live in association with the roots or leaves of plants, others live freely in soils and water; we shall discuss them again in Chapter 5. For present purposes the important point is that, in most soils, the supply of 'fixed' nitrogen (ammonia or nitrate) limits the productivity of that soil. Hence the number of animals, or men, that can feed from that soil depends on how rapidly the nitrogen cycle is 'turning': on how actively nitrogen-fixing microbes are performing.

Of course, the cycle may be bypassed to a limited extent. Artificial fertilizers increase soil productivity by bringing chemically fixed nitrogen to the soil. Thunderstorms, and ultra-violet light from the sun, generate oxides of nitrogen in the atmosphere without the intervention of living things, and rain washes these into the soil as nitrites and nitrates. But on a world scale, the earth's productivity of vegetation, and hence of food for men and animals, still depends on the activity of the nitrogen-fixing bacteria. In a year, something in the region of a thousand million tons of nitrogen pass through the cycle; C. C. Delwiche has calculated that every nitrogen atom in the atmosphere passes through organic combination on an average once in a million years. Obviously the microbes are of basic importance to the economy of living things on this planet.

But if the nitrogen-fixing organisms are of basic importance, one should not under-estimate the rest. The putrefying microbes return protein nitrogen to circulation by forming ammonia and, since most plants prefer to assimilate their nitrogen as nitrate rather than ammonia, the two groups of bacteria which convert ammonia to nitrate (collectively called 'nitrifying' bacteria) perform an economically useful function. This is not an unqualified virtue, however, because nitrates are washed out of soils by rain much more easily than ammonia; in recent years there has been a tendency among agricultural chemists to advise the use of ammonia fertilizers, which plants can manage with perfectly well, together with chemicals that inhibit multiplication of nitrifying bacteria.

Another biological cycle of basic importance is the carbon cycle. This, as far as higher organisms are concerned, is intimately involved with the cycle of changes undergone by oxygen. All living things respire; in effect, respiration is the transformation of the carbon and hydrogen compounds that constitute food into carbon dioxide (CO_2) and water, usually with the aid of the oxygen of air. Thus living things tend to remove oxygen from air and replace it by carbon dioxide. The reverse process, that of 'fixing' carbon dioxide as organic carbon and of replenishing the oxygen of air, is conducted by green plants: they reduce CO_2 to form the constituents of their own substance with the aid of energy derived from sunlight and in so doing they release the O of H_2O as oxygen (O_2). Today, on a world scale, these processes are in balance, such that the atmosphere consistently contains about 21 per cent of oxygen and 0·03 per cent of CO_2. The main contribution of microbes to this cycle is less fundamental than in the nitrogen cycle: in decay and putrefaction they break down residual organic matter such as wood, faeces and so on and thus return carbon dioxide to the cycle. But in so doing they often provide an important diversion of the carbon cycle in that their carbon turnover need not necessarily be tied to the oxygen cycle. We shall meet in Chapter 2 the 'anaerobic' bacteria, which have no need of oxygen for their respiration and which can produce such materials as methane, hydrogen or butyric acid from organic matter. They are most important in deposits of organic matter to which oxygen does not readily penetrate. On a world scale, of course, the products formed by anaerobic bacteria are oxidized by other microbes, using oxygen, to yield finally CO_2. Thus the carbon is returned to circulation and the cycle proceeds. The turnover rate of the carbon cycle over-all is about ten thousand million tons of carbon a year. On land, most of the CO_2-fixation is conducted by higher plants, but in the sea microbes are still the most important CO_2-fixers: microscopic algae and diatoms, microbes that float in the 'plankton' layer of the sea surface, form the bulk of the organic matter that fish feed upon. One can represent the carbon cycle so:

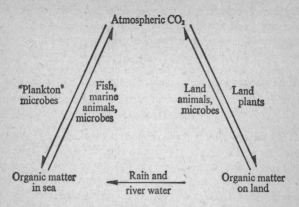

Atmospheric CO_2

"Plankton" microbes

Fish, marine animals, microbes

Land animals, microbes

Land plants

Organic matter in sea

Rain and river water

Organic matter on land

The microbes of plankton use sunlight, as land plants do. We shall encounter, in later chapters, several groups of microbes that can fix CO_2 using chemical reactions, not sunlight, but, though they may have been important during the early history of life on this planet, they contribute little to the carbon cycle today except in certain very special environments.

Elements such as hydrogen, iron, magnesium, silicon, phosphorus are all part of the structure of biological molecules and undergo comparable cyclical changes. The phosphorus cycle, particularly, is somewhat worrying because it involves a net transfer of something like 13 million tons of phosphorus a year from the land to the sea. Microbes play a certain part in this and the other cycles just mentioned, but their part is not a major one and we shall not discuss them in detail. However, there is one cycle of great importance that we should not neglect, if only because it depends exclusively on microbes. The element sulphur is a component of protein and of certain vitamins – living creatures contain between $\frac{1}{2}$ and $1\frac{1}{2}$ per cent sulphur – and the biological sulphur cycle is of critical importance in maintaining supplies of that element. But before we discuss it we must introduce a technicality that will be important here and later in this book: the concepts of 'oxidation' and 'reduction'.

Coal, which is carbon, becomes 'oxidized' when it is burned, and the chemical energy of this reaction is dissipated as heat. The process is called 'oxidation' because oxygen atoms are added to the carbon atoms to give carbon dioxide:

$$C + O_2 \longrightarrow CO_2$$

If insufficient oxygen is available, some carbon monoxide is formed:

$$2C + O_2 \longrightarrow 2CO$$

(This, incidentally, is the poisonous component of motor exhaust fumes.) Thus there are degrees of oxidation in that carbon can be partly or wholly oxidized; in a similar way, other elements may form stable compounds in several degrees of oxidation.

Food consists of carbon compounds which, when used by the body, are oxidized to give carbon dioxide and water. A typical example is glucose, which has the formula $C_6H_{12}O_6$:

$$C_6H_{12}O_6 + 6O_2 \longrightarrow 6CO_2 + 6H_2O$$

Some of the energy of such a reaction appears as heat; much of it goes to drive the various chemical reactions that keep the body functioning.

Microbes live by comparable oxidative reactions, but there are some that can conduct such processes without using oxygen gas. The sulphate-reducing bacteria, for example, use sulphate:

$$\text{Carbon compound} + CaSO_4 \longrightarrow CO_2 + H_2O + CaS$$

Calcium sulphate thus becomes converted to calcium sulphide. This process is called a 'reduction'; generally speaking, if some chemical is being oxidized, another is being reduced. (In burning, for example, the oxygen is 'reduced'). The denitrifying bacteria reduce nitrates in a rather similar way:

$$\text{C-compound} + NaNO_3 \longrightarrow \text{Na carbonate} + N_2$$

Things get a little complicated when chemists refer to reactions that do not involve oxygen at all as 'oxidations' and 'reductions', but this only means that the reactions in question have the same general character as those that do concern oxygen. Compounds of iron, for example, can exist as 'ferrous' salts (sulphates, nitrates

21

and so on) or 'ferric' salts; the ferric group are all more oxidized than the ferrous ones from the chemist's point of view, though they need not necessarily contain more oxygen. (Or, indeed, any oxygen at all: ferric chloride – $FeCl_3$ – is more oxidized than ferrous chloride – $FeCl_2$).

Microbes can make use of all sorts of oxidative reactions to obtain chemical energy for growth, movement and multiplication, including, as we shall see in Chapter 2, the conversion of ferrous compounds to ferric. Since oxidations are coupled with reductions, they bring about some interesting reductions, too, and in appropriate circumstances one can find one group of microbes conducting reductions and others oxidizing whatever they have reduced. This occurs particularly clearly in the biological sulphur cycle, which is 'turned' by a group of soil and water bacteria called the 'sulphur bacteria'. (In fact, they have little or no biological relationship; the main thing they have in common is that their metabolism is based on the sulphur atom.) Here is the sulphur cycle:

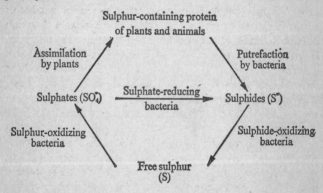

(Notice that sulphur appears in two oxidation states: sulphur itself is more oxidized than sulphide, though containing no oxygen, and sulphate is even more oxidized.)

In this cycle the sulphur of animal protein comes from plants, which get it from sulphates in soil. In decomposition and putrefaction of dead material, bacteria release the sulphur as sulphide,

22

which is a 'reduced' material. Other bacteria can oxidize this to sulphur, yet others oxidize it further to sulphate, which plants can re-use. The sulphate-reducing bacteria can bypass the top part of the cycle, reducing the sulphate back to sulphide; they obtain energy to do this by oxidizing organic matter, and thus a microbial sulphur cycle can go on without involving higher organisms at all. Such microcosms of sulphur bacteria are often encountered in Nature, in sulphur springs, in polluted waters and so on and, as we shall see in Chapter 9, may have been the dominant living systems during the early history of this planet. They are called 'sulfureta' (singular: sulfuretum) and are responsible for a variety of economic phenomena that will appear in later chapters of this book. We shall meet the individual bacteria of the sulphur cycle later.

Microbes, then, play an important part in the cyclical changes that the biological elements undergo on earth. In this sense, then, they are of transcendental importance in the terrestrial economy, because without them higher organisms would rapidly cease to exist. Yet they couple these basic activities with a number of minor functions which may be valuable, trivial or a thorough nuisance to mankind. Disease, for example, is caused by microbes. From a biological point of view disease is valuable in that it limits excessive animal populations, but the reader need hardly be told how thoroughly inconvenient it can be to civilized man today. Pollution and putrefaction are all very well in their place – our sewerage systems depend on them – but out of control they can be both nasty and destructive. Microbes ferment foods, yielding delicious delicacies and wines; but tainted food is dangerous. Microbes aid our digestion and nutrition, but may upset our stomachs in a strange land. Over geological time microbes formed several of the world's most valuable mineral deposits, but when they corrode steel and concrete we do not welcome their peculiar propensities. And so it goes on: microbes are neither generally good nor generally bad; they can be either. The important thing, which is not widely realized, is that they have an enormous effect on the economy and well-being of mankind. That, in fact, is what this book is about. How do microbes come into our lives? What do they do? And why? These are far-ranging questions, because, as the patient reader will learn, it might be more pertinent to ask whether there are any aspects of our daily lives in which microbes are not involved. We shall have to skip and skim in places, but in a book intended to introduce readers to an unfamiliar subject this is, I think, excusable. Let us start, therefore, by 'meeting' that huge group of invisible or scarcely visible creatures we call microbes.

CHAPTER 2

Microbiology

I was involved in the formation of the National Collection of Industrial Bacteria, a sort of 'bank' established in Britain from which strains of industrially significant microbes can be obtained. It has quite an important function: not only does it act as a reserve of organisms used in industry and non-medical research, but it also keeps typical bacteria involved in spoilage and deterioration, so that technologists can obtain reference strains to compare with those which may be causing trouble. In the early days of the NCIB's existence, parties of visitors used to come round, and on one occasion a small party of civic dignitaries and their wives, visiting the locality from France, came to see us. I never clearly understood why; it seemed a rather soggy sort of entertainment for the local municipality to arrange. However, I well recall the alarm shown by the wives, when, not having at first understood the word *bactéries*, they suddenly realized they were amid a collection of *germes*. As one woman they pulled out handkerchiefs, covered their noses, and left as soon as they politely could.

Laymen always associate bacteria, microbes and germs with disease. Microbes seem to have a faintly alarming or disgusting aura, and the fact that by far the majority are nugatory or even beneficial is rarely understood. Yet it is so. One's hands, hair, mouth, skin and intestines are teeming with bacteria; all but freshly cooked or sterilized foods are contaminated with living bacteria and their spores; drinks, soil, dust and air have populations of microbes, the majority of which are harmless and many of which are beneficial. Disease-causing (pathogenic) bacteria are the minority, except where sickness is prevalent.

The fact that we eat, sleep, live and breathe microbes has only

25

slowly been realized during the last hundred or so years and has, as we shall see in the next few chapters, led to the enormous advances in hygiene and medicine of the twentieth century. We discussed some of the impacts of microbes on man's existence in the first chapter, and we shall look at these in greater detail later on. In this chapter I propose, as it were, formally to introduce some of the microbes we shall encounter later, to familiarize the reader with the way in which they are classified and what generally they do, and to show how their study has crystallized into a branch of biology known as microbiology.

Though microbes had been known before the late nineteenth century, the subject of microbiology can fairly be said to have been created by Louis Pasteur. Pasteur, who was a French chemist, proved that fermentation and putrefaction, hitherto believed to be purely chemical processes, were due to microbes. The manner of his proof is now a matter of history, with which we shall not be concerned; from the point of view of the development of microbiology the important point was his realization that the air contained a menagerie of microbes likely to fall randomly on any susceptible material and to putrefy or ferment it. Consequently, scientists who wish to study and understand these microbes need to develop special methods for sorting out, conserving and keeping separate different types of microbe. Since the individual microbes are invisible to the naked eye, and are very numerous, it has rarely been practicable to take one microbe and study it. For, in the first place, it is inconveniently small, and secondly, if it does not die, it turns into two new ones, then to four and so on. The microbiologist, generally speaking, is obliged to study great numbers of microbes at once and deduce an average behaviour for the whole lot; therefore he must be at pains to see that they are all as nearly the same as possible and, above all things, that the pure 'family' (usually called a species or strain) is not contaminated with little strangers from his hair, skin or the air.

How he does this we shall discuss in Chapter 4. For present purposes the essential point is that the techniques of microbiology are, on the whole, very different from those of the rest of biology. You can take a dog, dog-fish or plant and observe it in a variety of ways, doing a variety of things. While you *can* do this with a microbe, it would not, at present, get you very far. Just as chemists deal in the behaviour of millions upon millions of molecules, and rarely derive information from the study of single molecules, so microbiologists study microbes in thousands of millions, and rarely have recourse to the individual germ. This is not a matter of choice in either instance: the techniques are, at present, just not available for fruitful study of the unitary bodies of the two sciences. For this reason, microbiology is a science defined more by the techniques it uses than by the subjects it covers. Indeed, when 'macro'-biologists come to study the individual cells of multicellular organisms, as in the use of tissue cultures, they adopt many of the techniques of microbiology.

As a general principle, one can say that microbiology is concerned with organisms that consist of one cell or a very few cells. Since cells are small, a microscope is almost always necessary to see microbes. The subject, naturally, overlaps into the provinces of botany and zoology, but it is fair to say that the microbiologist's primary concern is with that great group of unicellular living things known to biologists as the *Protista*.

At this point it is necessary to classify the main types of microbe that will concern us in later chapters, and here another difference from conventional biology arises. The classification of plants and animals have what biologists call 'phylogenetic' significance: creatures closely related in the evolutionary sequence of living things are classified close together, more divergent types further apart, so that one is made aware at a glance that cows, for example, are closer to buffaloes than to horses, but that all three are closer together than they are to dogs; yet all four form a group separate from frogs; and so on. With microbes the groupings are far less well defined. We can say that algae and viruses, for example, are far apart; but within the bacteria, for instance, even organisms that look and behave in similar manners may have evolved from different ancestors. Some phylogenetic classification of microbes *is* possible, but it is very tentative, and generally microbes are classified according to what they do, not according to some hypothesis about how they came to do it.

With that little homily over, we shall look at the classification of microbes as conventionally accepted today.

Algae (pronounced with a hard 'g'; singular: alga)

These are unicellular plants of the kind that one sees on the walls of goldfish aquaria, which turn ponds and water butts green. Seaweeds and many pond weeds are in fact multicellular algae, but these are normally the province of the botanist. Typical unicellular green algae are *Scenedesmus* and *Chlorella*. The latter is an extremely common inhabitant of green water, and consists of single egg-shaped cells, about 10μ (0·01 mm) long, capable of swimming around ('motile' in biologists' jargon) with the aid of two hair-like appendages ('flagella': a plural noun of which the singular is 'flagellum'). The cells are green, and the green colour is due to chlorophyll, contained in a portion of the cell called the 'chloroplast' (in *Chlorella* the chloroplast occupies almost all of the cell). There is a nucleus, as in the cells of higher organisms, and a cell wall composed of cellulose. Like plants, the green algae need light to grow, and with it they reduce carbon dioxide to sugars and starch and so they multiply. They do not use organic food at all: light, CO_2 and certain minerals are all they need for growth. Creatures that use exclusively mineral matter for growth are known to microbiologists as 'autotrophs', and the green algae come in a particular class of autotrophs called 'photo-autotrophs' because of their need for light. The antonym of autotroph, 'heterotroph', pertains to organisms that require organic food (as you and I do). We shall need these words in later sections.

A group of algae exists called the 'blue-green' algae because several of their members have a blueish tint to their green colour (others are reddish or brown). They have no clear chloroplast, usually lack a distinct nucleus and have some other rather distinctive biological characters. To microbiologists they are of interest because they seem to be closely related to certain bacteria, and may represent a phylogenetic link between bacteria and algae.

Protozoa (singular: protozoon)

These are single-celled animals of which the schoolchild's amoeba is a typical example. They are heterotrophs, and are in fact the most complex of the microbes. For some reason they tend to be neglected by microbiologists (possibly because a specialized type of zoologist, the protozoologist, exists and regards them as his special province!), but they have in fact been extremely valuable in nutritional and genetical research. *Paramoecium*, the slipper animalcule, was probably one of the first microbes to be observed by Antonie van Leeuwenhoek, the discoverer of microbes, in the seventeenth century. *Astasia*, a motile ovoid protozoon, is interesting because it has a nearly identical cousin, *Euglena*, which possesses a chloroplast. This creature thus bridges the gap between algae and protozoa and, hence, that between plants and animals. Protozoa cause one or two fairly rare diseases in plants, animals and men, but as far as we know they have a relatively small impact on mankind compared with other microbes. Therefore, though they will crop up occasionally in later chapters, we shall say no more about their classification here.

Fungi (pronounced with a hard 'g'; singular: fungus)

Mushrooms and toadstools are familiar to botanists, both amateur and professional, but rarely provide material for study by microbiologists. Moulds, mildews, rusts and yeasts, however, are very important and, because of their simple structure and metabolism, have become honorary microbes to the microbiologist despite the fact that many of them are not unicellular. The common bread mould, *Neurospora*, forms green spores which give the characteristic colour to mouldy bread (though a relative, *Eurotium*, is often present too). Blueish colours are often due to *Aspergillus;* mouldy cheese often features the justly famous *Penicillium*. Yeasts, used in baking and brewing, are fungi, and ordinary soil is rich in small, thread-like fungi of a simple kind called actinomycetes. These creatures are essentially plant-like:

they grow as threads that sometimes branch and they spread by forming spores (analogous, in a general sense, to forming seeds), but they lack chlorophyll. Hence they cannot photosynthesize. They are heterotrophs: they need organic material in order to grow and are therefore normally found on decaying organic matter of almost all kinds. They are particularly versatile at breaking down such resistant materials as wood, leather and so on, as we shall see in Chapter 7.

Certain fungi live in association with special algae, forming the composite creatures called lichens. In these circumstances, aided by the autotrophic abilities of the algal partner, they can grow in extremely barren environments such as the roofs of houses, bare rocks and so on. Quite what benefit, if any, the alga receives from this partnership is obscure.

Bacteria (singular: bacterium)

This is a collective name for the traditional 'germs'. They are microscopically small creatures, related to fungi, usually 1 to 2μ in length or diameter. They have almost no visible internal structure. They were the first disease-causing microbes to be identified, though we now recognize pathogens among the fungi, viruses and protozoa as well. They are generally so small that they can only be seen clearly with the most powerful of optical microscopes and, though there are many thousands of species and strains known, they tend all to look much the same. Three main shapes are known: rods ('bacilli'), spheres ('cocci') and commas ('vibrios'); some of the rods are filamentous. Rather less common shapes are S-shaped forms ('spirilla') and corkscrew or wavy forms ('spirochaetes'). When bacteria multiply, they do so by simply growing to a maximum size and splitting into two; sometimes the two daughter cells fail to separate and they grow in clusters or chains. Some are motile; some form spores and can then resist heating or drying. Sexual reproduction does not occur among bacteria, though certain strains are now known to undergo a primitive kind of sexual congress.

The bacteria are mostly heterotrophic: dependent on pre-formed organic matter for their food. They occupy a rather central position among the protista because there are bacteria related to most of the other main groups. Certain bacteria, for example, contain a specialized type of chlorophyll and conduct photosynthesis. They resemble the blue-green algae and can be autotrophic. Others are distinctly fungoid in character and the various types merge imperceptibly into the actinomycetes. Many microbiologists, indeed, classify actinomycetes as bacteria. Some bacteria are so small that they are practically invisible even under the most powerful optical microscope. Mycoplasmas are fragile, shapeless specks of protoplasm that fall between bacteria and viruses (below); they resemble certain forms ('L-forms') that true bacteria may occasionally take up and they cause diseases among cattle; some contain chemicals called sterols, which indicate a biological relationship to protozoa and animals. Bdellovibrios are probably true bacteria, but they are about an order of magnitude smaller: they are tiny comma-shaped creatures, 0.1 to 0.3μ long, that exist in soil and are parasitic on normal soil bacteria. One can culture them on other bacteria.

Virus (singular: virus)

Though the correct plural name of this group should be 'virus', I am going to be like almost everyone else and call them 'viruses'. These creatures are between ten and a hundred times smaller than bacteria, from 0.2 to 0.02μ long. They have become important in recent years as the major causative agents of disease: as we shall see in the next chapter, most of the bacterial diseases are now under control but the viruses remain largely unconquered. The borderline between viruses and bacteria becomes rather indistinct at the size level of mycoplasmas and bdellovibrios, but if we regard these as bacteria, the most complex viruses are probably the *Rickettsiae*, round particles of about 0.2μ in diameter that cause diseases such as scrub typhus or trench fever in both man and animals. Viruses are responsible for many plant diseases (wilts, scabs and so on); diseases such as poliomyelitis and the common cold in man; foot and mouth, among other

31

diseases, in cattle; diseases of fish and doubtless of other organisms. They also attack bacteria, and the viruses responsible for diseases among bacteria have been given the special name of 'bacteriophages' by microbiologists. There is a class of bacterial viruses called 'temperate 'phages' which seem to live harmlessly in their host until some stress causes the infection to develop.

Viruses lie on the borderline of living things. They have, for example, no metabolism of their own: they do not respire, break down carbon compounds, fix CO_2 or do anything like that. When they infect a creature, they pervert its own metabolism so that it synthesizes more of the virus. When the host dies or, in the case of higher organisms, when the infected cells die and break up, many hundreds of virus particles are liberated and can spread the infection further. When they are not infecting a host, viruses behave like stable chemical molecules. They do not die and, in fact, some viruses have been concentrated, crystallized and stored for years in the laboratory. If you can take a crystalline substance from a bottle, infect an organism with a trace of it and later harvest relatively vast quantities of those crystals from the infected creature, are those crystals living or dead? Since there is no straight answer to this question we shall leave it to examiners and linguistic philosophers to chew over; as far as their impact on mankind is concerned they are only too alive and, in this book, we shall treat them as microbes.

Sub-viral particles

At the time of writing (early 1967) there have been reports of particles, smaller by an order of magnitude than viruses, which have rather similar properties and cause degenerative diseases in man and animals. Scrapie, a disease of the nervous tissue of sheep, is caused by such an agent; it has some remarkable properties including resistance to boiling and ability to survive two years' exposure to the strong disinfectant formalin. Disseminated sclerosis and a tropical disease of man called kuru may be caused by similar agents; so little is yet known about these creatures that we can do little more than mention them here.

*

An important property of microbes is their capacity to exist in association with other organisms. We have already met the lichens, combinations of algae and fungi, and in Chapter 5 we shall recognize the importance of bacteria that live in the intestines of animals. We shall also encounter the special groups of nitrogen-fixing microbes that live in the roots of plants and then – and only then – fix atmospheric nitrogen and thus supply the plant with an essential nutrient. Even more intimate associations may exist; bacteria may form an integral part of the protoplasm of protozoa, and harmless viruses may become part of the genetic apparatus of bacteria. Ultimately, as we shall discuss in Chapters 10 and 11, it becomes possible to imagine that many of the characters of highly developed organisms were derived from associated microbes at earlier stages of their evolution.

The way in which microbiologists classify microbes is extremely important to the specialist, for the obvious reason that one cannot study microbes usefully until one can pin-point what one is talking about and dealing with. Yet for a survey such as this we must disregard the intricacies of microbial classification because we are more concerned with what microbes do. That is why the foregoing treatment of microbes has been cursory and restricted to outlining the major types that we shall encounter later on. Microbial classification is a difficult and changing science, and the reason why this is so illustrates one of the most important properties of microbes from our point of view: their adaptability. If you take a microbe which, for example, cannot grow with the milk sugar called lactose, and then grow a culture of, say, a few thousand million progeny from it, about one in a hundred thousand of those progeny is likely to be able to use lactose. The progeny of these variants will all be able to use lactose. Supposing, to take a different example, one has a population whose growth is stopped by a certain amount of penicillin. If one gives the population a little penicillin, but insufficient to prevent them all from growing, the few persistent organisms will multiply and their progeny will be found to be resistant to much more penicillin than was the parent population. If one performs the process again and yet again, stepping up the penicillin concentration each time, one can 'breed' strains of microbes with enormous drug resistances. Finally, as the third example, if one takes bacteria that are normally simple, discrete rods and grows them in an environment that they can manage with, but which is not the best for them (starve them of magnesium, for example, or have a trace of disinfectant present), their appearance will be quite altered: they may form long, snaky filaments, develop weird protuberances, and even make the environment coloured; their chemical composition will also change and in many ways they will seem to be quite different organisms. These examples should be sufficient to show how the properties of microbes can often depend on how they have been treated or where they came from. The mutability of microbes is so great that the central problem of microbial classification is less that of giving the little beasts names than that of discovering what characters are truly immutable and truly distinctive.

From a practical point of view the adaptability of microbes means that, in almost any terrestrial environment, one will find living or dormant microbes capable of all kinds of biochemical activity. The chemical versatility of microbes, as a group of organisms, is possibly their most impressive feature, and for the rest of this chapter we shall look at the range of these abilities.

*

We have looked briefly at the 'biological' classification of microbes, a system that resembles in principle the horse-dog-frog classification of chordate animals even if it has less phylogenetic significance. But there are other ways than the conventional one of classifying animals and these can be very useful in special contexts. An obvious one is to do so according to environment: there are arctic, temperate and tropical animals acclimatized to diverse ranges of temperature; there are desert animals accustomed to extreme dryness and aquatic animals enjoying extreme wetness. One useful classification of animals makes use of their eating habits, so we have carnivorous, herbivorous and omnivorous animals. Yet another system uses the duration of their activity: one has nocturnal or daytime creatures and those that become dormant – hibernate – for cold or dry seasons. Other minor classifications include parasitic or non-parasitic, wild or tame, fierce or timid. These classifications all have their uses, and they cut completely across the 'natural' or 'biological' system. In general biology they are usually of secondary importance, but in microbiology, because of the deficiencies of the more formal system that I mentioned earlier, they are often the more important. For our purposes they will certainly be the more useful and we shall now look at some of them. Let us start by looking at the classification of microbes according to the sort of environment in which they flourish.

Men and other mammals, as most people know, require very precise physical and chemical conditions to live at all. Their temperatures must lie within the range 35 to 40 degrees Centigrade and they must breathe an atmosphere of 20 per cent oxygen with $0·03$ per cent CO_2 at a pressure around 760 mm. of mercury. Temporary deviations from these conditions can be tolerated, but their bodies in fact have built-in mechanisms to maintain such an environment: temperature regulation and ventilation rate adjust automatically to cold, heat or carbon dioxide changes. The salt concentration (salinity) of the blood is also closely regulated by the kidneys; the breathing rate and kidney function control the acidity of the blood. Mammals, in fact, only withstand the fluctuations of the terrestrial environment by controlling their internal environments very closely. Cold-blooded creatures have wider tolerances of temperature but are otherwise pretty exacting; plants tolerate, and indeed flourish in, atmospheres with excessive carbon dioxide and, in some instances, they tolerate salty, acid or very dry soils. But again they need air, light and an equable temperature to do well. Plants and animals have learned to grow and multiply on dry land, but they do this by controlling

35

the state of their interiors rather minutely so as to guard their cells against external fluctuations.

Microbes are mainly aquatic. Some filamentous fungi grow in air, on damp materials such as decaying bread, but all bacteria, protozoa, algae and viruses, all the truly unicellular protista, require a watery environment in which to grow. A microscopic film of water on a leaf, on skin, in soil or on a jelly is sufficiently aquatic for most of them, but they never grow actually out of water. However, though they may not grow out of water, they do not necessarily die when dried. Many bacteria and moulds form spores, resistant bodies which will withstand desiccation not just for years but for decades. Dr Peter Sneath produced the most impressive death curve known to microbiology when he examined soil samples attached to ancient pressed plants kept at Kew: he found live bacterial spores in specimens dating back to the seventeenth century (but no earlier). The tomb of Tutankhamun was sterile, as regards bacteria, when, in 1923, it was opened for the first time in 3,000 years, so it seems that, though bacterial spores last many years, they do not last for ever. Viruses do not form spores, but they survive drying if there is a little protein around in the fluid from which they dried (as there always is on droplets from a sneeze, for example). Once dried, they last indefinitely as far as we know, and it is a pity that techniques for recognizing unknown viruses were not available (indeed, still are not) when Tutankhamun's tomb was opened.

Most microbes that do not form spores die if they get too dry, but even some of those can be protected if there is some protein around: a few bacteria will survive, for instance, in mucus dried on a handkerchief. (Handkerchiefs, like drying-up cloths, are among the most infectious of civilized appurtenances from the microbiological point of view; but more of that in Chapter 3).

Spore formation by moulds and bacteria, dormancy as a result of drying, and the property some bacteria and protozoa possess of forming relatively resistant bodies called cysts, together comprise an important general property of microbes: that of going into a state of suspended animation when conditions become adverse. In Chapter 1 we noted that microbes could be detected many miles up in the stratosphere. They are, in fact, nearly all spores of the moulds *Cladosporium* and *Alternaria*, with dormant bacteria of the *Micrococcus* group, blown there by winds from the lower atmosphere. It is improbable that microbes actually multiply in the airborne state, though such a thing could conceivably happen on a wet dust particle of suitable character and buoyancy. Dormant microbes are very important in dispersal, being the main form in which microbes become spread around everywhere.

Many microbes are killed by freezing, but, here again, protein can protect them and so, it seems, can soil. The permafrost zones of the Arctic and Antarctic zones contain viable bacteria and fungi, and a most curious fact about them is that many of the bacteria are thermophilic. This means that they require an uncommonly high temperature to grow: 55 to 70 degrees Centigrade is commonly provided in laboratories. The hottest hot bath that one can comfortably bear is between 45 and 50 degrees; at the temperatures at which thermophilic bacteria grow, normal creatures would rapidly scald and die. Thermophilic bacteria are normal inhabitants of hot springs, hot artesian wells and other geothermal environments; this is comprehensible enough, but why should they be present in ordinary temperate soils, and even in the permafrost? This is still one of the more baffling problems of microbial ecology. In practice, as we shall see later, it means that hot environments such as central-heating systems, cooling towers and so on are as liable to microbial contamination as any other environment.

Thermophilic creatures are restricted to the microbes, and some exceptional bacteria show quite extraordinary heat tolerance. At the elevation of Yellow Springs National Park, U.S.A., water boils at 92 degrees Centigrade; in the boiling water of some of the springs there are dark deposits of small, rod-shaped bacteria multiplying at that temperature. Professor T. D. Brock of Indiana University has studied the microflora of that area: a filamentous bacterium called *Flexibacterium* flourishes up to 83 degrees, the temperature limit for blue-green algae seems to be 75 degrees, fungi and true algae are found up to 60 degrees, protozoa to 50 degrees, insects to 40 degrees. Obviously the more complex the creature, the lower is its maximum temperature.

Heat above about 80 degrees is lethal to most microbes, even most thermophiles. However, the spores of certain bacteria called clostridia are very resistant even to heat. Boiling water, for instance, will kill spores of the bread mould in about 10 minutes, whereas spores of some clostridia will stand six hours' boiling; some will even survive five minutes' pressure cooking in live steam at 120 degrees.

Salty water tends to kill microbes, which is why foods such as bacon and fish can be preserved by pickling in brine. Strong syrups have similar effects. The sea is sufficiently salty to kill most (but by no means all) fresh water bacteria and viruses (a circumstance for which the inhabitants of Great Britain have cause to be grateful, because their islands are situated in what is now a sea of dilute sewage). Yet there exists a whole microbial flora adapted to life in the sea, and a branch of microbiology ('marine microbiology') has grown up around their study. Even pickling brines and preserving syrups become infected with specialized bacteria, moulds and yeasts that can grow in such strange environments. A familiar example in the home is jam that has gone mouldy and begun to ferment. Microbes that withstand strong salt or sugar solutions are called 'strong halophiles' by microbiologists; as well as being found in foods and brines, they crop up in natural salt pans: the red-brown colour of many brackish lakes in the Middle East is due to a halophilic alga called *Dunaliella*.

We spoke just now of bacteria in the sea. Most of the sea is very cold and only the upper layers (the 'thermosphere') change temperature according to the seasons. Below a certain level (called the 'thermocline'; its depth depends somewhat on latitude and season) exists the 'psychrosphere' where the temperature lies between 4 and 10 degrees Centigrade at all times. More than 90 per cent of the volume of the Earth's oceans is psychrosphere. In addition, for every ten metres, approximately, the pressure in the sea increases by about one atmosphere. What, then of the microbes which inhabit this zone? As the reader may guess, they are peculiar, and in particular, most are psychrophilic and many are barophilic. These words mean that they only grow at low temperatures and high pressures. For many years the existence of true psychrophilic (low temperature) bacteria was doubted, and the main reason was that microbiologists simply forgot to refrigerate their samples while transferring them from the sea to the laboratory. So these bacteria, which die fairly rapidly at temperatures above 20 degrees, had mostly died by the time the samples could be examined properly; only their hardier neighbours survived. Barophilic microbes are even more difficult to study: specially strong apparatus is necessary to reproduce the pressures of 500 to 1,000 atmospheres encountered in, for example, the deep Pacific trench and it is almost certain that many of the microbes that inhabit such deep sedimentary oozes have never been detected. Only those that tolerate a brief exposure to 'low' pressure can readily be cultured, even in specialized laboratories. An interesting feature of growth at high pressures is that, at such pressures, bacteria show increased heat resistance: thermophilic, barophilic bacteria from an oil well have been grown by Professor ZoBell under a pressure of 1,000 atmospheres at 104 degrees: well above the boiling point of water at ordinary pressures.

At the opposite extreme of pressure, few normal microbes mind a near-vacuum, provided it is wet. Most anaerobic bacteria (see below) can be cultured in vessels that have been evacuated and contain nothing but a little water vapour over the culture fluid, a property which can be very convenient in a laboratory, but a thorough nuisance when they get into 'vacuum-packed' foodstuffs.

Bacteria and most viruses do not tolerate acids. Even acidity as weak as that of vinegar prevents the growth of most bacteria. This is why pickling works: the normal putrefactive bacteria cease growing, though certain acid-forming bacteria survive and, in fact, aid the pickling process by forming acid (see Chapter 5). Yeasts and moulds, on the other hand, somewhat prefer mild acidity, doubtless because their normal habitat is fruit juices, plant exudates and fermented matter. Strong mineral acids such as sulphuric or hydrochloric are, however, lethal to most microbes and it is therefore curious to discover that there exist micro-organisms that can not only tolerate sulphuric acid solutions but actually generate them. The sulphur bacteria called thiobacilli, which we shall meet again in Chapters 6 and 7, oxidize sulphur or pyritic ores to form sulphuric acid, and couple these reactions to the fixation of carbon dioxide – much as green plants couple the trapped energy of sunlight to a similar process of CO_2-fixation. They are autotrophs, but different from those that we met under the heading 'algae' earlier in this chapter, because they couple a purely chemical, not a photochemical, reaction to biological syntheses and growth. Such creatures are called 'chemo-autotrophs', to distinguish them from 'photo-autotrophs', which, like plants, use sunlight.

Thus we can classify microbes according to their temperature relationships into thermophiles, mesophiles and psychrophiles, according to salinity into normal organisms and halophiles, according to pressure into normal and barophilic, according to resistance to heat and drying in terms of whether they form spores or not, according to their tolerance of acidity (the 'acid' microbes are called 'acidophilic'). These classes have obvious analogies to the arctic-temperate-tropical, the desert-aquatic and other classifications of animals mentioned earlier; let us now look at a classification according to nutritional habits, because this is much more important among microbes than is the carnivore-herbivore division among animals.

From the nutritional point of view microbes span the gap that distinguishes plants from animals, and include categories of nutrition that do not occur at all among higher organisms. Most notable of these are the autotrophic types of metabolism such as that of the thiobacilli just mentioned. We shall say more about chemo-autotrophy later. To return to this matter of acidity: when thiobacilli generate acid, in sulphur springs or in the seepage waters of mines containing pyrites, they prevent the growth of common microbes. However, there develops in such waters a whole micro-flora of acid-tolerant creatures: yeasts, actinomycetes, bacteria and even some protozoa, all depending primarily on the CO_2 fixed by the chemo-autotrophs that grew there in the first place. Just as heterotrophs such as man and animals depend on plants to live in the neutral (or, strictly, very faintly acid) conditions of this planet, so, in specialized acid environments, a microbial microcosm can develop analogous to ours but independent of sunlight.

The thiobacilli are part of a fairly small group of chemotrophic microbes. As we saw just now, they couple the oxidation of sulphur compounds to CO_2-fixation. Other reactions that can be used by bacteria for chemo-autotrophic growth are the following:

> Oxidation of hydrogen to water (by *Hydrogenomonas*).
> Oxidation of ammonia to nitrite (by *Nitrosomonas*).
> Oxidation of nitrite to nitrate (by *Nitrobacter*).
> Oxidation of ferrous ions to ferric (*Thiobacillus ferro-oxidans*).
> Oxidation of methane to water and CO_2 (by *Methanomonas*).
> Oxidation of sulphide to sulphur (*Thiovulum* and some other sulphur bacteria).

If the reader is dismayed by the chemistry implied by these reactions, he need not be. There is no point in writing out 'correct' chemical equations for these processes (they are mostly obvious and elementary anyway, provided one remembers they are taking place in water), because the essential point is that a number of purely chemical reactions exist which microbes can use as alternative energy sources to sunlight for the primary synthesis of biological material. All the processes listed assume the presence of air, and autotrophic reactions that need neither air nor sunlight are, as far as we know, rare. However, one or two well established instances exist. The bacterium *Thiobacillus denitrificans*, while able to grow at the expense of sulphur oxidation in air, can, if no air is available, oxidize sulphur while reducing the nitrate ion. The sulphur goes to sulphuric acid and the nitrate to nitrogen gas; the organism couples this interaction to the reduction of CO_2. An organism called *Micrococcus denitrificans* can conduct a similar process using hydrogen to reduce nitrate.

Some bacteria need both light and a chemical reaction for autotrophic growth. The coloured sulphur bacteria, which we shall also meet in Chapter 6, oxidize sulphide to sulphur provided they are illuminated, and in these circumstances they fix CO_2 and grow. The importance of this process is that air is unnecessary: provided both light and sulphide are present, they grow in the total absence of air. Microbes that grow without air are called 'anaerobes' and are, as we shall see shortly, very common. But anaerobic autotrophs seem rather rare and, with the exception of *Thiobaccillus* and *Micrococcus denitrificans*, they seem mostly to require light. Several types of bacteria exist which make use of light for growth, as plants do, but they are peculiar in two ways. For one thing, they need some organic matter, which plants do not, and, again unlike plants, they do not grow photosynthetically in air. (One has to make the reservation that they do not grow photosynthetically in air, because they can usually grow in air if there is no light.) These bacteria are always coloured, though they are not necessarily (or even commonly) green. Red colours (due to relatively large amounts of carotenes, which swamp the green chlorophyll) are very common among such bacteria.

Chemo-autotrophy is restricted to the bacteria and is not encountered among the fungi or the protozoa, nor, of course, the viruses. A few blue-green algae can oxidize sulphide, but the majority of algae are ordinary photo-autotrophs, like green plants.

While we are dealing with the chemical versatility of microbes we should mention here the iron bacteria. This is a group of bacteria, often filamentous or in the form of twisted, branching stalks, that occur in iron-rich waters. The brown 'iron' deposits on rocks and stones in mountain streams are often formed by these bacteria, which oxidize dissolved ferrous ions to the ferric form. At one time this reaction was thought to permit chemo-autotrophic growth, but the evidence for this seems now to be unsound. Yet microbiologists may well be mistaken, because the process seems to be of little use unless, as has been suggested, the precipitate tends to concentrate organic matter by adsorption (just as charcoal adsorbs smells) and so enables the bacteria to feed more easily.

One aspect of the metabolism of microbes, which has no analogy among higher organisms yet which provides an important way of categorizing them, is their respiration – or lack of it. We mentioned a while ago the class of bacteria called anaerobes, which live without air. All higher organisms require air (or at least an inert gas with 21 per cent of oxygen) or else they die. Certain plant tissues (e.g. seeds) can respire for a while without air and some primitive animals (nematodes, insect larvae) seem able to tolerate considerable oxygen starvation. But basically their metabolism is based on the use of oxygen to oxidize foodstuffs. Yeasts, some moulds and many bacteria (but not, generally speaking, protozoa and algae) can grow anaerobically, which means without air. (Viruses, of course, don't care: they use their hosts' metabolisms anyway). Anaerobic bacteria are quite as common and widespread in Nature as aerobic ones. They grow anaerobically in one of two ways, either by splitting the food molecules into smaller fragments so as to yield energy without the participation of oxygen, or by using an alternative oxidizing agent to oxygen. We can call these processes 'fermentative' or 'oxidative' respectively.

A typical fermentative reaction occurs in the alcoholic fermentations brought about by yeasts: fruit sugars (mainly glucose) are decomposed by the yeasts to alcohol and carbon dioxide, a sequence of reactions that provide enough energy for the yeasts to grow and multiply and which involves no air. Many moulds and bacteria, if deprived of air, can conduct such fermentations, forming CO_2 together with products such as lactic acid, succinic acid, butyl alcohol in addition to ethyl alcohol. Most of these microbes can use air if it is present, in which case the glucose and other products become oxidized completely to CO_2. Other bacteria exist, however, that can only grow if air is absent and these are called 'obligate anaerobes' to distinguish them from the optional 'facultative anaerobes'. Members of the genus *Clostridium* (the 'clostridia' mentioned earlier) do not grow unless air is absent and thus they flourish in polluted or putrescent environments where other microbes have used up all the available air. They ferment sugars and amino-acids, derived from carbohydrates and proteins, and, particularly when using protein, produce some evil-smelling and even poisonous by-products such as the ptomaines (amines formed from protein). Clostridia are characterized

43

by forming spores, and this property confers on them the resistance to heat and desiccation which, as we shall see in later chapters, makes them dangerous in food technology. But obligate anaerobes that do not form spores are known, such as the *Bacteroides* found in the intestines of cattle and in milk. The rumen or first stomach of ruminant mammals has no air normally and is rich in fermentative bacteria; it is one of the few environments in which anaerobic protozoa may be found.

The second class of anaerobes, the oxidative anaerobes, function rather differently, and are exclusively bacteria. Instead of oxygen, they use an ion such as nitrate, sulphate or carbonate to oxidize organic food, and this material becomes reduced. We encountered two nitrate-reducing bacteria earlier: *Thiobacillus denitrificans* and *Micrococcus denitrificans*, the only authenticated anaerobic chemo-autotrophs. Quite a number of ordinary bacteria can use nitrate in place of oxygen for respiration, generally reducing it only to nitrite and not to nitrogen gas, but, in dung heaps, compost heaps and polluted muds, bacteria which reduce nitrate to nitrogen flourish. They are important in the nitrogen cycle (see Chapter 1) as 'denitrifying bacteria'. Most denitrifying bacteria are facultative: they can use oxygen if it is available. This is not true of the bacteria that use sulphate or carbonate. The sulphate-reducing bacteria, the microbes we first met in Chapter 1, are very strict anaerobes which, while they are not killed by air, cannot grow in its presence. What they do is reduce sulphate to sulphide while oxidizing organic matter to acetic acid and CO_2; they thus produce a horrible smell and, since sulphide reacts fairly rapidly with oxygen, they remove oxygen from any neighbourhood in which they get established. This property is at the bottom of the extraordinary variety of economic nuisances they cause – and the few benefits they have engendered – as we shall see in Chapters 6 and 7.

Let us pause a moment here and consider the sulphate-reducing bacteria in slightly more detail, because they will appear often in this book and they illustrate well the way in which the classifications we have been discussing cut across each other. They are, as I said, strict anaerobes, because they 'breathe' sulphate instead of oxygen; but within this restriction they have representatives in several of the categories we have discussed. One of the main groups (called *Desulfotomaculum*) forms spores, the other (*Desulfovibrio*) does not. One species of *Desulfotomaculum* is thermophilic; some of the *Desulfovibrio* group are halophilic. Representatives of the groups are to be found in environments ranging from brackish, super-cooled Antarctic waters to hot artesian springs; barophilic types have been found in deep Pacific sediments. Bacterial sulphate reduction is believed to be one of the commonest biological processes on earth, although, because of its anaerobic nature, it mostly occurs deep in seas, in soils and in polluted waters.

Carbonate reduction is also an extremely anaerobic process. The marsh gas that bubbles up when polluted mud at the bottom of a stagnant pool is disturbed is methane (CH_4) and it is formed by the action of bacteria (one group is called, rather obviously, *Methanobacterium*). Some of these organisms form methane from other carbon compounds by fermentative reactions, but others actually couple the oxidation of such compounds to a reduction of carbonate to methane. The methane bacteria, like the sulphate-reducing bacteria, are very widespread and are even more sensitive to oxygen. (They find a warm, anaerobic habitat in the stomachs of ruminant mammals.) They have only rarely been cultured in the laboratory in the absence of other bacteria to help them along. They should not be confused with the methane-oxidizing bacteria, mentioned earlier among the chemo-autotrophs, which need air and which couple the oxidation of methane, in air, to CO_2-fixation and growth.

The categories we have used so far to discuss microbes, such as the aerobes and the anaerobes, the thermophiles and the psychrophiles, the autotrophs and the heterotrophs are, as I said earlier, often more useful to microbiologists than the 'biological' classification into algae, fungi, bacteria and so on. This is particularly true when one is discussing their impact on mankind – as, rest assured, we shall shortly start doing – because, though one would ideally wish to know exactly what all the types of microbe in a certain environment are, one can often say useful things about the microbiology of an environment without such detailed knowledge. To give a simple example: if sulphate-reducing bacteria are becoming dominant in a certain environment, then a fairly predictable sequence of changes in the chemistry and microbiology of that environment is going to take place no matter to what genus and species the actual bacteria belong. Information about genera and species becomes important at a more detailed level – when one has to make a choice among possible counter-measures, for example. The variety of categories used by microbiologists may seem confusing at first, though I have tried to show that they are in principle no different from categories of animals, such as herbivorous *versus* carnivorous, or tropical *versus* temperate. However, I undertake to remind readers of the details of this chapter when they arise elsewhere in this book (reminders are also available in the glossary) and I shall bring it to a close by drawing one important moral about the behaviour of microbes.

What we have been discussing, and what makes these various classifications of microbes so important, is the extraordinary chemical versatility of microbes. We have seen how microbes can utilize quite curious chemical reactions for growth and multiplication, and so far we have discussed mainly reactions involving primarily mineral or inorganic substances such as sulphur and iron. We have been entirely concerned with major nutrients, materials that provide energy, and have said nothing about the fixation of nitrogen, for example, which, as we saw in Chapter 1, is a basic process in the biological economy of this planet. Nor can we say any more of such processes here, except to point out that, where higher organisms other than plants need fixed nitrogen, amino-acids, vitamins, fats and so on in their diet, microbes range from those that can synthesize all of these things from mineral sources to those that are so exacting that one wonders they survive at all. *Mycobacterium leprae*, the causative organism of leprosy, has still never been cultivated away from living tissues, and many disease-causing organisms need quite complex brews if they are to be cultivated in the laboratory. One can almost say that, whatever minor nutrient one mentions, there will be microbes that need it and others that do not; the only exceptions seem to be vitamin C (ascorbic acid) and the fat-soluble vitamins which, as far as we know, are not *required* by any known bacteria, fungi or algae. (The position regarding protozoa is uncertain: representatives of the group may need steroid materials, which are analogous to fat-soluble vitamins, and some mycoplasmas certainly need them.) Viruses, of course, fall outside this discussion because, in a sense, they require no nourishment at all.

The basic foodstuffs of animals are carbohydrates, proteins and fats, but many organic materials having comparable compositions cannot readily be used. The cellulose of plants, the lignin of wood, the chitin of crustacean shells, the keratin of hair, processed materials such as leather, paper and so on are either not eaten or are discharged undigested (except, as we shall see in Chapter 5, when the animal carries commensal microbes within itself to effect their digestion). The range of organic matter suitable as food for animals is in fact rather limited. This is not so for microbes. Many fungi utilize the cellulose and lignin of wood and break down paints, leather, paper. There are bacteria that decompose cellulose, and bacteria or yeasts that metabolize waxes, hydrocarbons such as petroleum, kerosene, petroleum grease. Asphalt, coal and road-building materials are slowly attacked by certain bacteria. The gases hydrogen and methane may be utilized by certain bacteria; even polythene, unknown to the living world before this century, is attacked by some soil microbes. Equally curious are the organisms that attack strong poisons. Phenol, for example, is a powerful disinfectant, yet there exist strains of bacteria that grow readily with it. Others can metabolize and grow with antibiotics and a mould exists that can grow with cyanide as its main source of carbon: cyanides are possibly the most universal poisons for terrestrial living things. Fluoracetamide, which is a powerful, universal poison used sometimes as an insecticide, caused deaths of cattle in 1963 when a field in Smarden, Kent, was accidentally contaminated with it; microbes have since been obtained from soil that decompose it and actually grow at its expense. Most of these microbes only tolerate small concentrations of the toxic substances – if they get too much phenol, say, or cyanide, then they, too, are killed. But provided they are not over-fed, as it were, they convert these materials to harmless waste products. This property is vitally important in the disposal of certain industrial wastes.

After some acquaintance with the chemical versatility of microbes, the microbiologist tends to be more surprised by organic materials that are not attacked by one or another creature: at present fluorinated plastics and certain detergents, plus pure carbon in the form of graphite or diamond, seem definitely immune, but few other substances are. We shall see in Chapter 7 how such materials as iron, steel, concrete, stone or rubber, while not necessarily consumed by bacteria, may be corroded or decomposed as a result of their activities.

Finally, though we have mentioned bacteria that consume and detoxify poisons such as phenol, we should also refer again to the general ability of bacteria to acquire resistance to toxic substances. We mentioned at the beginning of this chapter how one could train bacteria to resist, for example, penicillin, and this provides quite a good general illustration. There exist in nature bacteria which can grow in the presence of penicillin because they contain an enzyme, penicillinase, which enables them to destroy penicillin. Such organisms have caused trouble in hospitals. Bacteria trained to resist penicillin, however, do not make penicillinase; they adjust their metabolism in such a way as to avoid the damage penicillin would have done, and by similar adaptive processes one can get microbes adapted to sulphonamide drugs, flavin disinfectants (such as 'acriflavin') and various antibiotics. Copper sulphate is a powerful general poison for living things, yet at Rutgers University, New Jersey, U.S.A., there is a strain of mould that grows in 20 per cent copper sulphate in weak sulphuric acid provided a little sugar is present! The creature has developed a mechanism for keeping the copper outside its cell walls.

I could continue listing the variety of chemical activities that microbes are capable of, and the toxic environments they will tolerate, almost indefinitely, but not only would such a list become wearisome; I also realize that a quite detailed acquaintance with the biochemistry of ordinary multicellular living things is necessary to appreciate quite how impressive this diversity of microbial behaviour is. Yet, essentially, all terrestrial living things have similar biochemistries. The chemical mechanisms whereby they build up and break down proteins, carbohydrates and fats, the ways in which they control these processes, even the ways in which they use or store energy, all these are similar in most of their chemical details. Microbes are no exception (leaving out – as usual – the viruses, who get a host organism to do these things for them). The distinctive features of microbes are that they can make use of unusual and ingenious methods of obtaining energy in order to drive a fairly conventional metabolism, and that they can adjust themselves to run such a metabolism in circumstances that would be lethal to higher organisms. They can be found all over this planet, can grow and perform chemical transformations in what seem, from an anthropomorphic point of view, the most unlikely places. For this reason they have a profound, and often unrealized, effect, not only on the 'Balance of Nature', but on the existence of mankind and on man's economy. Microbiology is the study of microbes as a pure science; the study of their impact on man and other higher organisms, with which this book is concerned, has been called *economic microbiology*. Though economic microbiology is not a subject taught at schools and universities – aspects of it crop up in hygiene, industrial microbiology, agricultural bacteriology and so on – it is in fact a good example of the sort of hybrid of pure science and technology that Britain is so lamentably backward at developing: we seem to be good at very pure science, not *too* bad at wholly applied technology, but frightful at bringing the two together.

CHAPTER 3

Microbes in Society

We ended the last chapter on rather a bleak note: commenting on the apparent inability of the British to bridge the gap between pure science and its applications. This comment, like all generalizations about societies and social behaviour, may be true in general but is often found faulty in specific instances. A glaring exception is in that most personal and important technology called Medicine – for Medicine is not a science, despite the fact that its practitioners are called doctors. It is a model example of a technology: the application of various branches of science to one facet of the human condition. It is, historically, one of the most admirable examples of science and its application progressing hand-in-hand; even today it is almost unique among technologies in that a fundamental discovery in, say, a biochemical or physical laboratory, may find application in medical practice within weeks instead of years.

The reason is simple to see. We all hate being ill, whether we are doctors, scientists, treasury officials or laymen, and we will support with positive enthusiasm research intended to cure or alleviate this condition, whereas the study of quasars or the ecology of plankton might cause us reservations. Microbiologists have particular cause to be grateful for the self-interest that underlies the relative affluence accorded to medical research because, since microbes are the cause of most illnesses, microbiology has progressed very rapidly in the last half century, particularly in its medical aspects. Naturally, this imbalance has left non-medical microbiology in a somewhat neglected state, as will become obvious in later chapters of this book, but though 'pure' microbiologists have at times been critical of the narrowness of their more medical colleagues this fact should not blind us to the enormous contribution the old 'Path. and Bact.' type of scientist has made to the science as a whole.

In this chapter we cannot hope to survey medical microbiology even superficially. Microbes cause disease in men, animals and plants; for a catalogue of which microbes cause which diseases the reader must look elsewhere, in the technical literature of medicine, veterinary medicine and agriculture. We shall mention instances of specific diseases, and the microbes that cause them, but for the purpose of this book we shall be more concerned with why microbial diseases happen at all, how they are spread and how they may be avoided or treated.

Disease is a sort of parasitism, but an inefficient sort. The microbes that live on the human skin, in the mouth and in the intestines are parasites: they make use of their host as a supplier of food and warmth and provide little or nothing in return. (Some intestinal bacteria actually contribute B vitamins, as we shall see in Chapter 5, thereby graduating to the status of symbionts). Though unusually heavy blooms of skin, mouth and intestinal bacteria can cause rashes or discomfort, these parasitic microbes generally cause the host no harm at all, and they probably do some good by consuming materials that would otherwise support the growth of more damaging microbes. As parasites, these microbes are perfectly adapted to their hosts: they live in their little microcosms peacefully causing no one any harm, and this is the case with the normal commensal microbes found in association with all living creatures. Disease occurs when a microbe finds its way into a host, or some part of a host, to which it is imperfectly adapted yet within which it finds it can grow and flourish. When this happens, the biological defence processes of the host are brought into play and, if these are overstrained or unsuccessful, the host sickens and may die. Now, it is obviously a poor sort of parasite that kills its host. From an evolutionary point of view, when the host dies, the parasite's own microcosm is destroyed and all the parasites dependent on it are likely to die too. Thus the most perfectly adapted parasites, as we said before, cause little or no damage and it is the poorly adapted and inadvertent parasites that are dangerous and sometimes lethal.

If diseases are due to parasitic microbes growing in the wrong host, or in the wrong part of a host, then it should be possible to find a host, or part of a host, where they are harmless. In many instances this is true. The bacterium called *Bordatella pertussis*, which causes whooping cough, can be isolated from most healthy throats, and so can the *Streptococcus* species that cause sore throats and tonsilitis. They seem normally to be in a sort of balance with the hosts' defence mechanisms: seemingly without effort, the host keeps them at bay and only when some variation in the condition of the host occurs will disease strike. In the case of whooping cough, for instance, it is usual for children to have this disease some time in early life and subsequently to be immune, or so lightly susceptible that subsequent infections pass unnoticed, because at the time of the first infection the body developed defence mechanisms against *Bordatella* which it can return to for the rest of its life. What precisely those mechanisms are we shall discuss later.

Pneumococcus, the organism that causes classical pneumonia, can certainly be isolated from the lungs of healthy people, so, sometimes, can *Mycobacterium tuberculosis*, the bacterium that causes consumption. The skin is usually populated by a tiny spherical germ, *Micrococcus pyogenes* variety *albus* (the 'white staphylococcus') which is quite harmless, yet among them we will often find a few of its yellow brethren (*Micrococcus pyogenes* var. *aureus*) which can cause pimples, boils and more drastic skin conditions. For some reason that is not understood – and, since this type of skin infection is prevalent during adolescence, it is probably a change in the host and not the microbe that allows it – hair follicles or sweat glands can become infected with the yellow pyogenic (pus-forming) cocci and the familiar, unpleasant sequence of rash formation, inflammation, and eventual exudation of a mass of pus and debris takes place.

In the intestines we have quite a balanced microbial flora and, despite modern hygiene in handling foods, and general cleanliness of habits, there is little doubt that these bacteria get passed round from individual to individual in families and communities. So our bodies develop immunity to the local intestinal microbes and we all live together in relative harmony. Travel abruptly to another country, however, and be a little incautious in eating or drinking over the first few days, and a sometimes catastrophic re-arrangement of the intestinal flora may take place. How many gastronomic delights have been spurned after one tasting by travellers who did not realize that *Escherichia coli* from Paris, Rome, Cairo, Bombay, was not quite the same, as far as their bodily immunity was concerned, as *Escherichia coli* from, say, Finchley, London, N.3? There are, of course, troublesome intestinal bacteria to be found abroad, those causing dysentry, typhoid and paratyphoid, even cholera, but it is almost certain that the majority of 'Gyppy tummy'-like diseases suffered by travellers are not caused by virulent pathogens; they are mostly due to ordinary, locally harmless, microbes that have suddenly found a host whose immunity to them is faulty.

If I may digress into quackery for a moment – and I must assure the reader that it is quackery, for I have no medical qualification – there is a simple routine for travellers which will considerably lower his chances of getting this kind of vague intestinal infection. There is no real chance of avoiding these microbes, so the thing to do is to admit them in as small doses as possible, while avoiding non-microbial disturbances of the gut, so as to build up a normal immunity painlessly. In practice this means that one should avoid gastronomic excess during the first few days. Drink the local water, for instance, but in small amounts at first; choose freshly cooked dishes, wash fruit and so on; in a few days you should be able to gorge yourself gluttonously on the local delicacies with no more disastrous consequences than you should reasonably expect in your own home.

We have become side-tracked from our discussion of where pathogenic bacteria go when they are not being pathogenic. With some, then, we know they are carried around by healthy people who have become immune. With a killer disease such as typhoid, immune carriers can be extremely dangerous and anti-social. The case of 'typhoid Mary' is celebrated in medical history: a New York cook, who, though immune to typhoid herself, managed to infect numerous Americans in the twenties and who, refusing to believe that she was the source of the trouble, insisted on returning to her former trade under assumed names, with disastrous results. She was at large for twenty-three years after her recognition as a typhoid carrier, but was eventually detained. Nowadays, with the aid of antibiotics, carriers of typhoid can be cured, but even this is a long and tedious process, most unwelcome to the unfortunate carrier, who feels perfectly well throughout.

In some instances the reservoirs of disease are not men but animals. *Brucella abortus*, which causes undulant fever in man, is a pathogen of cattle, and *Pasteurella tularense*, the cause of a rare but highly lethal disease called tularaemia, is endemic among certain rodents (e.g.: ground squirrels in California) and transmitted to man by tick bites. Foot and mouth disease, a virus infection of cattle, may occasionally infect man. Sleeping sickness, an African disease of cattle, is caused by a parasitic protozoon called *Trypanosoma* and is transmitted to man by the bite of the tsetse fly; *Plasmodium*, the protozoon that causes malaria, is by now well known to be transferred from patient to patient by mosquitoes; recently virus diseases, forms of dengue, have been found to be transmitted by mosquitoes, too. Salmonellosis is the general name for intestinal infections related to typhoid that can infect man (paratyphoid is a disease of this kind); the reservoir of infection is cattle and, sometimes, ducks, and transmission of disease may take place by way of infected milk or eggs respectively. I think the widespread belief that ducks' eggs should only be used for baking arises from the fact that cases of paratyphoid-like diseases have been traced to them. The risk is, in fact, extremely small.

Rodents such as mice and rats can harbour and transmit microbes that cause gastro-enteritis, and the association of rats with bubonic plague (caused by the bacterium *Pasteurella pestis*) is now a matter of history. In 1665 London suffered from the Great Plague, during which the bulk of its population died of the Black Death – the medieval name for bubonic plague. The nursery rhyme *Ring-a-ring o' roses* originated then, enshrining the folk-medicine myth that a posy of aromatic herbs and flowers, by disguising the stench of death and decay, somehow protected against the plague. In fact, rats only carry plague from place to place; the infective agents are rat fleas, which transmit the disease from infected rodents to man. Even today bubonic plague persists in parts of Asia and, at the time of writing, it is becoming serious in Viet Nam, with over 2,000 cases diagnosed in South Viet Nam in the first six months of 1965. War, strife and the plague go together: in 1947, 57,000 people died of plague in one Indian state during upheavals following on independence.

Though animals, insects and carriers can act as reservoirs of infection in many instances, a number of other diseases cannot be accounted for in this way. Venereal diseases, virus infections such as the common cold, poliomyelitis, influenza and so on, seem to have no clear origin or reservoir. In these cases it is probable that, in ordinary communities, there are at all times a number of people with clinical infections who act as reservoirs of disease. There is reason to believe that syphilis, a venereal disease caused by a curly bacterium or spirochaete, was unknown in Europe until Columbus's crew brought it back from Haiti in the late fifteenth century. It remained unknown among the South Sea Islanders until the visit of the Endeavour, captained by Captain Cook, in 1769. The disease is only, or almost only, transmitted by sexual intercourse and, having been introduced to Polynesia by the Europeans, it rapidly became endemic in that part of the world, with the ghastly degenerative consequences, both physical and mental, that characterize its later stages. The common cold, too, is probably kept in circulation by persons who contract mild infections during the summer and, in special environments, it can die out altogether. Persons who spend a year or two in the Antarctic research stations usually cease having colds within a few weeks, despite the climate, but the arrival of a supply ship can trigger off a new round of colds throughout the whole community; the Islanders of Tristan da Cunha proved remarkably susceptible to colds and bronchial disorders after their transfer to Britain in 1961 when their local volcano became over-active. This probably contributed as much as beat music and the stresses of our society to their understandable desire to return to their island.

The reserves of infective microbes provided by any densely populated society are quite dismaying when one considers the virus diseases. One can recognize the influenza virus, for example, by the kind of immune reaction that patients who have suffered from it develop, and over the last thirty years it has become clear that not one type, but a considerable variety, of viruses cause respiratory diseases ranging from a mild cold to influenza. Moreover, in studying these viruses, many others have been found that seem to cause no disease. The common cold is a subject dear to the hearts of most of us, particularly in winter, so I shall attempt some indication of the complexity of the problem involved.

The throat can harbour a great number of viruses, which fall into three main groups. 'Adenoviruses', particularly prevalent in the tonsils, can cause sore throats, and at the last count (late 1965) twenty-eight different types were known. In the mucus normally coating the tissue of the nose and throat are found 'myxoviruses', viruses that may be recognized relatively easily in the laboratory because they cause blood cells to clump; among them are the influenza and mumps viruses, as well as organisms that cause mild, influenza-like diseases. Then there are innumerable types of very small virus that have been called 'picornaviruses' and a sub-group of these, the 'rhinoviruses' includes some of the causative organisms of the common cold. Unhappily there are at least thirty types of rhinovirus. A second group of picornaviruses is the enteroviruses, also found in the throat but distinguished by being found in the intestinal tract as well. Some of these cause sore throats and chest infections (e.g.: the thirty known types of Coxsackie virus, named after the town of Coxsackie, U.S.A.); others, the echoviruses, either cause respiratory infections or seem to have no harmful function at all. One is forced to the conclusion that, among viruses, there exists an enormous variety of types of which only a few are pathogenic but that, unlike the larger microbes where one kind of organism generally causes one kind of disease, many different types of viruses can cause similar diseases. This conclusion is rather depressing from the point of view of developing immune reactions: if there are thirty kinds of common cold one can have, and we know that immunity to colds does not last long, what prospect is there for control of this trivial scourge? No doubt an answer will be found, but the reason why progress is slow should now be fairly obvious.

Why do microbes grow in the throat, intestines, or wherever we find them? In general, we do not know the answer to this question, but there are one or two instances in which we do. We mentioned earlier the bacterium *Brucella abortus*, which can cause undulant fever in man. This microbe, however, more usually causes contagious abortion in cattle, a disease in which the pregnant cow aborts a stillborn calf. When this happens the *Brucella* is found to inhabit almost exclusively the placenta, the organ attaching the embryo calf to its mother's uterus; the rest of the cow, and the calf, is relatively free from the pathogen. A few years ago Professor Harry Smith and his colleagues discovered the reason for this. *Brucella*, normally, requires a number of vitamins and such trace materials in order to grow properly, and among these is a sugar-like substance called erythritol. Erythritol is fairly rare in animal tissues but, for reasons that we do not wholly understand, it is plentiful in the calf's placenta. Hence the infection flourishes there but not elsewhere, and, since the placenta is, as it were, the embryo's life-line, it dies, and duly the mother's uterus expels it.

The reason for the action of *Brucella* in contagious abortion is a particularly clear example of what is called the specificity of infections: the fact that microbial diseases are often localized. By injecting erythritol artificially into experimental animals, for example, Professor Smith and his colleagues were able to induce a generalized brucellosis. Microbes grow in a special location, and perhaps cause disease, because some nutrient they need can be found only there, or because something they dislike is absent. Another example of the former case is *Corynebacterium renale*, which causes kidney disease in cattle. It grows only in kidneys because it has a particular affinity for urea which, as a component of urine, is primarily concentrated in the kidney. An example of the latter case, where microbes flourish because something they dislike is absent, is gas gangrene, a putrefactive disease of wounds that can occur after serious injury. The microbe responsible, *Clostridium welchii*, is fairly common in polluted waters and soils, but is normally harmless because it is an anaerobe: it does not grow if air is present (see Chapter 2). However, it forms spores which survive in air. Wounded tissue usually has its blood supply interfered with, if only because the small blood vessels are damaged and inflammation and swelling tends to squeeze them tight so that the flow of blood is restricted. Consequently the supply of oxygen brought by the blood to wounded tissue may be low and, if the wound is extensive, conditions in the damaged tissue may become quite anaerobic. If, now, spores of *Clostridium welchii* have got in accidentally from external contamination, they find the situation much to their liking and grow, producing incidentally a substance (a 'toxin') which is highly poisonous to tissue and which extends the area of damage rapidly. A curious development of this principle – the ability of normally harmless anaerobes to grow in tissue that is deficient in oxygen – has been made use of in the treatment of cancer. According to a report published in 1966, cancerous tissue can be deficient in oxygen because it grows relatively rapidly, and regression can be induced by deliberately infecting certain cancers with the normally harmless *Clostridium butyricum*. The 'cure' is apparently incomplete and impermanent at present.

In gangrene the microbe is what one might call an 'unintentional' pathogen: the fact that a product of the microbe's growth is toxic to the host is unfortunate for him but irrelevant to the microbe, which is normally non-parasitic and, so to speak, uninterested in finding a host. Tetanus, caused by *Clostridium tetani*, has a similar origin: a soil clostridium grows in wounded tissue because it becomes anaerobic and, quite incidentally, forms the powerful poison that causes lockjaw. In this case the patient will die by the time the symptoms of tetanus are detectable, which is why anyone suffering a deep wound in country or farmyard areas should immediately have prophylactic treatment against tetanus unless they have been properly immunized already – as most country children are these days.

An extreme case of this kind is the 'disease' known as botulism.

Here the microbe, an anaerobe called *Clostridium botulinum*, does not grow in the host at all: it grows in infected canned or preserved meat or fish. But in growing it produces a toxin which is one of the most powerful poisons known to man, which rapidly kills anyone who eats the food. The organism itself does not grow at all when eaten. Fortunately modern methods of food preservation are such that botulism is extremely rare, otherwise we should all have to be immunized against botulinus toxin.

We have talked glibly about the body's defence mechanisms against microbes and about immunity to infection. What does this mean? The answer is fairly complex; in fact the body has at least three lines of defence. The first is an enzyme called lysozyme, which is found in saliva, tears and nose mucus, and has the property of dissolving many bacteria. The body's second line of defence is based on the fact that the blood contains certain white corpuscles (leucocytes) which are rather like domesticated protozoa and live in the blood stream. Some of them, known as phagocytes, actually eat up and digest any extraneous microbes that get in. If a slight wound occurs the damaged tissue causes these phagocytes to congregate near the site of damage and thus be ready to forestall infection. The body also has a system of cells, centred on the liver, called the reticulo-endothelial system, from which it can generate reserves of phagocytes if need be.

This is all very well, but a bacterial infection of the blood, for example, once well established, involves billions upon billions of microbes, far more than the phagocytes could possibly cope with. How, in such circumstances, does the body cope? The short answer is, of course, that it does not, at least at first. Massive microbial growth only occurs if the body's initial defences have been broken down, and then one is very ill and, if the bacteria produce particularly nasty toxins, one may die. If one recovers, the reason is that the third defence mechanism has been successful: the body has made certain proteins called antibodies which, dissolved in the blood stream, react with the invading microbes and cause them to coagulate in lumps. In this condition they do less harm and are more easily ingested by the phagocytes. The serum of the blood is now immune to the particular microbe and this immunity can be retained, sometimes only for a few months, sometimes for many years, even a whole lifetime. Colds and influenza, for example, seem to generate rather short-lived immunities; mumps, measles and such childhood ailments seem to cause lifelong immunity. Immunity is very specific: immunity to a virus such as that of mumps confers no immunity at all to that of poliomyelitis, though both diseases are due to myxoviruses. One of the few exceptions to this is the cross-immunity that exists between cow-pox and smallpox: vaccination is in fact the practice of deliberately infecting people with the almost harmless cow-pox virus, to which they develop immunity and which also renders them resistant to the far more dangerous smallpox. 'B.C.G.' vaccination against tuberculosis makes use of a live but harmless culture of the tubercle bacillus to induce immunity against natural, virulent tuberculosis; the Sabin poliomyelitis vaccine is a live, non-virulent strain of the virus. But generally the medical profession, quite reasonably, prefers to induce immunity to disease by injecting microbes that have been killed in such a way that they can still provoke the immune reaction. Injections against bacterial diseases such as typhoid or diphtheria are of this kind.

Immunity can be developed against the toxins formed by microbes as well as against the microbes themselves, and a serum that has developed such an immunity is said to contain 'anti-toxins' or to be an 'anti-serum' against such a toxin. Anti-sera against tetanus and botulism are induced in horses and used in emergencies where there is a risk of these diseases; in such cases the patient acquires no permanent immunity to the disease, but in an emergency this does not matter.

Diseases such as mumps, measles and influenza have no re-liable anti-sera as yet but, since most of the population is immune to these diseases most of the time, pooled sera from numbers of people will, if injected into a sufferer, alleviate the disease to a large extent by providing partial immunity. This is the logic of the use of γ-globulin, a form of pooled serum obtainable from blood banks, to treat such diseases in patients (such as adults with mumps) where it could be dangerous to let the disease take its natural course.

The specificity of immune reactions is extremely valuable to the microbiologist and, in fact, sometimes provides him with the only available method of recognizing organisms. In 1964 there was a frightful outbreak of typhoid in Aberdeen, apparently because, when some infected canned corned beef had been cut on a mechanical slicer, the slicer had become infected and contaminated other cooked meat that was sliced on it. As a result, the organisms became spread widely among the customers of one particular food store, causing an explosive epidemic that reached over 400 cases before it was contained. The whole story was a fantastic sequence of mishaps: it seems almost unbelievable, for example, that the original beef could have been as heavily infected as it was, yet not have been obviously 'bad', but later experiments, in which tins of meat were deliberately infected with typhoid bacteria alone, looked perfectly wholesome for three months. The manner in which the source of infection, a cooked-meat counter, was tracked down was also an impressive piece of detective work. (In one family, for example, everyone was infected except one person who, it transpired, hated corned beef and had eaten none). But most impressive to the layman was the identification of the infective organism as a South American strain, and the consequent discovery that the original reason for infection of the beef was failure to use chlorinated water to cool the cans at the original South American factory. This identification was done by means of anti-sera: different strains of typhoid bacteria (*Salmonella typhi*) generate appreciably different antibodies, and a collection of anti-sera to various known strains is kept at the Government's Enteric Reference Laboratory in North London. Once a culture from the Aberdeen outbreak was available, its identification as a South American strain was a matter of routine. The way in which microbes react with anti-sera, and the sort of anti-bodies they generate, is called by microbiologists their 'antigenic pattern', and collections of anti-sera to both medical and non-medical bacteria exist which are used entirely for identifying and typing various microbes. The antigenic pattern of a strain of microbe may be said to have something of the quality of a fingerprint in man for identification: if one has it on a file somewhere, the chances of recognizing the culprit are extremely high.

Once the source of the Aberdeen typhoid outbreak was tracked down, the means by which it spread was obvious. People actually ate the bacteria along with cold meats which had become contaminated by the slicer. Once the organisms got inside the patients, they multiplied and the disease took its normal course, leading to fever, vomiting, diarrhoea and so on.

Not all diseases are spread in so clear-cut a fashion. Smallpox, for instance, has been eliminated from Britain by almost universal vaccination at a young age, but it is re-introduced accidentally now and again, usually by visitors from the Far East who may be incubating the disease when they arrive. Though it is known to be transferred from patient to patient by physical contact – to be contagious – it also spreads in an unpredictable way without contact. Diseases that do this are called infectious diseases, and with smallpox the manner in which it gets around is so random and haphazard that we have no clue to the way in which it spreads. Poliomyelitis is rather similar in its behaviour: there seems to be a tendency to contract the disease, at least in the temperate countries of the northern hemisphere, during late summer and autumn, and quite frequently only one person in a family or group will get it, though all have, as far as one knows, been equally exposed to infection. In the case of poliomyelitis the route of infection is still unknown, but it seems likely that the virus is air-borne, floating around on dried droplets of breath, saliva or other body exudates. Colds and influenza are certainly spread in this manner, and are highly infectious. One well-aimed sneeze from a snuffly baby, as is well known, can lay low a whole group of admiring adults, and it seems very likely that dried mucus from a cold, preserved in a pocket handkerchief, can remain infectious for a long time and can even re-infect the original sufferer. Many families know well that, in a bad winter, they can keep what seems to be the same infection travelling round from person to person from November to April, becoming, to their friends and relatives, a snivelling group of red-nosed horrors. Yet when the Common Cold Research Unit at Salisbury tries to reproduce this sort of dissemination in laboratory conditions, they find it very difficult. Does a family really keep the same cold running all winter? Or do they just become unusually susceptible to various colds that are doing the rounds? We do not yet know, but until we do, it is sensible to switch to disposable paper handkerchiefs as soon as a cold develops, and to BURN them when used: not to put them in litter bins, waste-paper baskets and so on.

Many bacterial and most virus diseases are infectious. The protein of mucus, present in cough or sneeze droplets, preserves the microbes from the lethal effects of drying. Most streptococcal throat infections are spread this way. But another important route of infection is through the intestinal tract, and an understanding of why this is so reveals some disconcerting truths about our social and domestic behaviour even in this relatively hygienic age.

Most people, nowadays, cover their mouths when they cough or sneeze into a handkerchief, and they know why they do this: to protect others from the infectious aerosol of droplets that a cough or sneeze generates. Fewer people, though still a great number, understand that they must wash their hands when they have used the toilet. Toilet paper, after all, is permeable to bacteria, and excrement, not to put too fine a point on it, is a pullulating mass of bacteria and viruses, many of which are potentially pathogenic. Few people realize, however, that when a used toilet is flushed, a turbulence and spray of water and excrement is generated comparable to a sneeze: in any toilet one can isolate faecal clostridia and streptococci from the ceiling, walls and door handle as well as around and beneath the seat. British water closets certainly generate such infectious aerosols; it is probable that the vortex type favoured in the U.S.A., depending on a swirl rather than a splash to flush the closet, is less generous in the matter of dispersing faecal microbes around the room. Moreover, most public, and domestic, lavatory suites are designed with the wash-hand basin in a separate room from the toilet, which is convenient if two people wish to use the two facilities at the same time, but which means that the occupant of the W.C. must use an unwashed hand to operate the flushing system and open the door. The idea that washing facilities should always be available in the same room as the W.C. is penetrating only very slowly to this country, though it is realized fairly widely in the U.S.A. and Scandinavia. Incidentally, it is in Sweden that I have encountered the only sensibly-designed toilet paper: a 2-ply roll of which one ply, the outside, was the traditional British type, smooth, impermeable (but relatively useless for its main purpose), and the inner ply was the soft, absorbent type which is now increasingly popular because of its good wiping properties, though it is extremely permeable to microbes. This combination, used the right way round, is probably the most hygienic material available for European practice.

While we are on these important if unsavoury matters, let us consider the average gentleman's public urinal. Urine is, in fact, normally a sterile fluid. Unless one has a kidney or urethral infection there are no bacteria in fresh urine. The great Lord Lister, the pioneer of elementary hygiene in surgery and hospital practice, used fresh urine as a readily available sterile fluid in some of his crucial experiments on the spread of airborne bacteria. A urinal, however, is far from sterile: it is a culture of bacteria especially rich in types capable of growing in urine and of releasing ammonia from the urea therein. The customary design of urinals is such as to ensure a generous splash-back of these bacteria on to the shoes and trouser-legs of anyone using them, again contributing to the spread of both pathogenic and harmless bacteria. The cup type of urinal, by reducing the splash, is to be preferred from the point of view of hygiene.

The British are a dirty nation, as anyone who has travelled northwards or westwards knows. (But those who travel south or east reach an opposite conclusion, and we should be grateful that, despite our national reputation for dirtiness, our disposition to litter public places and foul our public conveniences, we nevertheless reach a high level of hygiene by world standards.) Other nations survive in apparent good health; if we spray ourselves regularly with a fine mist of faeces, does it really matter? Are we not thereby building up an immunity to infections to which we would otherwise succumb? The answer, of course, is that one can certainly be too fussy about these things. Some exposure to infection is essential for the acquirement of immunity. But countries with lower hygienic standards than ours still have diseases such as typhoid, dysentery and cholera endemic among their populations, and it is mainly due to our fairly elementary standards of hygiene that we are now free of these scourges. But, with the increasing freedom of travel among nations, diseases of this kind are carried anew with greater and greater ease to parts of the world that had eliminated them. It would probably be impracticable, at least during this century, to eliminate cross contamination by faecal microbes altogether, but some common sense in the design and use of lavatory facilities is essential if Britain is to preserve its freedom from the nastier infections that may spread from the intestinal tract.

Typhoid, cholera and dysentery reach epidemic proportions when drinking water becomes contaminated with faecal organisms, and this is why public health authorities spend so much effort observing the faecal pollutions of potential water supplies. In fact, water-borne diseases are rare in Britain, and the main routes of cross infection are probably air-borne droplets of breath, contamination of foodstuffs by careless hygiene in handling (notices saying NOW WASH YOUR HANDS are still mandatory in the staff lavatories of the catering industry) and carelessness in day-to-day hygiene. Cracked tea-cups harbour mouth pathogens in the cracks, an infected cut finger can spread pathogenic micrococci on prepared food and cause food poisoning; even that domestic stand-by, the drying-up cloth, can spread more bacteria on a newly washed plate or glass than the detergent removed. Fortunately they are mostly harmless, or the market for washing-up machines would be better than it is.

Certain diseases, notably skin diseases, are contagious: they only spread by contact between the infected part on one patient and the susceptible part of another. The disease called ringworm, due to various fungi collectively known as *Microsporon*, is an example of this kind, and so is the common athlete's foot. Perhaps the most socially troublesome of the contagious diseases are the venereal diseases, which infect the genital organs and which are transmitted during sexual intercourse. Gonorrhoea ('clap' in vernacular) is a painful disease caused by a fragile coccus of the *Neisseria* group and can be cured fairly readily by modern chemotherapy, but during certain campaigns towards the end of the Second World War so much do-it-yourself therapy was practised by the troops that drug-resistant strains of *Neisseria* emerged and, had not new drugs effective against the resistant microbes been developed, a critical situation could have arisen. Syphilis ('pox' in vernacular) caused by a spirochaete *Treponema pallidum*, is a more drastic disease, because it is less easily detected and, if it proceeds unchecked, leads to physical, nervous and mental deterioration of a kind that cannot be cured. We saw earlier how it was introduced into the South Sea Islands by Europeans in the eighteenth century; it has been endemic there for generations, often retarding the mental and physical development of the population and providing a serious trap for visitors who, from Gauguin onwards, enter with too great enthusiasm into the free sexual *mores* of such societies. Venereal diseases can be cured if they are detected in time, but their involvement in the sexual conventions and taboos of Western societies makes them a particularly intractable problem of social hygiene. The type of person likely to contract a venereal infection is, at least in Western society, not likely to be very responsible about noticing the disease in its early stages, about persisting with treatment and avoiding passing it on. Therefore foci of infection persist, notably in ports or areas with a considerable depressed or migrant population, and such foci can be the despair of social workers, doctors and medical officers of health. Moreover, the last decade or two has been a period in which the sexual, religious and social tenets of Western society have been questioned by adolescents rather as an earlier generation questioned its political assumptions in the twenties and thirties of this century. No doubt the upshot of the developing 'new morality' will ultimately be constructive, but an immediate consequence has been a marked increase in sexual permissiveness and hence in the spread of venereal diseases among adolescents. Patients are now coming from ordinary middle-class families here, in the U.S.A. and in Scandinavia. Whether the 'new morality' is to be deplored or encouraged is outside the scope of this book; here we can only hope that whatever advances in enlightenment it may bring, education in sexual hygiene will be among them.

The spread of infectious disease is normally an accidental process, though deliberate transfer of infection is sometimes encouraged. German measles (rubella) is a mild disease in childhood, but if it is contracted by an adult woman in the early stages of pregnancy it can have a teratogenic effect: it can cause deformity in the foetus. Therefore the parents of young children sometimes encourage them to play with infected playmates in the hope that they will get the disease over. I have done this myself. (My daughters remained doggedly healthy, developing the disease at an extremely inconvenient time many months later.) Others have encouraged mumps in this way, because the disease can have drastic effects on adults but is rarely serious in children. (I did not encourage mumps; they nevertheless caught it and duly infected me . . . .) But though the deliberate spread of disease among men has never been practised on a large scale, it has not escaped military minds as a possible weapon in warfare. Bubonic plague, due to the bacterium *Pasteurella pestis*, decimated populations spontaneously in the Middle Ages as we saw earlier, and the deliberate spread of comparable pestilence among an enemy could be an effective and demoralizing form of attack which would leave their industry and wealth relatively undamaged. An example is the atrocity story told of the early American pioneers, who are alleged to have sold bankets infected with smallpox to the Red Indians, knowing well that they had no natural immunity to the scourge. Biological warfare, as the process is called today, would require a highly infectious microbe, rapid and serious in its action, against which the home troops and civilian population could be immunized. It would most probably be a virus because, as we shall see later, most bacterial infections are susceptible to drugs and antibiotics whereas viruses in general are not. It would be spread as an aerosol, because it would thus reach more people and be less easily controllable than if food or water were infected or if infected pests such as insects or rats were distributed. It would

67

be cheap: a modest laboratory and the necessary know-how is all that would be needed to produce the weapon (though to deliver it is another problem altogether).

One can argue that, in these days of atomic holocaust, biological warfare is a relatively humane form of warfare. For, however lethal the agent developed, there would still be a sporting chance that some representatives of mankind would survive, simply because there has not been a disease yet to which a few members of the population do not have a powerful resistance. This is not necessarily true of atomic warfare, which could in principle make the planet uninhabitable by men and higher organisms for years and even decades. But, in practice, it is not at all a likely weapon to be used. The problems of preparing enough of the microbe, of immunizing one's own population and then distributing it in such a fashion that the aerosol travelled the right way, are enormous, even given the massive resources that modern military organizations can command. A weapon that returns like a boomerang if the wind changes does not really commend itself to the military mind; moreover, as we shall see shortly, most airborne microbes are killed by sunlight, so that effective biological warfare would probably only be practicable during the hours of darkness.

In my opinion biological agents, along with death rays, laser beams, neutron bombs and so on, belong more to the realms of science fiction than to practical warfare. But my opinion is not widely shared and the prospects of such weapons are certainly dismaying. The fount of human imbecility seems inexhaustible, so Governments are probably right to foster germ warfare laboratories, so long as scientists can be persuaded to work in them.

We mentioned just now that aerosols of microbes are killed by sunlight, and this brings us to the question of why diseases are seasonal. There are many answers to this question: one's natural resistance depends on one's nutritional status, on what other stresses one is putting up with (mental stress included), but such laboratory tests as have been conducted have provided very little evidence to support the popular view that damp and cold enhance one's susceptibility to disease. Instead it seems more likely that a damp atmosphere prolongs the life of microbes in an aerosol, and so does a low degree of illumination; consequently, in winter, when the air is humid and the hours of daylight are short, persons living in communities get a heavier dose of live, infective organisms at all times and thus stand a greater chance of catching disease. Sunlight kills most pathogenic microbes quite rapidly at ordinary temperatures when they are airborne in partly dried droplets (though spores are killed much more slowly) and the main lethal effect is due to the ultra-violet component of solar radiation. Ultra-violet lamps can be used indoors to sterilize the air in operating theatres, pharmaceutical and microbiological laboratories. Even in diffuse daylight there is an appreciable amount of light of the effective wavelengths, though scarcely any penetrates glass in these conditions. Certain bacteria exist which are resistant to the sterilizing effect of daylight – they are, generally speaking, rich in the pigment carotene, which is also present in plants and protects the delicate chlorophyll pigment of leaves against damage by light – but happily they are not ordinarily pathogenic. As far as infective microbes are concerned, they mostly do not form spores, so the open air in daylight is a fairly safe place even in winter. Snow and sunshine, with its high incidence of ultra-violet radiation, is most hygienic. No doubt this is the reason why a hard but sunny winter seems to entrain fewer respiratory infections than the typical British winter, cold, wet and grey.

Dryness, as we mentioned earlier, also hastens the death of air-borne microbes. Though they survive for a while in dry conditions, they die off more rapidly than if the relative humidity is high. An interesting factor in the spread of infection in crowded communities is electric discharge. The London Underground railway, particularly in winter, might be expected to be a hot-bed of all possible diseases, with literally millions of people crowded into it, twice daily, throughout the year. In fact it is not so. The air in the average tube system is remarkably free of live microbes, and the reason seems to be that the frequent electric discharges produced by the trains generate ozone and oxides of nitrogen, both of which are quite good aerial disinfectants. The late Professor D. D. Woods, a most distinguished chemical microbiologist, used to relate how, in the early days of his career, he was astonished to find the air in his laboratory in a London hospital was virtually sterile *even with the window open*, when all sorts of spores and airborne microbes could be expected to drift in. The reason, he discovered, was that his window was close to the main outlet of the ventilation system of the London Underground! So many aspects of urbanization seem to enhance the risk of disease; it is refreshing to encounter one that operates the other way. And it is interesting to speculate that, should the metropolitan underground transport system ever desert electricity for another power source, a consequence might be an epidemic of respiratory infections unparalleled even in these bronchitic islands.

We have discussed, so far, where the microbes of disease come from, why, as far as we know, they cause diseases, how they are transmitted and how our natural defences act against them. In this chapter the case against the microbe has so far been very strong, and before we turn to the subject of chemotherapy, of how we can aid our natural defences in coping with infectious microbes, we ought perhaps to say a word about the harmless microbes that abound in civilized communities. The skin, for example, is populated by the completely harmless white staphylococcus mentioned earlier in this chapter, and a brisk interchange of this microbe occurs among people all the time. Micrococci live in the normal nose and throat, and by serological methods it is possible to distinguish types and show that, on the whole, people retain their personal strains for many years. One is, as it were, adopted by a strain of micrococcus in early life which, in some completely mysterious way, repels other people's strains. The mouth has a flora of lactobacilli, a milk bacterium which we shall meet again in Chapter 5, together with a fearsome-looking spirochaete (*Leptospira buccalis*) which is apparently quite harmless. On these feed a protozoon, *Entamoeba gingivalis*, which is probably beneficial in keeping the microbial population within bounds. The film that develops on the normal teeth and gums, and which is removed when one cleans one's teeth in the morning, consists entirely of microbes. Under the microscope it has a most alarming appearance to the uninitiated – but is entirely fascinating to those who realize that this busy little microcosm is just as it ought to be.

Caries, the ordinary form of tooth decay, is due to acids formed by some or all of the mouth bacteria, but, since they form acids whether tooth decay appears or not, caries is probably caused primarily by the host's failure to cope with its normal population of microbes rather than by the appearance of new pathogenic types. Fluoride deficiency, particularly in early life, undermines the resistance of the teeth to the acids produced by mouth microbes; fluoride is mainly obtained from drinking water and most water supplies in Britain are now known to be deficient in fluoride. It is a tragedy that, at the time of writing, handfuls of faddists throughout the country are ruining the next generation's teeth by opposing fluoridation of local water supplies.

We shall see in Chapter 5 how the bacteria normally present in our intestines contribute in important ways to our nutrition; these are probably the most useful of the microbes that habitually live with us. It is probable, as we saw earlier in this chapter, that there are numerous harmless viruses in the intestinal tract. The urethral tract should be sterile, but the vagina in females normally contains micrococci living harmlessly in its exudates. Sweaty areas, such as under the arms or between the toes, tend to be richer in microbes and the characteristic 'stale' smell of sweat is due to microbial action on sweat; some of the components of sweat have an anti-microbial action and help to keep the microbes down but they are not wholly effective. Deodorants do not in fact deodorize; they contain disinfectants that prevent the development of microbes that would cause the odour. Babies develop nappy rash, not because urine is intrinsically harsh to their skin, but because bacteria grow in the wet nappy and form ammonia from the urea of urine. It is the ammonia that causes the rash, being a strong skin irritant. We live, in fact, with great numbers of personal microbes; they are ordinarily harmless and only become a nuisance if we behave in an unhygienic manner.

With that genuflection, as it were, to the harmless and even desirable microbes that live with us, we shall return to the pathogens and the question of how the natural defences against microbial invasion can be aided.

The belief that specific substances exist that will cure disease has existed from time immemorial. The beneficial effects of herbal extracts, crushed oyster shells and alcoholic drinks on fevers and distempers, though often imaginary, form part of a strong tradition of folk medicine that persists to this day. In the seventeenth and eighteenth centuries, cookery books would contain as many recipes for dishes that would cure disease as for dishes of gastronomic interest; I encountered a particularly unpleasing example some years ago in a seventeenth-century recipe book: it recommended snail water, the liquor obtained from prolonged steepage of live snails in water, as a certain cure for phthisis (tuberculosis). Some of these folk-medicine cures undoubtedly had beneficial effects, but little logic underlay the discovery and prescription of such remedies until the end of the nineteenth century. At this time the germ theory of disease was widely accepted, structural organic chemistry was advancing with incredible speed, and the stage was set for the emergence of *chemotherapy*, the science of controlling disease by specific chemicals. Paul Ehrlich, a German, was probably the father of chemotherapy; his most spectacular discovery, in 1910, was the drug 'salvarsan', or 'Ehrlich 606' which proved very active against syphilis. Previously, the only cure for this disease, and a most risky and uncertain one it was, was to feed the patient with poisonous derivatives of mercury. If the patient did not die, there was a fair chance that the spirochaetes would, and that he would be cured. A similar situation arose in the treatment of trypanosomiasis ('sleeping sickness', caused by a protozoon) with arsenical compounds, so Ehrlich had set about preparing, quite deliberately, an organic material containing arsenic that would remain active against the trypanosomes yet be less lethal to men. Salvarsan, which chemists represent by the formula:

was the 606th compound to be investigated; it was not very active in trypanosomiasis but proved most effective against syphilis.

Ehrlich also noted that dyes, which bacteriologists were using to render these microbes visible under the microscope, were taken up very strongly by bacteria. If the dyes could be made poisonous, could they not be used to cure microbial diseases in the living patient? Acriflavine, a yellow dye that is still used for treating superficial wounds and skin conditions, was introduced by Ehrlich; it is a powerful bactericide but is too poisonous for internal use. Other dyes such as methylene blue proved to have some microbicidal action (they are still used occasionally) but were still rather toxic. Domagk, in 1935, made the most spectacular advance in this direction by obtaining the first chemotherapeutic agent that was strongly active against bacteria, Prontosil:

A certain ingenuity went into the development of prontosil, because, though it has the chemical structure of a dye, it is not in fact coloured. Domagk and his colleagues had realized that the property of being strongly absorbed by microbes was the important chemotherapeutic factor, not the property of being coloured. This ingenuity proved somewhat misplaced when it was found that Prontosil broke down in the patients' liver to sulphanilamide:

73

a compound which is nothing like a dye, but which was just as active as Prontosil. This discovery released the flood-gates, as it were, leading to the development of a variety of exceedingly potent anti-bacterial drugs called the sulphonamides in English (sulfa-drugs in American). These have the general formula:

$$RNH{\cdot}SO_2 \text{—} \hexagon \text{—} NH_2$$

where R can be any of some two or three hundred atomic group-ings, depending on the particular properties required. They could be 'tailor-made' in chemical laboratories so as to stay in the gut or be absorbed in the blood stream; they were often more active against microbes than the original Prontosil; many of them were less poisonous to humans than the original materials.

Today it is difficult to recall the impact the sulphonamides made in 1935–7. Pneumonia, which had been the major killing disease in Britain during the twentieth century, abruptly became almost trivial. Puerperal fever, a systemic infection due to the bacterium *Streptococcus pyogenes*, which was often contracted during childbirth, showed a dramatic drop in incidence and mortality. The sulphonamides were indeed a triumph for the chemotherapist.

Yet, for the scientist, there was this small, niggling query. They were nothing like dyes. Why, then, were they so marvellous? The answer, found by D. D. Woods working in Sir Paul Fildes's laboratories in the 1940s, was quite unexpected. Woods found that certain materials, such as serum, contained a substance that made bacteria immune to the sulphonamides, and eventually he isolated it. It proved to be a simple compound called *para*-amino benzoic acid:

$$HOOC \text{—} \hexagon \text{—} NH_2$$

Now, a peculiarity of the effect of p-AB (which we shall call it for short) was that, if there was only a little sulphonamide present, only a little p-AB was needed to neutralize its effect on bacteria, but if a lot of the drug was present, a lot of p-AB was needed. A sort of competition seemed to exist, as far as the microbes were concerned, between p-AB and the drug. Woods also noticed that the formula of p-AB was rather like that general one we have written for the sulphonamides, and he proposed the following hypothesis to explain the situation. If all microbes are assumed to need p-AB in order to grow, perhaps sulphonamides seem so like p-AB to the microbes that they try to use them instead, and thus fail to grow. This theory has two obvious consequences. First, that sulphonamides would be found not to kill microbes, but just to prevent them growing; secondly, that sooner or later some microbe might be found that would be unable to make the p-AB it needed and would require to be provided with it for growth. In the second instance, p-AB would turn out to be a vitamin for some microbe.

Both of these deductions proved brilliantly correct. Sulphonamides do not kill bacteria: in the infected patient they stop their growth and give the body's defence mechanisms time to deal with them. And several microbes are now known that require p-AB as a vitamin. The discovery of p-AB as a vitamin led to enormous advances in both microbial and general biochemistry, stretching into realms of biosynthetic chemistry that we cannot possibly deal with here. From the medical point of view it opened a new, rational approach to chemotherapy: if one knew the sort of vitamins and growth factors needed by microbes, one could make chemicals in the laboratory that were rather like them (called in laboratory jargon 'structural analogues') and hope they would inhibit microbial growth and thus be valuable chemotherapeutic agents.

This hypothesis proved abundantly true in most respects. The forties and early fifties were a period of intensive research into microbial nutrition; vitamins and vitamin-like compounds were discovered and isolated, structural analogues prepared and, in test-tube experiments, these frequently proved to inhibit microbial growth in the competitive manner that the sulphonamides showed. It is ironical to have to record that not one of the drugs made was of practical chemotherapeutic value. They were too toxic to man, or his kidneys eliminated them too well, or his blood and tissues contained too much of the vitamin they were antagonizing, or the infective bacteria did not need the vitamin. One of the few successful drugs made according to the rational approach proved not to obey the rule at all. It arose from studying analogues of vitamin B_2 (riboflavin) which is required by many microbes. By altering analogues in various ways a group of research workers at Imperial Chemical Industries' laboratories ultimately developed a drug, paludrine, which was highly effective against malaria. But by then it had been so much altered that it had no competitive action against B_2 at all.

The next major advance in chemotherapy, really a step back to the early thirties, occurred in quite a different way. Most people are familiar with the story of penicillin: how Fleming recognized it when a stray mould grew in a culture of micrococci and started to dissolve it; how he attempted to isolate the active material, failed and gave up; how Chain, a refugee working at Oxford, took up the problem and succeeded in extracting the material, how it proved fantastically active, more so than any drug known hitherto, and was prepared in milk churns at Oxford; how, because the Second World War was on, development was transferred to the U.S.A. with the ludicrous result that, after the war, the British had to pay patent royalties to use methods of making it developed there; how it became universally available after the war, but its use led to the appearance of penicillin-resistant strains of microbe and penicillin-sensitive patients. This story – or these stories – with their ramifications into politics, personality, vested interest and carelessness, deserve a book to themselves; they cannot detain us here. Penicillin is one of a class of products made by moulds called antibiotics. They have strong anti-bacterial actions and this property is probably of value to moulds in nature, since moulds and bacteria tend to compete for the same types of nutrient.

The discovery, development and success of penicillin led to a burst of research activity on the part of the pharmaceutical industry during which literally millions of moulds, actinomycetes, even bacteria and algae, were screened for anti-microbial activity. A few dozen antibiotics turned up, of which about six are of real value: streptomycin, aureomycin, chloramphenicol, and the tetracycline group. We shall say more about them in Chapter 6; for the purposes of this chapter we shall note that, like sulphonamides, they tend not to kill bacteria but only to stop them growing. Quite how they act is not certain; what seems clear is that they all act in different ways. With penicillin we have a clear indication that it prevents bacteria from making their cell envelope properly.

Here we must say a little more about drug resistance in microbes, which we first discussed in Chapter 2. Microbes can acclimatize themselves to such substances as sulphonamides and antibiotics if they encounter them in small doses. Therefore, when using these drugs in practice, it is important to give as massive a dose as the patient will tolerate right at the start and to sustain a high level throughout the treatment. If a patient relapses, or develops a new infection after treatment with one of these drugs, an entirely different drug should be used lest the infective microbes be resistant to the earlier one. We mentioned earlier the disastrous effect of ill-considered use of sulphonamides to treat gonorrhea during the Second World War. This is the reason why antibiotics and sulphonamides are not, and should not be, made available except on prescription. The sort of penicillin-resistant bacteria that appear in practice, as distinct from in the laboratory, seem to be those that are able to destroy penicillin and, in recent years (as we shall see in Chapter 6), partly synthetic penicillins have been made industrially that are insusceptible to penicillinase, the enzyme that destroys ordinary penicillin. These new products therefore work on the naturally resistant strains so, with this drug, the problem of resistance has receded – for the time being. But among the anti-malarial drugs resistance is again becoming a serious problem. Quinine, the traditional remedy for malaria, has been replaced in general use, since the Second World War, by two synthetic drugs: chloroquine and amodiaquine.

These, unlike quinine, are prophylactics (they protect against the disease) as well as remedies and, for two decades, they proved remarkably successful. Unfortunately, in the mid-1960s, reports have appeared from places as distant from each other as Brazil, Colombia, Malaya, Cambodia and Viet Nam, of infections resistant not only to these drugs but to others like them. The basic reason for this seems to be careless use of the drugs in therapy; now, in some localities, it is becoming necessary to return to the traditional quinine, to which resistance is very rare. Drug-resistance is today one of the focal points of research in chemotherapy.

Nevertheless, chemotherapy, at least in regard to bacterial and protozoal infections, has made dramatic strides in the last few decades. In retrospect it seems something of a comedy of errors – Ehrlich missed the importance of salvarsan for two years because he was concerned with trypanosomiasis, and it was his colleague Hata who realized its value in syphilis; the sulphonamides were developed as dyes, and were successful for the wrong reasons; the 'structural analogue' theory proved perfectly correct but only really useful retrospectively; the best-ever antibiotic, penicillin, was the first one to be discovered. Yet it was one of the most productive comedies of errors in the history of mankind: not only were the resulting advances in medical, biochemical and chemical knowledge quite spectacular, but the bacterial and protozoal diseases have, as a result of chemotherapy, largely come under control. Tuberculosis, pneumonia, typhoid, plague, anthrax, venereal diseases, cholera and so on are all curable, given accurate diagnosis and facilities; even the dreaded leprosy can be controlled. Though these diseases certainly persist in many of the lesser developed parts of the world, they are no longer the scourges they were even thirty years ago.

Our *bêtes noires* are now the virus diseases. Although the 'rational approach' was unproductive, it is still true that sulphonamides and antibiotics act by interfering with the *growth* of microbes. The microbes, in an infection, are growing rapidly whereas their hosts, if they are growing at all, are growing (in a relative sense) minutely slowly. Hence these drugs, though they may act on both host and microbe, influence only the microbe's growth seriously and thus they enable the host to recover. Viruses, however, grow in quite a different way from other microbes. They actually get inside the cells of their hosts and pervert the metabolism of those cells. They cause a defect in the mechanism controlling the cell's own machinery, so that it uses its metabolism to make the wrong thing. Thus, instead of keeping themselves in good repair, the cells make lots more viruses. One can put this point another way: the way a cell functions is controlled by its genetic structure, which means that the precise chemical composition of its genes 'programmes' it for the period of its existence. Genes consist of substances called nucleic acids and so, mainly, do viruses. A virus infection 'programmes' cells to make more viruses and thus the chances of an effective chemotherapy of virus diseases are rather slim, because any effective agent would be equally damaging to the healthy cell. But all hope is not lost: nucleic-acid analogues have been made that were active in practice against smallpox, and the American firm Du Pont de Nemours has produced a chemical of weird structure (admantidine hydrochloride) which is active against a type of Asian flu (type A_2). It seems to prevent absorption of the virus by the host tissue. Clearly there are still possibilities for development along these lines. Mainly, however, it is the natural defences that are our bastion against virus infections, and a pretty soggy sort of bastion they can become during a cold, damp British winter. In the last five or so years scientists have been aware of a substance, interferon, which the cells make when they become infected by a virus and which interferes with the establishment of the viruses in the tissues, but, apart from the fact that it is a protein, its chemical nature is obscure. At the time of writing, it is a promising line of research, but its practical value is, so far, slight.

CHAPTER 4

Interlude: How to Handle Microbes

The time has come, I think, to say something of how all these things are known. So often, in books of this kind, the author tells his readers the results of scientific progress, paints a sort of panorama of present-day knowledge, without giving them any idea of how this progress came about, of how the knowledge was obtained. This, you may say, is just fine: as a lay reader you are prepared to take my authoritative word that everything written in this book is based on sound, well-conceived experiments.

Would that it were! The trouble with science is that its day-to-day aspects are extremely uncertain. Occasionally great and obvious advances in knowledge take place, but generally research and its applications progress by repetitious and tedious experiments, almost always giving negative or useless results, from which, slowly and over a long period, a picture of the behaviour of whatever-it-is the scientist is studying emerges. No scientific finding is 100 per cent certain; the majority of observations that find application are more than 90 per cent certain. Today, living in a society that depends for its existence on a highly developed technology, it is most important that laymen should be able to view critically the results of scientific research – or at least the claims made for them by journalists, scientists and scientific administrators. It would be very surprising, for example, if some of the information I have written in this book is not falsified by recent research before it is published. How, then, is one to judge what is likely to be well-established and what is a little dicey?

The answer, which applies to scientists as much as to laymen, is to develop a feeling for the subject. That may seem a highly unscientific statement, but I make no apology for it, for it is not as unscientific as it sounds. If one knows something of the way in which experiments are done, one can distinguish those that are rigidly precise from those that are merely suggestive. Since scientists make use of both, a knowledge of the sorts of experiments on which a subject is based gives one, in due course, a sort of instinctive understanding of what beliefs are reliable and what should be accepted with reserve, to be modified or abandoned in the light of future experiments.

The whole of microbiology is based on the belief that living matter does not generate itself from non-living matter: that a truly sterile broth, for example, will never go bad if it remains uncontaminated by a microbe. This belief, which was not widely accepted before the late nineteenth century, rests on a number of very simple experiments in which broths were sterilized and left, exposed to air and warmth, in vessels designed so that air-borne microbes could not enter them. Some of John Tyndall's original broths, set up in the late nineteenth century, may still be seen at the Royal Institution off Piccadilly in London. Yet the chances are that life originated spontaneously on this planet at some time, as we shall see in Chapter 10, so the view that spontaneous generation does not now occur does not imply that it never could occur. It implies merely the acceptance of a belief that it is an event of such extreme improbability, in this day and age, that it may be disregarded for the purposes of ordinary scientific research.

The principle that sterilized material will, if suitably protected, remain sterile unless one infects it is basic to microbiology. Microbiologists prepare sterilized broths, sometimes jellified, in which microbes can grow, and infect these with particular strains and species so as to keep them 'pure', which means uncontaminated by other microbes. These are called 'cultures' of microbes, and every now and again a small portion of the population is transferred, or 'sub-cultured', into a new lot of broth or jelly to keep the strain live and multiplying. The compositions of these broths range from a simple solution of a few chemicals, through soups and milk preparations, to most complex brews of blood, meat and vitamin supplements. Whole textbooks have been devoted to their preparation and we shall not discuss details of them here, but there are certain basic principles used to devise such broths that are important. First, however, let me introduce the technical word 'medium', which is used a lot by microbiologists. A medium (plural: media) is an environment, usually a broth or a jelly, in (or on) which microbes are allowed to grow. Most microbes require, in order to grow, a solution containing traces of elements such as iron, magnesium, phosphorus, sodium, potassium, calcium, a source of nitrogen such as an ammonium salt and some kind of carbohydrate food: sugar, for example. A balanced chemical fertilizer mixture of the kind used in horticulture will, for example, make a fine medium for many bacteria, if a little sugar is added, and if such a solution were to be infected with a grain of soil and put in a warm place, a positive menagerie of soil bacteria, mostly little rods called *Pseudomonas*, would rapidly grow. Since they would be using dissolved oxygen to oxidize the sugar, they would rapidly exhaust their supplies of dissolved air, except at the surface of the liquid, so that deep in the culture medium anaerobic bacteria such as *Clostridium* would start growing. One would soon have a horrible, evil-smelling mess, probably bubbling as the anaerobes generated carbon dioxide from the sugar; the microbial population would be very mixed and of little use to anyone who wished to learn something about the types of organism present.

Microbiologists use two general techniques to obtain pure cultures of a single type of microbe. The first is called *enrichment culture*, a procedure that makes use of a *selective medium*. Supposing, for example, one wants some nitrogen-fixing bacteria. One could make up the sugar medium as we have described, but leave out the ammonium salt. In these circumstances, if it were infected with a little soil, only those microbes that could use atmospheric nitrogen could grow, and thus the culture would become rich in nitrogen-fixing bacteria. Once they started growing, of course, some of the nitrogen fixed would become available to other microbes in the soil inoculum, these would start to grow and the population would become pretty mixed. But it would be enriched in nitrogen-fixing bacteria, at least to start with. If one wanted sulphur bacteria, one could leave the ammonium salt in but add sulphur instead of sugar; some ferrous sulphate in place of the sugar would encourage iron bacteria. Instead of changing the composition of the medium one could change its acidity: a weakly acid sugar medium favours the growth of yeasts and moulds rather than bacteria. Or one could exclude air, simply by using a bottle filled to the brim and stopped, and so enrich the medium in anaerobes. (With a sugar medium, however, this is not a very good idea, as clostridia often generate gas and blow the stopper out.) A little sulphate in such a medium enriches the population in sulphate-reducing bacteria; nitrate selects for denitrifying bacteria. Use of a high temperature selects for thermophiles; heat your soil before inoculating the medium and only microbes that form heat-resistant spores will grow.

Obviously the possibilities of enrichment culture are almost limitless; the reader may devise for himself media suitable for enrichment culture of microbes utilizing alcohol, disinfectants, rubber, shoeleather, plastics and so on. Not all the obvious media work, and, correspondingly, one can observe microbes in natural environments that respond to no simple enrichment technique. But, generally speaking, enrichment culture is the primary step used by scientists who are seeking pure cultures of microbes.

Medical microbiologists, however, do not make much use of enrichment culture methods, for the simple reason that their enrichments have been done for them. An infected patient is already an enrichment culture, so that the medical scientist jumps at once, as it were, to the second step: that of isolating a pure strain of the enriched microbes.

Once one has an enriched population or, in other words, has obtained a culture of microbes containing a majority of the organisms one is interested in, how does one get the population pure? The easiest way to do this is to use a jellified medium, and to spread a tiny drop of the enrichment culture over it in such a way that each individual microbe is well separated from its neighbour. When the jellified culture is allowed to grow, each separate microbe will multiply to form a colony of similar microbes, and those colonies that are widely separated will come mainly from the predominant organisms in the enrichment culture. It is then a simple matter to infect a new culture with a fragment of one of those 'pure' colonies and thus obtain a pure culture of microbes.

This is the principle of a process called 'plating'. Microbiologists generally use covered dishes called Petri dishes (after their inventor) containing media set with a gelatinous seaweed extract called agar, for plating cultures; for anaerobes they use tubes of media set with agar. Other procedures, such as micromanipulation, can be used to obtain pure cultures; they all depend on causing single microbes from large populations to form colonies of progeny well separated from their neighbours.

For plating to be successful, not only must the medium be suitable to the microbes in composition, but the medium, glassware and instruments must be sterilized. In addition, the operations must be carried out so as to reduce the possibility of contamination by airborne microbes to a minimum. Such 'aseptic technique', in microbiologists' jargon, requires working conditions to be pretty free of draughts and both media and glassware must be pressure-cooked or sterilized in ovens for some time. Not all media can be pressure cooked, because cooking may decompose their constituents and make them unsuitable for fastidious microbes. In such cases a very fine filter may be used to remove extraneous microbes, or irradiation with γ-rays or ultra-violet light may be used. Sterilization by γ-radiation is used to provide sterile plastic ware for microbiologists, because plastics, though cheap and disposable, rarely stand the temperatures needed for heat sterilization. Pressure cooking, in live steam above the boiling point of water, or baking at high temperatures, may seem rather drastic procedures to eliminate microbes that are mostly killed at temperatures above 50 degrees centigrade, but it is necessary because, as we saw in Chapter 2, the spores of certain microbes can be very heat-resistant. It so happens that the common airborne bacteria include some of the toughest spore-forming types.

Enrichment culture and simple colony isolation will yield pure cultures of most microbes capable of growing on laboratory media, but some microbes are not domesticated so easily. *Mycobacterium leprae*, the bacterium that causes leprosy, has never been grown away from living tissue, and pure cultures of protozoa have often been obtained in association with live bacteria on which they feed. Particularly intransigent in these respects are the viruses, which just have to be grown on living tissue. They can be separated from bacteria and other microbes quite easily: a filter of suitable fineness will let viruses through but hold up all larger microbes. But once filtered, viruses must be provided with living hosts in which to multiply. Tissue cultures, fertile chicken's eggs or cultures of bacteria are most often used; animal hosts are sometimes necessary and in at least one case – the common cold viruses (see Chapter 3) – human volunteers are the best means of culturing them. The isolation of pure lines of such viruses depends basically on diluting enriched populations such that only a few infective units remain which, since the population was enriched initially, are presumed to be similar and representative of the predominant type. With exigent viruses, such isolations can be very difficult and, indeed, one can be pretty sure that many more viruses exist than have ever been cultured in the laboratory.

The situation with viruses exemplifies an extreme case of a question that is true of microbiology in general: how far can one be sure that the behaviour of microbes that one can grow in the laboratory parallels their behaviour in nature? The answer is that one cannot be sure. The late Professor Kluyver, a distinguished Dutch microbiologist, used to argue that all cultures of bacteria are 'laboratory artefacts': strains whose characters had been altered by making the adjustment to grow in laboratory media. He was, of course, quite right. As we saw in Chapter 2, microbes have remarkable properties of adaptability, and the microbiologist must always keep in mind the reservation that the behaviour of his material in his laboratory might be quite misleading as regards its behaviour in its natural habitat. A simple example is that the typhoid bacterium, *Salmonella typhi*, almost always needs to be provided with the amino-acid tryptophan for growth when it is freshly isolated from a patient with typhoid. It readily loses this character in the laboratory – apparently it learns to make its own tryptophan very easily – and almost the only way to make it regain a need for tryptophan is to infect an experimental animal with the strain and re-isolate it.

Since microbes cause disease, this sort of question becomes particularly important in medical microbiology. Is a microbe obtained from a diseased patient really the cause of the disease? In some cases there is little doubt: bacteria obtained from blood, which is normally sterile, may justly be regarded as the cause of a septicaemia. But in mouth disorders, for example, there are so many microbes around already that, unless a quite unusual type is present, it is difficult to be certain which is causing damage. Indeed, in this particular instance there is still no general agreement about which of the flora of the mouth are responsible for tooth decay. One of the earliest bacteriologists, Dr Robert Koch of Berlin, crystallized this dilemma in a set of conditions known as Koch's postulates: a microbe may be accepted as the cause of a disease if (1) it is present in unusual numbers when and where the disease is active, (2) it can be isolated from the diseased patient and (3) it causes disease when inoculated into a healthy subject. These conditions, for obvious reasons, are not easy to apply in practice, but if they are not adhered to the scientist can be badly misled. The common cold, now known to be a virus infection, causes secretions which encourage the growth of all sorts of bacteria, some harmless, some irritant. In the early years of this century these bacteria were thought to be the cause of colds, but they are now known to be secondary bacterial infections developing as a result of the primary viral infection. Intestinal disorders cause gross changes in the intestinal flora which are often a consequence rather than a cause of disease. Koch's postulates apply throughout microbiology and are by no means restricted to its medical aspects; we shall discuss in Chapter 7 the corrosion of stone, a phenomenon that certainly can take place through the agency of sulphur bacteria but which often has nothing to do with them. Koch's postulates, regrettably, are sometimes forgotten even by those in the best position to make use of them.

Having obtained a pure culture of microbes, the first thing one generally does is to look at it. Are the microbes rod-shaped, spherical, twisted or comma-shaped? Do they swim about? Lie in chains or clusters? Form filaments? Form spores? Do they show an internal structure, granules and nucleus? One can conduct cultural tests: do they grow in milk, broth, a simple sugar and salts mixture? Do they form gas and/or acid? What do their colonies look like on jellified media? An important test for bacteria was devised in 1884 by Christian Gram, based on whether the organisms, killed and dyed, did or did not retain the dye after washing with alcohol or acetone. This test, the 'Gram reaction' is still very valuable for dividing bacteria into two great groups, which, by some coincidence that is still not clearly understood, correspond in several other important properties: Gram-positive bacteria (those which retain the dye) tend to be particularly sensitive to drugs such as penicillin and sulphonamides and to have other physiological properties in common. Tests based on appearance, culture and staining reactions give, with the aid of published keys and guides, some idea of the nature of the microbe and, if that is his aim, the microbiologist can follow up these clues with more tests, including those with anti-sera (see Chapter 3), and identify the microbes completely. But again we must emphasize the element of uncertainty mentioned earlier: if the microbe is a well known and important one, such as a *Salmonella*, it may be possible to obtain a very precise identification, but if it is one of the myriad of rod-like bacteria that inhabit soil, for example, it is likely that only a rather vague classification will be reached.

Often a microbe does something useful, makes an antibiotic, a vitamin or other chemical, in which case the scientist may wish to grow large amounts of it. Mass culture of microbes on a production scale is called 'fermentation'. This is an incorrect name, actually, because fermentation strictly refers to the transformations of substances brought about by microbes growing in the absence of air – the classical example is the fermentation of sugar to alcohol by yeasts – but today industrial microbiologists refer to any large-scale cultural process, with or without air, as a fermentation. In principle all fermentations are laboratory culture procedures scaled-up, but this can be easier said than done. The engineering problems of handling, containing and sterilizing large volumes of culture fluid, and of incubating, harvesting and extracting the products are so great that a whole technology called 'biochemical engineering' has grown up around it. Even the procedure of supplying air to several thousand gallons of microbial culture is more of an engineering feat than it sounds: on that scale the microbes tend to consume oxygen faster than the engineer can persuade it to dissolve. Biochemical engineering has really only developed into a distinct discipline during the last two decades, largely as a result of the expansion of industrial microbiology consequent on the development of antibiotics; here we can do little more than note its existence, but we should mention one important concept which is now being accepted among biochemical engineers: continuous culture.

Suppose you are an industrialist producing yeast for the baking industry. By traditional methods you have to keep a stock culture of yeasts, grow a large 'seed' culture from it, prepare however many thousand gallons of medium your fermentor holds, sterilize it, inoculate it, wait for it to grow and harvest it. Then you must clean up and start again. How much better if the culture grew continuously! This is what happens in continuous culture: a fermentor is designed with an overflow, so that sterile medium is pumped in at a rate that is rather slower than the fastest that the microbes can grow. Once established, the culture continuously overflows into a collecting vessel and can be harvested continuously; the microbes, so to speak, grow as fast as they are fed. The process has the advantage that the production process can be automated, the plant works night and day, and, once established, it is less prone to contamination than traditional procedures. The main objection to its adoption by industry on a large scale is a mundane one: that fermentation industries have invested a lot of capital in batch fermentors and are loath to write off such expensive equipment while it can still be used.

Continuous culture is of great value in research, too. If the microbes are growing as fast as they are fed, one can choose which of the nutrients fed to them shall be the one that limits their growth. If a bacterial culture is grown in a simple medium of sugar and salts one can, by keeping the concentration of sugar low and seeing that the salts are plentiful, arrange things so that the bacteria use up all the sugar provided. The concentration of bacteria in the culture is determined by the concentration of sugar in the medium provided; in microbiologists' jargon the sugar is said to limit their growth. If, now, one grows similar bacteria in a medium with plentiful sugar but limited by the supply of ammonium, one obtains ammonium-limited organisms. And one finds they are different in several ways. They are rich in carbohydrate and are 'tough' – they do not die easily. Their enzyme balance and chemical composition has changed. By choosing diverse limiting nutrients, one can alter the biochemistry of microbes to remarkable extents. This gives microbiologists an experimental control over the physiology of their material which is unique in biology and which is still producing valuable basic knowledge.

Continuous culture makes use of the fact that microbes need certain nutrients to multiply, and that their growth can be controlled by adjusting the supply of these nutrients. Many microbes need quite complicated nutrients, such as amino-acids or vitamins, and it is often difficult for analytical chemists to analyse foodstuffs and other materials for such compounds. Microbiologists have used microbes for this sort of analysis: if one has a material containing vitamin B_{12}, for example, and one wishes to know how much it contains, one of the simplest ways is to add a little to a culture of microbes that require B_{12} and see how well they grow. This process is called 'microbiological assay' and it is the only method of measuring amounts of some of the vitamins. Microbiological assay was responsible for the unexpected discovery that sewage is one of the richest sources available of vitamin B_{12}; protozoa are particularly useful for B_{12} assay, and they have also been proposed as screening agents for testing cancer-producing substances. A decade ago most of the amino-acids were assayed with microbes, but today chromatographic analysis has been developed to such an extent that microbiological methods for amino-acids are obsolete.

Microbes, like all living things, die. Cultures have therefore to be sub-cultured to keep the strain alive, and this can be tedious if one has a large collection of microbes. There are, however, two ways in which they can be preserved without sub-culture: deep-freezing or freeze-drying. Both of these operations must be carried out in rather special ways, but if they are done properly the microbes go into a state of suspended animation and can be stored for very long periods. To deep freeze a live bacterial culture, for example, the organisms are suspended in quite strong (10 to 20 per cent) solutions of glycerol (but a number of other compounds of the class chemists call 'non-polar' are also effective). When such a suspension is frozen, nearly all the bacteria remain alive, whereas most would have died in an ordinary medium. If they are stored at a really low temperature, at –70 degrees Centigrade, or better at –200 degrees Centigrade, they only die very slowly. In this respect they are like the tissue and blood-cells which can be cold-stored in glycerol in 'banks' for surgery or blood-transfusion, but the whole living microbes can be so stored. Protozoa, perhaps because of their greater internal complexity, do not respond well to such storage.

Protein, such as white of egg or blood serum, also protects against freezing damage, and so do sugars. If one suspends bacteria in a mixture of serum and the sugar glucose, it is not only possible to freeze them without damage, but also to dry them, provided the material does not thaw during the drying process. The ice in the frozen mixture must be sublimed off under a high vacuum. This process, known as freeze-drying, is very useful because, once dry, the cultures need not be refrigerated. It is used by culture collections such as the National Collection of Industrial Bacteria referred to at the beginning of Chapter 2. If one orders a culture of bacteria from such a collection, one receives a little ampoule containing a speck of a dried serum-sugar mixture with the dormant microbes in it; on transfer to a suitable sterile liquid medium they will revive and multiply.

Freeze-drying has only been widely adopted for about sixteen years and, though some microbes are known to die out over several years even when freeze-dried, others that were dried in 1950 are still alive. (Or perhaps I should say capable of being revived so that I do not beg the question whether a freeze-dried population is truly alive!)

Microbiologists, industrialists and research workers may wish to keep their microbes alive, but in many day-to-day circumstances the problem is the converse: how to kill them. We have referred to sterilization throughout this chapter; how, in fact, does one sterilize something? We mentioned pressure-cooking and baking, and touched upon filtration and γ-irradiation, but these are of rather limited general application. Disinfection is quite a serious problem in general hygiene and is often carried out rather inefficiently, so I shall survey the question briefly here. For completeness I shall repeat the processes mentioned earlier.

Pressure cooking: In hospitals and laboratories, instruments, culture media and infected material are sterilized in large pressure cookers filled with steam – called autoclaves – so that everything reaches a temperature of 115–120 degrees for at least 15 minutes. This is long enough and hot enough to kill even the most heat-resistant spores, but one must remember that, even in steam under pressure, the middle of a heap of blankets, or of a large bulk of liquid, takes a long time to reach the temperature of the steam.

Steaming: All vegetative microbes, that is microbes that have not formed spores, are killed by steam, so if one steams a material, waits for the spores to germinate and steams it again, the chances are that few if any spores will remain. This process is used as a rough-and-ready method of sterilizing dental and surgical instruments, and sometimes for delicate media that would not stand pressure-cooking.

Pasteurization: Milk and some other foods can be spoiled by steaming in the sense that their flavour is impaired. If they are heated to about 70 degrees for a short time, all vegetative microbes are killed and only spores remain. Thus, though they are not sterile, they last longer than they otherwise would have done without going bad. Beer, cheeses and milk are often protected, though hardly sterilized, in this way.

Ultra-violet irradiation: We mentioned in Chapter 3 the lethal

91

effect of sunlight on airborne microbes. The most active wavelengths are in the short ultra-violet range, around 260 mμ, and by irradiating transparent objects with a UV-lamp one can sterilize them. The air in operating theatres, and in bottling plants in the pharmaceutical industry, can be sterilized in this way; the radiation is rather damaging to human skin and particularly to the eyes.

γ-irradiation: This is as lethal to microbes as to any other living things, though highly resistant species such as *Micrococcus radiodurans* exist. Such radiation can be used to sterilize opaque but heat-sensitive materials, electronic parts of space vehicles, for example. The process is used to sterilize certain research materials such as the plastic Petri dishes mentioned earlier and has possibilities in the food industry.

Filtration: Very fine filters are available that will sterilize liquids by filtering out microbes. They are rarely used outside the laboratory except in preparing sera for injection.

Chemical sterilization: Here we come to the major domestic method. Disinfectants, such as phenol ('carbolic acid') and its numerous proprietary variants, are simply poisons that are more lethal to microbes than to people and animals. Chlorine is a good disinfectant which is used in domestic water supplies; while it cannot be used in concentrations that would completely sterilize drinking water, it keeps gross microbial contamination under control. In swimming pools it is used to prevent cross infection in crowded conditions; it is useful in preventing transmission of infection between adults and bottle-fed babies. Yet it must be used sensibly: I have seen a mother religiously sterilize bottles and teats with Milton, pasteurize the feed and then, at the last moment, touch the teat to her hands or lips to see if the temperature is correct! Thus they neatly sub-culture their skin or mouth flora into their baby. Splash, by all means, but do not touch, should be the rule.

The phenols are good general microbicides and can usually be used to swab floors and walls safely, but they are quite powerful poisons and should be kept away from skin and food. They do not, as many people believe, 'kill smells'; that belief has arisen because they have a strong smell of their own and, of course, by killing the bacteria responsible, they may stop the smell of putrefaction. Soaps and detergents are moderately good disinfectants, and there is a class of detergents, the 'cationic' or 'quaternary' detergents, which are excellent disinfectants for use on the skin. They form the basis of many proprietary creams. Disinfectant powders, as we saw in Chapter 3, are the basis of deodorant creams and powders: they kill the microbes that ferment sweat and cause it to smell.

Certain simple chemicals such as copper salts have some disinfectant action and are used in horticulture (as 'Bordeaux mixture'). They are rather poisonous.

Disinfectants need time to act. It is no good, for instance, pouring carbolic acid down a smelly sink and washing it away at once; likewise it is a waste of money to chlorinate a W.C. and immediately flush it. Because disinfectants are selective poisons they rarely act instantly. The quaternary detergents seem to be something of an exception to this rule, in that they act at once if at all, but generally it is wise, when using a chemical disinfectant, to expose the material being treated to the disinfectant for as long as is reasonable. They function, moreover, by reacting in a chemical fashion with the living microbes, so if there are a lot of other materials present for them to react with there will be less disinfectant available to kill the microbes. One would need far more phenol to kill ten million bacteria in soil than one would need to kill the same number of bacteria in water, simply because much of the phenol would react with the soil particles and be neutralized as far as the microbes are concerned. Or, to return to our earlier domestic example, a dirty baby's bottle with encrustations of milk will require much more Milton to sterilize it than a clean bottle, because the chlorine reacts with the milk solids as readily as with the microbes.

Disinfectants are rather different in principle from the antibiotics and drugs discussed in Chapter 3. They are general biological poisons which, as we saw earlier, kill microbes more effectively than they kill higher organisms. They are, to use microbiologists' jargon again, microbicides (a word analogous to insecticides) whereas many drugs and antibiotics do not kill microbes at all: they merely prevent them from multiplying. Though disinfection is an important and necessary part of the day-to-day hygiene of civilized communities, it is important not to get obsessed by it. As we pointed out in Chapter 3, we need some exposure to infection to develop any resistance to disease at all. Perhaps the mother who touched the baby's teat to her lips was effectively wiser than we who raise our hands in horror at the thought? The answer, of course, is that she was not, because she did it out of ignorance, and she might, for example, have had gingivitis. The wise thing is to know what one is doing and why one is doing it. One can take liberties with microbes if one knows one is doing so; to take them in ignorance is to court disaster. Where have you heard that before, you ask? It is as true of atom bombs as of microbes, so let us remember that scientists, while they may know more of their subjects than politicians or housewives, have gained with their knowledge a realization of how profoundly ignorant they really are. Science has made fabulous advances during the present century, yet each fragment of knowledge teaches us how much more we ought to know.

CHAPTER 5

Microbes in Nutrition

Few people can be unaware that beers, wines, cheeses and so on are prepared by allowing microbes to act on foodstuffs; even fewer can have failed to recognize that food goes bad through the action of microbes. But these two kinds of microbial activity are relatively minor aspects of the importance of microbes in the whole field of human and animal nutrition. In this chapter we shall naturally deal with food preparation; its spoilage will crop up in Chapter 7. Let us start at what is perhaps the most important stage in nutrition: the assimilation of food.

Assimilation, technically speaking, is the process that follows digestion. Once food is eaten, the digestive enzymes of the mouth, stomach and intestines break it down into chemical fragments that the organism can absorb into its blood stream and use for its biochemical purpose. Carbohydrates are broken down to sugars, proteins to amino-acids, fats are partly broken down, partly emulsified. Some components of food – woody matter, for instance – are not readily broken down by the digestive enzymes and it is here that microbes come in. Ruminant mammals, such as sheep or cattle, have a primary stomach (called the rumen) in which grass, which is almost the only food they eat, quietly ferments. The rumen is a sort of continuous culture of anaerobic microbes, including protozoa and bacteria, which collectively ferment the starch and cellulose of grass to yield butyric acid, methane and CO_2. Rumen juice is extremely rich in microbes – up to 10^{10} organisms/ml. is commonplace – and they are very active: an ordinary cow produces 150 to 200 litres of gas a day and a large, well-fed, lactating cow is almost a walking gas-works at 500 litres a day. Some of the microbes are quite difficult to culture in the laboratory because they are so sensitive to air: with all this gas production the rumen is completely anaerobic. This culture is diluted steadily by the animal's saliva, and by water from the grass eaten; thus the contents of a typical sheep's rumen are replaced once every day. The rumen discharges, therefore, mainly bacteria, butyric acid, gas and a few unfermentable fragments of the food. The animal assimilates almost entirely butyric acid and fragments of dead microbes, and, since butyric acid is equivalent to carbohydrate, it is the microbes that provide the animal with the vitamins and amino-acids necessary for its growth. Sulphate-reducing bacteria, which are also present in the rumen, assist by generating sulphide from any sulphates ingested with the grass, and a sheep can apparently use this sulphide to form part of its protein. In a similar way, wood-eating insects such as termites rely largely on populations of cellulose-decomposing bacteria in their guts to decompose wood into materials they can assimilate. An interesting microbiological example of this nutritional interdependence occurs in the protozoon *Crithidia oncopelti*. This unicellular microbe has symbiotic bacteria inside its cell, actually within its protoplasm, which apparently supply their host with an amino-acid, lysine, which it needs for growth. The bacteria are sensitive to penicillin but the protozoon is not. If *C. oncopelti* is freed of its bacteria with penicillin – 'cured' of its infection, so to speak – it dies unless it is provided with lysine.

Carnivores, and omnivores such as man, are obviously less dependent on microbes for their nutrition. For one thing, they tend to eat the sheep and cattle, thus by-passing the problem of converting cellulose and starch to protein. Though they eat vegetable matter, the cellulose, which constitutes the major part of it, is almost entirely excreted. However, the mouths and lower guts of men and animals are also microcosms of microbes. Man, for example, lives with two continuous cultures: the mouth and the colon. We discussed the flora of the normal mouth in Chapter 3; many of its inhabitants survive the acidity of the stomach and are to be found in the lower intestines: the lactobacilli and streptococci are usually there. But a new flora is also present: a rod called *Escherichia coli*; methane-forming bacteria; gas-producing bacteria of the group *Clostridium* and, usually, yeasts.

New types of lactic organisms and streptococci are also found and, sometimes, non-pathogenic protozoa. The combined activities of these microbes can, after a starchy meal for instance, cause discomfort because the gas they produce from incompletely digested food is the main source of flatulence or 'wind'. But while growing and fermenting, they synthesize several substances that are invaluable to our nutrition. These are all members of the B-group of vitamins and it is, indeed, quite difficult to render normal, healthy individuals deficient in B vitamins; during the last war, volunteers remained perfectly healthy for weeks on diets of polished rice which ought to have given them beri-beri in a matter of days. Given a brief course of a sulphonamide drug, which killed off much of their intestinal flora, they rapidly succumbed to deficiency diseases. This is the reason why doctors, if they know their job, look out for vitamin deficiencies in patients that have been treated with antibiotics: though the important site of action of the antibiotic may have been elsewhere, the drug usually has a fairly drastic effect on floras of the mouth and intestine. Mysterious gut disorders and irritations that sometimes occur after a course of antibiotic often have a similar origin: the intestinal flora becomes unbalanced as the population returns to normal and produces troublesome physical reactions.

One of the important vitamins synthesized by the intestinal flora of both man and animals is vitamin B_{12}. This is a complex chemical containing the metal cobalt which, among other functions, is concerned in blood formation; its discovery revolutionized the treatment of pernicious anaemia. The intestine contains organisms that synthesize B_{12} and also organisms that break it down, and in young animals the amount of B_{12} actually assimilated depends on the balance between these two types. In the early days of antibiotics, the left-over mould, being a perfectly wholesome form of vegetable matter as far as anyone could see, was tested as feed for pigs and chickens. It seemed a near-miraculous discovery, like having one's cake and eating it, when such animals were found to grow and put on weight dramatically. They did not grow into giants, but they reached adult weight uncommonly rapidly and economically: antibiotic wastes appeared to be a sort of Food of the Gods. The precise mechanism of this action is still uncertain, but the major factor is simple: the bacteria that destroy B_{12} are more sensitive to antibiotics than those that make it. The wastes used as feeds contain traces of the original antibiotic and the upshot is that the B_{12} balance in the animal's intestine is shifted in favour of assimilation by the animal. This is not the whole story: antibiotic residues usually contain B_{12} themselves which, though it is of a slightly different chemical composition from the usual bacterial vitamin, assists the animal's nutrition. Antibiotic residues containing traces of antibiotics are now routinely used in intensive animal husbandry and have, in fact, given rise to anxiety in that their widespread use increases the risk of selecting antibiotic-resistant pathogens. In the light of their effect in cheapening food and making a decent standard of protein food available to more and more people, one can argue that the risk is worth taking, but such arguments neglect the point that the proportion of patients showing penicillin sensitivity has steadily increased during the two decades for which it has been in general use. Some 7 per cent of patients in the U.S.A. now react allergically to this antibiotic. The probable origin of such sensitivity is the continuous consumption of small amounts of penicillin in, for example, milk, and this can lead to an allergic response when the person receives the large dose needed to treat disease. The widespread use of antibiotics in food production is dangerous, not only because it can cause selection of antibiotic resistant bacteria, but also because it decreases the effectiveness of our medical resources against other microbes.

An understanding of the function of microbes is extremely important in agriculture. Obvious examples occur in the disease of farm animals. Drastic measures are necessary when virus diseases such as foot-and-mouth disease or fowl pest get established: with such scourges there is nothing to be done but to massacre and destroy the infected cattle or poultry, as the case may be. There are about 200 recognized microbial infections of farm animals, including such drastic diseases as tuberculosis, brucellosis, trypanosomiasis and rinderpest; in 1956 the U.S. Department of Agriculture estimated that livestock production could be doubled in the developing countries if control of communicable microbial infections could be made adequate. Within limits, quarantine regulations and chemotherapy keep these diseases under control, but occasional epidemics can occur and the situation will not be satisfactory until they can no longer happen. In the 1960s there was an outbreak of African swine fever, a virus infection of pigs, that obtained a foothold in Spain and Portugal and seriously threatened the European bacon industry. African horse sickness has appeared briefly in the Middle East, and also a South African strain of the foot-and-mouth virus. The rapidity and ease with which people and animals can travel about the world today make these persistent foci of infection a source of danger not only to the developing countries but also to more developed communities. The question of the control of livestock diseases is one of the urgent topics being faced by the Food and Agriculture Organization of the United Nations.

These matters are probably familiar, in principle if not in detail, to any intelligent reader of the newspapers. What is less well known, perhaps, is the importance of plant pathogens in crop production. Plant diseases, spread by insects or transmitted from root to root in soil, can cause enormous losses in agriculture: a figure of $1,900,000,000 was quoted in 1965 as the annual loss to the U.S.A. due to plant pathogens. Rusts, primitive types of fungus that damage cereal crops, destroyed enough cereals in New South Wales in 1947–8 to feed 3 million people; in 1956 nearly 40 per cent of the rice crops in a part of Venezuela was damaged by *Hoja blanca*, a fungus; in 1935 a third of the banana crop of Jamaica was destroyed by a fungus ('Panama disease' caused by *Fusarium oxyspora*). Catastrophes of these kinds look remote as paper statistics, but in practice, particularly in the more backward countries, they mean that great numbers of people will go hungry, starve and possibly die. Generally speaking, crops have a natural resistance to pathogens, and disastrous infection results from bad or unfortunate husbandry: proper attention to the organic content and alkalinity of soil can often prevent infections spreading drastically. In recent years the possibility of using antibiotics on crops has been seriously considered and they are, in fact, effective. However, they are prohibitively expensive for all except the richest countries, who normally have least need for them. The use of other dressings, sulphur dressings, Bordeaux mixture, and so on, to prevent fungoid blights in horticulture and viticulture is, of course, traditional, and it is interesting that sulphur dressings are effective because of a microbe. *Thiobacillus*, the sulphur bacterium which we first met in Chapter 2, slowly oxidizes the sulphur to sulphuric acid on the surface of the plant, gently producing an environment that is too acid for the development of pests such as the fungus *Oidium*, yet insufficiently strong to damage the grapes.

Biological control of plant pathogens and other agricultural pests, by deliberately encouraging microbes antagonistic to the pest, is still in its infancy. But few Western Europeans can be unfamiliar with the dramatic 'biological warfare' conducted (unofficially, in fact) against rabbits over the last fifteen years. In May 1952, a few rabbits in Eure et Loire, France, were infected with the virus disease myxomatosis and released; by the end of 1953 the disease had spread through twenty-six departments of France and reached Belgium, Holland, Switzerland and Germany, killing 60 to 90 per cent of the rabbit population. In due course it reached Britain and it is now endemic throughout Europe. Resistance to the disease is acquired by rabbits very slowly and, though it is a disgusting disease in its symptoms, there is no doubt that the post-war revival of European agriculture would have been much slower without it. In some areas productivity increased three-fold. In the well-fed communities of Europe today, we can afford to share the doubts of animal lovers about destroying the rabbit, once an engaging feature of the country scene, and officially the deliberate spreading of myxomatosis is frowned upon in Britain. But the farmer has no such doubts: in 1964 I was told that the black-market value of a well-myxomatosed rabbit was fifty pounds.

Smaller pests also can be controlled with microbes. There exist predaceous fungi that trap and digest potato eel-worms in the soil, and there are several preparations of bacteria available that can be used against insects. *Bacillus thuringensis* is packaged commercially for use against caterpillars – it destroys several species effectively – and attempts have been made (unsuccessfully, it appears) to control locusts with a species of *Cloaca* called '*Coccobacillus aericlorum*'. Care must be taken to use pure strains: *Bacillus cereus* is very like *B. thuringensis* but can be pathogenic to man. The use of insect viruses in this context would be very promising, because their dispersal by techniques developed for biological warfare should be reasonably simple. Research in this direction is very timely as people begin to realize how persistent chemical pesticides and fungicides can be and how dangerous both to man and to the natural ecology.

We mentioned the importance of the nitrogen-fixing bacteria to agriculture in Chapter 1. Generally speaking, the important process is symbiotic nitrogen fixation, that is, the process whereby the microbe 'infects' a plant and settles in a 'nodule', and the combination of plant and microbe fixes nitrogen. The best-known combinations are the leguminous plants, clover, lucerne and so on, with their associated bacteria *Rhizobium*. Since some strains of *Rhizobium* form more effective nodules than others, inoculation of leguminous crops with good strains of rhizobium is common and sensible agricultural practice. But though the legume + rhizobium pair is the most useful agricultural combination we should not forget that other symbiotic systems exist and can be more important in nature. The alder has a symbiotic nitrogen-fixing microbe that is probably fungoid (an actinomycete) and this enables it to colonize arid and mountainous areas. Shepherd's purse and Bog myrtle are hardy plants that colonize poor soils – heath or bog lands – and when such plants become established they create more fertile conditions and enable other plants to establish themselves. Nearly 190 non-leguminous plants and shrubs are known that fix nitrogen with the aid of nodules. Certain lichens, those combinations of a blue-green alga and a fungus which we met in Chapter 2, can, if the algal partner is a blue-green type able to fix nitrogen, render a tiled roof so fertile that ordinary flowering plants will grow on it – thus gracing the rural English scene. In 1883 the volcanic island of Krakatoa in the Malayan archipelago more or less exploded, killing many thousands and causing, incidentally, splendid sunsets (due to atmospheric dust) for many years after. The volcano virtually sterilized the island, and the first living things to return were the nitrogen-fixing blue-green algae. As these renewed the fertility of the soil, other plants, birds, insects and animals slowly returned and the island is now fully re-colonized.

The nitrogen-fixing bacteria are still fundamental to the world's food production, and in all but the most highly developed countries their activities still determine the amount of food produced. Many nitrogen-fixing bacteria are not symbiotic: *Azotobacter, Clostridium pasteurianum, Desulfovibrio* and one or two other free-living microbes fix nitrogen in the absence of a plant host and have no need of a nodule. One of these, *Beijerinckia*, has been considered important in the fertility of tropical soils. But the truth of the matter seems to be that they consume so much carbohydrate or similar carbon source to fix a little nitrogen that, from an agricultural point of view, they are not much use. There is just not enough carbonaceous matter available in ordinary soil to enable bacteria of this kind to fix useful amounts of nitrogen: if there were, other bacteria, non-nitrogen-fixing, would consume it more rapidly. Why they are such inefficient nitrogen-fixers is still an unsolved problem – indeed, they may be more effective in nature than in the laboratory, and their known inefficiency has not prevented agronomists, particularly in the U.S.S.R., from trying to improve farming yields by deliberately infecting the land with such bacteria. Great things have been claimed for soil dressings of 'azobacterin', a preparation of *Azotobacter* used in the U.S.S.R., but recently both Russian and Western scientists have questioned its value. The soils treated were often so poor that the peat on which the *Azotobacter* was usually added would probably have done quite as much good on its own, and the situation is additionally complicated by the fact that *Azotobacter* produces auxin-like substances – materials that stimulate plant growth without in fact augmenting their nitrogen content at all, and thus without augmenting their value as protein sources for food.

In the present state of knowledge it is safest to regard the free-living nitrogen-fixing bacteria as relatively unimportant to man's economy. The blue-green algae, however, are very important in the Antarctic, where they seem to be the primary source of soil fertility. In water-logged rice fields of the Far East they provide the main source of nitrogen for the crop. Their importance has been well understood in Japan, where Dr Watanabe has developed methods of 'farming' blue-green algae to produce a green manure for rice production. This is both a practical and an intellectually satisfying process: with the aid of sunlight Watanabe's microbes convert atmospheric CO_2 and nitrogen to the raw material of the basic food of the Eastern hemisphere.

Whole books have been written about the importance of microbes in agriculture, their effect on soil structure and fertility, their role in the decomposition and re-cycling of vegetable matter. As Professor Hugh Nichol pointed out years ago, the major raw materials of agriculture (soils and manures) are either microbial products or substitutes for microbial products. In a survey such as this we can only be selective and mention what the author regards as the highlights. After all, this chapter is concerned with nutrition and, though there would be virtually no science of nutrition without agriculture, there are other things than bread and meat ...

... Beer, for instance. It is curious that, when I mention to laymen the industrial importance of microbes, the first thing they think of is beer. The importance of yeasts in the production of fermented alcoholic drinks has particularly impressed itself on successive generations of mankind and if, in a serious book such as this, we cannot truly maintain that liquor is essential to nutrition, we must admit that it certainly enhances the pleasure of nourishing oneself.

Beer is produced by such a complex process that one wonders, when one considers it dispassionately, how anyone thought of it. Yet some kind of beer was made by the ancient Egyptians about 6,000 years ago, and the ancient Britons made a beer from malted wheat before the Romans introduced barley. Essentially the process of making beer is this: barley is caused to germinate by steeping it in water for a day or two and leaving it in a warm, damp place for between two and six days. This process is called 'malting'; gibberellins, mentioned later in this chapter, are used to control it. The grain sprouts, and develops enzymes that hydrolyze the starch stored in the seed to sugars, the malt is then killed by gentle heating but, since the enzymes are not wholly destroyed, breakdown of the starch to sugar continues to take place. It is then steeped in water once more, so that the sugars soak out, together with amino-acids and minerals needed by yeasts for growth. This extract, the 'malt wort', is in due course boiled, to inactivate the residual enzymes, and hops are added to impart a bitter flavour. Though this has only recently been realized, hops also introduce materials that hinder the growth of bacteria in the extract. When the wort is cool, yeasts are introduced and the whole is allowed to ferment for a week or so. The material is not stirred, so that, though the yeasts start off by growing aerobically, they rapidly exhaust the oxygen and the bulk of the population grows without air. In these circumstances they convert the sugar of the wort to alcohol and the gas carbon dioxide; they stop growing when sufficient alcohol has accumulated to be inimical to further growth. After a period of storage, to settle out the yeast, the fermented liquid may be drunk.

Many refinements are used according to the type of beer being brewed, but essentially only two types of yeast are used: *Saccharomyces cerevisiae* and its close relative *S. carlsbergensis*, selected for their tolerance of alcohol, their flavour and settling properties. A variety of treatments is used to stabilize the beer (so that it will last), to retain its gaseousness, to prevent precipitation on storage; in addition, extraneous bacteria, lactobacilli and acetobacter, have to be kept under control because they can spoil the beer by forming lactic or acetic acids. These matters form the bulk of the craft of brewing, for despite advances in our understanding of the process, brewing is far from being a science.

Wine, the fermented juice of grapes, is produced by a similar fermentation process, but nothing analogous to malting is required. Grapes are crushed, traditionally by treading with bare feet but nowadays mechanically, their juice is collected and fermented with 'wild' yeasts: yeasts that appeared naturally on the fruit, or which contaminate the wine vats from year to year. These yeasts are usually a close relative of *S. cerevisiae*, though wine specialists often call them *S. ellipsoideus*, and sometimes, mainly in California, pure strains are used (though not by producers of the great wines). Extraneous bacteria are kept down by 'sulphuring', treatment of the grape juice ('must') with sulphur dioxide (or with sodium thiosulphate, which forms sulphur dioxide in contact with the acids of grape juice), which is more toxic to bacteria than to yeasts. Part of the craft of wine making lies in adding enough sulphur to yield a good fermentation and yet not sufficient to spoil the taste. White wines, which are made from grape juice separated from the skin, pips and stalks at an early stage, often suffer from over-sulphuring, recognizable as a flat after-taste (as of a London fog). Red wines, which are red because the fermentation is conducted in the presence of skin and pips, so that colouring matters are extracted, seem less prone to troubles from over-sulphuring, possibly because they have a higher content of tannins than white wines: tannins are slightly anti-bacterial, so less sulphuring is necessary. *Rosé* wines are made by exposing the must briefly to the solid grape debris, and therefore they also are sometimes prone to over-sulphuring. The thought that *rosé* wine can be made by mixing red and white wine is, naturally, unthinkable to any self-respecting wine manufacturer; one must conclude that cheap *rosés*, particularly in France, are sometimes made unthinkingly.

The basic process in wine making is, just as in brewing, a yeast fermentation of a sugar solution. With certain wines, notably the Burgundies, the must is unduly acid because it has a high content of malic acid. In these circumstances lactobacilli, present on the fruit or in the vat, convert malic acid to the weaker lactic acid and thus lower the total acidity. Oenologists call this process the 'malo-lactic' fermentation. Part of the quality of the sweet white wines called Sauternes is due to the use of grapes that have been partly dehydrated as a result of attack by the mould *Botrytis cinereae*. As wine-making depends on a microbial fermentation, it should be possible to produce wine continuously by continuous culture techniques – and, indeed, in the Bodega Cyana region of Argentina this has been done. But the great wines, those with noble names such as *Chateau Latour*, *Chateau Lafitte*, *Chateau Mouton-Rothschild*, are artistic triumphs rather than works of craftsmanship, and their quality depends almost entirely on details of the viticulture, the clarifying procedures after fermentation, the storage and maturation procedures; these details require a degree of experienced human intervention that is still far beyond the capacity of an automated, continuous process. In maturation the microbes play little or no part, though the contaminant mould *Oidium* usually found on grapes is said to add important flavours to a good wine. During maturation certain interactions between fruit acids and alcohol take place, and a certain amount of precipitation of insoluble matter occurs; the 'crust' of a good, matured wine is a precipitate of tartrates and tannins. Red wines can improve steadily over up to fifteen years, though immediately after bottling they may deteriorate briefly (become 'bottle sick'). White wines show little improvement once bottled.

Reinforced wines, such as madeira, sherries, port, vermouths, are basically wines to which sugar, extra alcohol and sometimes herbs have been added. Microbes play no part in these treatments. In the case of sherries an interesting sort of continuous culture process is used called the *solera*. The wine, duly fermented, is admitted to a sequence of casks in tiers. One cask leads to the next, and as many as ten casks may be arranged in sequence. Wine is drawn off from the bottom cask, and the process of travelling from first to last cask may take several years. Each cask develops a floating scum or '*flor*' of yeasts, related to *S. cerevisiae* but called *S. beticus*, and though this microbe has little effect on the alcohol content of the wine, it adds certain flavours and aromas that give sherry its famous character. After withdrawal from the *solera*, sherry is sweetened with sweet, fresh wine and reinforced with brandy.

Brandy, and all other spirits, are distilled from wine or malted cereal fermentations. Microbes play little part in their preparation after the fermentation stage, and we shall not discuss them further here.

Champagne and other sparkling wines are of some special interest because they make use of a double fermentation process. Fermentation, as we saw, yields not only alcohol but the gas carbon dioxide and, indeed, the gas produced by a bubbly, fermenting vat of malt wort or must can be quite lethal if a worker accidentally inhales it. In the manufacture of champagne some of this gas is deliberately trapped in the bottle. White wine, suitably blended, is mixed with a little syrup and bottled in specially strong bottles with bolted-on corks. It is left in racks to ferment slowly (a special strain of *S. cerevisiae*, a 'champagne yeast', grows) and sufficient gas is formed to carbonate the wine while yet, if the process is performed properly, avoiding explosion. Over several months the bottles are slowly turned over in racks (called 'pulpits') until they are upside down – and the yeast and sediment have settled on the inside of the cork. At this stage the cork is removed and replaced rapidly, so that a plug of yeast and debris is expelled (sometimes the necks are frozen to facilitate the process) and an equivalent volume of syrup and brandy, in variable proportions, is introduced. This process produces a stable wine which retains its sparkle for a long time after opening; cheap sparkling wines are produced merely by high-pressure carbonization of still wines, as in the preparation of soda water. They tend to go flat rapidly.

'*Pétillance*', a slight prickliness found in some young, local wines of Portugal, France and Italy, can arise from a related cause: the wine has been bottled before fermentation was complete and a slow residual fermentation has mildly carbonated it.

Great wines are made from fermented grape juice, preferably by Frenchmen, though it must be admitted that creditable products are made by certain Rhinelanders, Italians, Yugoslavs, even Australians and Californians. Generally speaking, it is the character of the grape and the ability of the wine maker, rather than the microbe, that determine the quality of a wine.

Cider (from apple juice), perry (from pears) and a variety of fruit wines, root wines or beers and even flower wines can be made. All depend essentially on the fermentation of fruit sugars by yeasts and, except for commercial ciders and perry, the yeast

107

used is usually 'wild', that is, one that is introduced naturally with the fruit. *Pulque*, a Mexican beer produced by fermenting the juice of the cactus *Agave* (the spirit distilled from it, Tequila, is perhaps more familiar to Europeans), is viscous because it contains bacteria of the *Lactobacillus* species as well as yeasts. Home-made wines can have somewhat knock-out effects because wild yeasts may produce mildly toxic by-products of fermentation such as acetaldehyde; the results may be a source of transient pride to those who have so painstakingly manufactured them, but it must be admitted that the pleasure of home-made wines usually lies more in the sense of accomplishment than in their gastronomic qualities. Yet accomplishment is not to be sneered at and, if only to prove that even a cursory survey such as this can yield information of practical value, I include the following recipe for a flower wine which, at the appropriate season, can be prepared in the home and can be drunk within ten to fourteen days (it does not keep). It illustrates the principles of *champagnization* without any of its hazards and, most important, is a pleasant, low-alcohol drink which, because of its short fermentation period, has none of the side effects of more elaborate brews.

Elderflower champagne*

Collect, or cause your children to collect, about nine blossoming elderflower heads. Steep them in one gallon of cold tap water containing one lemon, cut up, two tablespoons of white vinegar and one and a half pounds of sugar. After twenty-four hours strain and bottle. Drink after it has become active – about ten days. Activity is signified by slight effervescence when the stopper is removed and a turbidity in the wine due to the growth of wild yeasts.

This wine illustrates three of the basic principles discussed. Acidity, provided here by the vinegar but normally present naturally in fruit juices, favours growth of yeasts and prevents growth of bacteria which would otherwise cause distasteful flavours. Secondly, the raw materials must be removed after brief steeping or they, too, introduce unpleasing flavours. Finally, confining the fermentation in stoppered bottles prevents the escape of carbon dioxide and makes the brew slightly gaseous (the principle

* A tested recipe, for which I am indebted to Mrs Beryl Kelly of Hove.

underlying champagne fermentation). It is advisable not to forget about the bottles or they may burst.

Fermented milk products have as long a history as wines and beers. Cheeses, for example, were offered to the Gods by the Ancient Greeks, possibly as a substitute for ambrosia. Milk is an ideal material for the growth of many kinds of microbes, and some, such as *Bacillus mycoides*, a causative organism of bovine mastitis, or *Brucella*, responsible for contagious abortion in cattle, can cause troublesome infections in men. Bovine tuberculosis used also to be a hazard of milk consumption, but modern dairy hygiene has virtually eliminated such risks. Careless handling in the home, can, however, re-introduce infectious organisms, and the economical practice of returning tasted but unfinished milk to the jug, particularly children's milk, is a cause of many minor domestic catastrophes. Fortunately for most of us, the commonest microbe to grow in natural milk is *Lactobacillus casei* (also called *Lactobacillus bulgaricus*), the formative organism of yoghourt. This bacterium, by fermenting milk sugar (lactose) to lactic acid, makes the environment more acid and thus unfavourable for the growth of pathogenic bacteria. Yoghourt contains, in addition, another microbe, *Streptococcus thermophilus*, which adds a characteristic creamy flavour; sometimes yeasts are present. The product is an extremely safe and wholesome food, widely eaten in the Middle East and Balkans, and becoming increasingly popular in Western Europe. 'Leben' is similar, an incompletely fermented sheep's or goat's milk; American buttermilk is partially fermented skimmed milk that has become viscous because of *Leuconostoc*, a filamentous relative of the lactobacillus. Butter owes its flavour to a slight growth of streptococci during its preparation (their growth leads to formation of a flavoursome chemical called acetoin) and most dairies keep 'starter' cultures that are good at forming this material.

Acidity causes milk to clot, and the clot, or curd, arising from ordinary milk fermentation is the basic material of cheese manufacture. Though traditionally prepared by a microbial fermentation, the curd is nowadays usually made artificially by treating milk with the enzyme rennin (obtained from the stomachs of calves), familiar to housewives as the 'rennet' used for making junkets. Essentially the curd is a mass of casein, the protein of milk, and after removal of the liquid (whey), cheeses are formed simply by allowing further microbial action to take place on the curd. As with alcoholic drinks, whole books have been written on cheese manufacture. Here we can only take a brief look at the subject.

Cream cheeses or *cottage cheeses* are simply the fresh curd, or one which has been allowed to age slightly so that the lactobacilli cause some decomposition of the protein. They do not last long. As such cheeses age, protein breakdown continues further, traces of ammonia are formed, more whey is released. The curd becomes more dense, forming a *curd cheese*, familiar as Cheddar, Cheshire and similar cheeses. In those delicious, unsavoury-looking cheeses such as Camembert, 'Carré de l'Est' and so on, decomposition proceeds nearly to the stage of putrefaction, aided by fungi such as *Oidium* which grow on the surface of the curd. Considerable amounts of ammonia and amines derived from amino-acids appear. Moulds related to *Penicillium* also grow in the veined cheeses, such as Stilton or gorgonzola, and in these cases they spread throughout the curd. The veins are due to the spores of the moulds, which are coloured. In *Swiss cheeses*, such as Gruyère and Emmenthaler, *Propionibacterium* grows in the curd, forming propionic acid, responsible for the characteristic flavour, and carbon dioxide, responsible for the 'holes'. *Processed cheeses* can be made from any of the above. They are normally homogenized with fresh curd, plus preservatives, and then pasteurized and packaged to prevent further microbial action. They are good, perfectly nourishing forms of food, but are generally of minimal gastronomic interest.

Cheese making, like wine making, is a craft of great subtlety and, even in these days of enlightenment about food processing, real Stilton, for example, is only produced near (but, curiously, not at) the village of Stilton, Huntingdonshire. The formative organisms of Camembert are available all over the world, from Australia to the U.S.A., yet somehow the perfection of the authentic Norman product is rarely reached; it is a happy circumstance for the inhabitants of these islands that the economical Normans choose to export the best of their products and that good, true Camembert is found far more often in Britain than in France.

The third major use of microbes in the food industry arises in baking. This process need not detain us long: yeast is allowed to ferment the sugars in dough for a brief period and the carbon dioxide so produced forms tiny bubbles which lighten ('leaven') the bread as it is baked. The process can be copied by adding a touch of baking soda, but the nutritional value of the yeast, an excellent foodstuff as we shall see later, is then lost.

A minor microbial fermentation, of some importance on the Continent, is the preparation of sauerkraut from cabbages. In this process the shredded vegetable is allowed to ferment by the agency of lactobacilli, closely related to those that conduct the yoghourt fermentation. The lactic acid formed preserves the vegetable against further microbial decomposition. Vinegar, widely used in pickling as well as in everyday food preparation, is a dilute solution of another important food acid: acetic acid. Much commercial vinegar is now produced synthetically, by appropriately diluting industrial acetic acid, but the traditional *vin aigre* ('sour wine') is made by the action of acetic acid bacteria (*Acetobacter* and *Acetomonas*) on wine. These bacteria usually grow spontaneously when wine is exposed to air, and oxidize its alcohol to acetic acid; traditionally vinegar is made by allowing rough wine to trickle down towers of birch twigs, or other woody materials, on which a film of acetobacters grows. Thus a sort of continuous culture is formed: the twigs allow access to air and from the bottom vinegar may be tapped off. Any alcoholic beverage can serve for vinegar manufacture: wine (or 'Orleans') vinegar should properly be made from wine, malt vinegar from beer and cider vinegar from cider. Many bacteria other than acetobacters are to be found in vinegar towers and the microbiology of the process is not understood in detail.

In agriculture the silage process is essentially a treatment of grass so that, as in sauerkraut, lactobacilli grow and the acid formed preserves the material from complete putrefaction.

111

Modern methods of food processing and treatment sometimes, though far less often than food-faddists would have us believe, lead to products that are less wholesome than they might be. White bread, for example, is well known to lack several vitamins (E and many of the B group) present in wholemeal bread. So the practice has grown up of manufacturing nutrients of this kind in order to replace those lost in food processing, to enrich foods of limited nutritional value, and for use in medicine. Lysine is an amino-acid derived from protein which human beings cannot synthesize: a certain amount must be provided in the diet, and it has been made industrially for the enrichment of bread. The process used is interesting because it makes use of two microbes in succession: one, a special strain of *Escherichia coli*, cannot make lysine because, as a result of a mutation, it lacks a certain enzyme. It can only make an immediate precursor of lysine called diaminopimelic acid (DAP for short). If, then, this mutant is grown with only a little lysine (for it has to have some, or it will not grow at all), its whole lysine synthesizing system works normally up to the DAP stage, but stops there, with the result that relatively large amounts of DAP collect in the culture. Another organism, *Aerobacter aerogenes*, contains plenty of the enzyme necessary to convert the DAP to lysine, so, in the industrial process, this organism is grown, killed with toluene, and the extracted enzyme used to convert the DAP, accumulated by the *E. coli*, to lysine.

This process is gratifying to microbiologists because, instead of arising from some traditional procedure which microbiologists later came to understand, it developed as a direct result of an increasing understanding of the biochemistry of bacteria. It arose particularly from fundamental work conducted by Dr Elizabeth Work at University College Hospital, London, who originally discovered DAP as a curious amino-acid encountered only in bacteria. It is rare for fundamental research to 'pay off' in so clear-cut a fashion.

Vitamin C, or ascorbic acid, is one of the few vitamins that can be consumed fairly safely without medical guidance, and it is widely used to accelerate recovery from illness as well as for the treatment of genuine cases of deficiency ('scurvy'). Industrially it is made from a plant product, sorbitol, by a series of chemical transformations, and for one of these steps the material is exposed to a bacterium called *Acetobacter suboxydans*, which oxidizes it more gently than is possible by conventional chemistry. Vitamin B_2, or riboflavin, is produced microbiologically using the yeasts *Eremothecium ashbyii* or *Ashbya gossypii*: in 1957 the latter microbe provided the U.S.A. with 400,000 pounds of riboflavin. Vitamin B_{12}, or cobamide, which we discussed at the beginning of the chapter, is essential in the treatment of pernicious anaemia, and, though it was originally isolated from fresh animal liver, it is now produced exclusively using microbes. The demand for it in medicine is small, but its use as a supplement to animal feed makes its commercial production profitable. The streptomycete *S. olivaceus* and the bacterium *Bacillus megaterium* have both been used to produce it industrially; recently the bacteria involved in sewage fermentation (Chapter 7) have been shown to form considerable amounts of B_{12} and extraction of sewage may ultimately prove the cheapest source of this vitamin. Carotene, a precursor of vitamin A, is present in certain coloured yeasts and bacteria; in Brazil it is being produced industrially with the aid of the fungus *Blakesiana trispora*. Ergosterol, a relative of vitamin D, is present in yeasts but this source has not been exploited industrially so far.

Though they are not strictly nutrients, we should mention here the gibberellins, which have proved valuable in agriculture. Originally discovered as the causative agents of a fungus disease of rice, they are substances that are excreted by a certain fungus, pathogenic to plants, *Gibberella fujikuroi*. They have a hormone-like action on plants, accelerating growth and cell division and, when uncontrolled, they cause rapid death of seedlings. Controlled application of gibberellins can, however, accelerate growth of crops, decrease the dormancy period of potatoes and so on; in brewing, gibberellin treatment to accelerate malting is now almost universal.

There are other microbial products that are important in food production. Citric acid is used in enormous quantities in the soft drinks industry. The current annual production in the U.S.A. is believed to exceed 100 million pounds, all of which is made by the action of the mould *Aspergillus niger* on sugar. The citric acid industry is one of the most secretive, and details of the process are difficult to come by, but essentially a mat of the mould is allowed to grow on a sugar solution, containing certain salts and at a controlled acidity, and after a few days nearly all the sucrose becomes citric acid. Lactic acid, which we met earlier in the milk fermentations, is also used in the soft drink industry, and, though it can be manufactured using whey as the raw material and *Lactobacillus casei* as the microbe, other strains of *Lactobacillus* adapted to raw materials such as maize sugar or potato sugars are also used industrially. Another substance which can be prepared from microbes is glutamic acid, used as an additive to enhance the flavour of packaged foods (as the 'sodium-half-glutamate' or 'monosodium glutamate' of dried soups, for example). Many bacteria and some moulds can be used to produce this material but most of the 15 million pounds consumed annually in the U.S.A. is still of plant origin (from sugar beet).

These examples show the importance of microbes in the assimilation of food, in food preparation and processing and, most important, in the basic processes of agriculture. If, then, we are so dependent on microbes for almost every aspect of our nutrition, why do we not dispense with agriculture, give up eating plants and animals, and live on microbes? The question, absurd as it may sound, is a perfectly reasonable one and has, in various forms, been asked many times. Yeast is one of the most nutritious of foods, being rich in protein and vitamins of the B group and having a reasonable quota of fats; waste brewers' yeast is marketed and used in most Western countries as a food supplement under various trade names. In many parts of the world, such as East Africa, parts of Malaya, India, Indonesia, China, there is not so much a food shortage as a protein shortage: most of the population get something approaching a reasonable minimum of carbohydrate, but nothing like the minimum of 16 per cent protein in the diet required by a healthy human (children need rather more, mature adults rather less). This protein shortage could be alleviated by converting spare carbohydrate to protein, and the obvious way to do this is to allow a micro-organism to grow on it, such as a yeast. During the Second World War a process was worked out in Britain for producing food yeast (*Candida utilis*) from molasses by a sort of primitive continuous culture procedure. The product had a pleasant taste, a sort of toasted, meaty flavour; experiments performed by the Medical Research Council, with the cooperation of the armed forces, showed that yeast could indeed provide much of the dietary protein of an ordinary man. A problem was that the yeast was so rich in B vitamins that, if it formed too great a part of the diet, there arose a risk of hypervitaminosis. The tests were so successful that, after the war, a plant was set up in Trinidad to prepare food yeasts from wastes of the sugar industry. The material was used in East Africa, India and Malaya but – and here is the human side of the problem – enormous resistance to its widespread use was encountered among even starving populations. Unfamiliarity, as most parents learn from their children, is an extraordinarily powerful deterrent to eating what is good for one. The food-yeast-production plan foundered, partly because of conservatism on the part of the consumers, partly for simple economic reasons: the demand for the protein, such as it was, was half a world away from the supply, and the consumers were far too poor to pay for a procedure requiring a moderately advanced technology. Molasses could be put to more uses, or even thrown away, more cheaply. More recently, in the 1960s, the expanding world population and renewed evidence of widespread protein shortages again forced food yeast upon the attention of microbiological technologists. The British Petroleum Company has a project for using petroleum fractions for the culture of yeasts, and has successfully grown various strains in water in which crude petroleum is emulsified. The yeasts utilize the waxy components of the petroleum and actually improve the fuel quality of the petroleum that remains after growth. Moreover, since the waxes are pure hydrocarbons, unlike the sugars of molasses, they are much richer in terms of carbon, so that one gets nearly twice as much yeast per pound of wax as one would per pound of sugar. The product is said to have a nasty taste of petrol, but this can be removed; its economic

115

basis is the sounder because it assists in the refinement of petrol as well as forming protein. Dr Champagnat, a leading protagonist of the process, estimates that diverting 3 per cent of the world's oil production to preparation of food yeast could double the world's protein supply. The Shell petroleum company has a comparable project for obtaining protein from natural gas. This gas is methane, so one can use it for the mass culture of methane-oxidizing bacteria, which could then be useful as an animal feed, a fertilizer or even a food supplement for humans. Dr Seymour Hutner has suggested that such bacteria might be used as food for the mass culture of protozoa, which in turn should be offered as fodder to fish and thus yield increased amounts of a protein food that is intrinsically agreeable to man.

Such projects for growing food yeasts or bacterial protein are short-term measures in the sense that they make use of plant material such as molasses, or of a fossil material such as petroleum or methane. On the one hand their yield is limited by the world's productivity of sugar, on the other we know that the oil and natural gas resources of this planet will last for only a few more generations. More satisfactory for the long-term interests of the earth's population are projects for the mass cultivation of algae, studied by the Carnegie Institute of Washington and the Tokagawa Institute of Japan in the 1950s. Algae, such as *Chlorella* and *Scenedesmus*, use sunlight and carbon dioxide as their main nutrients and thus take the place of plants. They produce greatly increased yields per acre, properly handled, and they are in many ways as valuable as yeasts: wholesome food supplements, though they would never, one hopes, be offered or accepted as a complete diet. The problem, which applies to all microbial foodstuffs which are required on a large scale, is that a fairly advanced technology is required to produce and harvest them, and communities enjoying such technologies have, so far, been able to corner enough of the world's more conventional food supplies to keep themselves reasonably well fed. The essential problem is simple: agricultural products, grain, meat or vegetables, are reasonably concentrated foods when produced; the best, richest cultures of yeast, *Chlorella* and so on contain less than one per cent of the harvest. The rest is water. Removing that water, by sedimentation, centrifugation or filtration is what requires the technology: it is an expensive and power-consuming process. Nevertheless, Professor H. Tamiya has calculated that *Chlorella* protein could be produced in Japan at less than one third of the cost of milk protein. Though, to the writer's taste, *Chlorella* recalls slightly fishy spinach, Dr Tamiya claims it can be made delicious and has given recipes for *Chlorella* cakes, biscuits and even ice-cream. But Japan is technologically the most advanced of the Far Eastern nations and, over-populated though it is, it has at the present time insufficient demand to make a *Chlorella* industry viable.

Microbes, today, may seem unpromising foodstuffs to the businessman, but people have got to be fed, or they fight. Microbes are already established constituents of animal feeds; it is probably just a matter of time before microbes become an accepted part of the diets of ordinary people.

*

In the last three chapters we have been rather subjective in our consideration of the microbes. We have looked at their role in our sickness and our health, we have considered how scientists handle them and we have concerned ourselves with their importance in what we eat and drink. These are certainly serious matters and concern every one of us directly. But the importance of microbes to mankind stretches far more deeply into our social structure and economy than such day-to-day considerations would suggest. In the next three chapters we shall look at microbes from the point of view of society rather than of the individuals who compose it; we shall consider their relevance in industrial production, in the manufacture, storage, distribution and disposal of products. Health and food will, of course, crop up again and again, but our attention will be mainly focused on the impact of microbes on the economic machinery that keeps society going.

CHAPTER 6

Microbes in Production

Microbes and Raw Materials

Despite the massive production today of fermented foods and drinks, of antibiotics, vitamins and chemicals through the agency of microbes, it remains true that the most important microbial products, as far as mankind is concerned, were laid down millions of years ago.

Industry consumes power, and it is nowadays a commonplace of sociology to express the standard of development of a country as the power consumed per head of the population. Power is needed for every facet of industrial civilization, from boiling potatoes to running a computer; this is why developing countries become so obsessed with hydro-electric schemes, power-stations and so on. Even food production, once it is mechanized, becomes a power-consuming process, and in a sense the world's food shortages mentioned in Chapter 5 are special cases of the world's power shortage. Manpower alone can support a small, agrarian community, but no sooner does social organization become complex than communities become dependent on machines and, therefore, on the fuel that drives those machines.

The major power sources of the world today are hydro-electricity and the 'fossil' fuels, coal, natural gas and oil. Industry uses these sources of power to transform natural materials such as wood, coal-tar products, metal ores and so on into economically useful products. It is possible to produce a valid, and very instructive, account of the world's economic situation in terms of the availability of power, and, looked at in that light, the recent development of atomic energy becomes something to be regarded with hope for the future rather than with the dismay with which contemporary politics surrounds it. Though we obviously cannot go into details of the world's power resources here, there are two basic principles that we should recognize.

The first principle is that concentrating a material is expensive and power-consuming. To take a simple example, if one wishes to obtain common salt from the sea, one has to evaporate away or otherwise remove about 32 grammes of water for every gramme of salt recovered. Now, no matter how one does this – by boiling, by using sunshine or by some sophisticated process such as electro-dialysis – a lot of power has to be used in getting rid of that water. If the power takes the form of sunshine, or a dry wind, then it is cheap – but one waits a long time for one's product and one gets it in small amounts. If one wants a lot and is in a hurry – and it is almost axiomatic that highly-developed civilizations want a lot of almost everything, in a frantic hurry – then it is cheapest to find a natural salt deposit and expend power in digging it out and carting it to where it is needed. To generalize, then, it is always more economical in terms of power to use as concentrated a raw material as possible. Given unlimited power we could extract all the raw materials of industry – iron, copper, nickel, sulphur, uranium and so on – from dilute sources such as the sea or ordinary rock and soil. But we do not have unlimited power, nor shall we have in this century. Therefore, to express the principle differently, any concentrated ore, such as a sulphur deposit, soda deposit or bed of iron ore, represents a saving of power.

Industry makes things from concentrated raw materials, and this brings us to our second principle. The effect of using materials such as iron, copper, sulphur and so on is to disperse them about the world and so to dilute them: the whole trend of industry is to take concentrated materials and, as a result of using them, to make them become diluted. We shall discuss several examples of these principles in this and the next chapter.

The first importance of microbes in industry, then, is that, over geological aeons of time, they have provided mankind with several concentrated reserves of industrially important materials. They were concerned in important respects with the genesis of the two fossil fuels and, as we shall see, were responsible for the deposition of several important minerals. A whole subject, called 'geo-microbiology', has grown up around the study of microbes in the formation and treatment of fuel and mineral resources; for the first part of this chapter we shall look at this subject and observe how microbes, millions of years ago, contributed to our basic industrial needs today.

Sulphur is perhaps the best-established of the microbiologically produced minerals. Nearly every major industry that exists consumes sulphuric acid for one reason or another – it is used for pickling metals, electro-plating, treating artificial fibres, preparing fertilizers, manufacturing all kinds of chemicals and pharmaceutical products, extracting ores, and so on. It has been said that the national demand for sulphuric acid in a country is a measure of its degree of industrialization. Much the easiest way of making sulphuric acid is to burn sulphur to form sulphur oxides and then to react these with water. One can make sulphur oxides by other means, such as burning iron pyrites (FeS_2) or heating calcium sulphate (the mineral 'gypsum') with coke and sand, but native sulphur is the most concentrated source of sulphur possible and, consistent with our first principle enunciated above, it is the most economical raw material from the point of view of the power expended in obtaining it. A little elemental sulphur is needed industrially as a vulcanizing agent in rubber production, for making matches, or in certain chemicals; a little is used in medicine and horticulture too, but by far the greater part is needed to make sulphuric acid. In this respect sulphur provides a very good example of our second principle: though used on an enormous scale, very little sulphuric acid appears in the final products of industry. One can think of electrical accumulators, which contain free sulphuric acid, or certain detergents which are organic derivatives of sulphuric acid, but by and large sulphuric acid is used during the process of production and does not form part of the finished product. Hence, when it is used, it goes, figuratively (and sometimes actually) down the drain. It is disposed of by some means or another and eventually finds its way into the sea, usually as sodium or calcium sulphate. A lot of sulphur disappears into the atmosphere. Nearly all fuels – coal, oil, wood, petroleum – contain sulphur compounds which, when they burn, pollute the atmosphere as sulphur oxides. (This is why curtain fabrics, stone and metalwork corrode so rapidly in towns; it is also one of the reasons why town dwellers are so prone to bronchitis, because sulphur oxides damage the lung membranes.) Over Britain, 5 million tons of sulphur pollute the air each year, ultimately being washed into soil, rivers and seas by the rain. It is probable that the sulphur cycle, which we discussed in Chapter 1, results in a net loss of sulphur from the land to the sea. In general, the pattern of sulphur movement today provides a very clear example of industrial civilization taking a concentrated natural resource and diluting it.

The demands of industrial countries for sulphur, which is mainly converted to sulphuric acid, are enormous. In 1951 the U.S.A. was consuming nearly 5 million tons a year and Britain needed nearly half a million tons – though, because of a world sulphur shortage, it was not getting it. The world's deposits of native sulphur are mainly located around the Gulf of Mexico, in Texas, Louisiana and in parts of Mexico itself. Other deposits exist, in Sicily, Iceland, North Africa and the Carpathians, but something like 95 per cent of the world's supplies come from the Gulf area. The mineral is located in rather confined deposits, called domes, and is always found associated with calcium sulphate and, usually, oil is not far away. The question arises, how did it get where it is, and why is it always associated with a particular geological pattern? The answer, which seems to be reasonably well established, is that it was formed as a result of intense microbial activity during a geological era of warmth and sunshine, probably while a sea was drying up. The Caribbean is known to have stretched far into the Southern States of the U.S.A. and into Mexico some 200,000,000 years ago (whether it was the Permian or the Jurassic period is still uncertain) and it was probably about that time that the world's major deposits were laid down. Sulphate-reducing bacteria in the drying, concentrating sea used organic matter for the reduction of calcium sulphate in the water to calcium sulphide. This in its turn became oxidized to calcium carbonate and free sulphur, probably through the agency of the photosynthetic sulphur bacteria. Hence the sulphur cycle, which we met in Chapter 1, progressed as far as sulphur but no further, so that sulphate was reduced and sulphur accumulated. The reason why it did not progress further is almost certainly that there was no air available: the drying up of the sea caused organic matter to become concentrated, whereupon microbes grew and used up all the dissolved oxygen. In addition, the coloured bacteria generated more organic matter photosynthetically from CO_2, using sunlight, so a huge, anaerobic salt pan developed, with calcium sulphate crystallizing out and sulphur sedimenting; deposits of microbial organic matter also formed which, later, may well have contributed to oil formation.

How do we know this? There are two lines of evidence, one of which is that, in certain parts of the world, one can see such a process happening even today. In Libya, in North Africa, there are a number of lakes (near the hamlet of El Agheila) where warm artesian water, rich in calcium sulphate and containing hydrogen sulphide, comes to the surface through springs. One of these, called Ain-ez-Zauia, is about the size of a swimming pool and is slightly warm (30 degrees Centigrade); it is saturated with calcium sulphate and contains about $2\frac{1}{2}$ per cent sodium chloride – a reasonable approximation to a warm, drying-up sea, if a little weak in salt. Under the Libyan sun, this lake produces about 100 tons of crude sulphur a year, formed as a fine, yellow-grey mud which is, in fact, harvested by the local Bedouin. (They export some to Egypt – or did when I was there in 1950 – and use it as medicine themselves.) The way in which the sulphur is formed is this: sulphate-reducing bacteria reduce the dissolved sulphate to sulphide at the expense of organic matter formed by coloured sulphur bacteria, which in their turn have made the organic matter from carbon dioxide using sunlight and sulphide, some of it from the spring waters, some formed by the sulphate reducers. Thus we have sulphur formed from sulphate by two inter-dependent types of bacteria, the whole process being propelled by solar energy. The bed of the lake consists of a red, gelatinous mud made up almost entirely of coloured sulphur bacteria; the bulk of the lake is a colloidal suspension of sulphur rich in sulphate-reducing bacteria; the whole system smells strongly of hydrogen sulphide.

In fact, we took samples of this lake back to a British laboratory in 1950, artificial lake water (corresponding to the analysis of the real thing) was prepared, and a small mock-sulphur lake of about 10 gallons set up in which, when illuminated, the red gelatinous mud grew and sulphur was formed; by altering the conditions somewhat it was possible to accelerate sulphur formation quite considerably.

Lakes and sulphur springs of this kind exist in various parts of the world and the fact that one can isolate the appropriate bacteria from then, and even duplicate biological sulphur formation in the laboratory, is strong circumstantial evidence in favour of the belief that this is how the majority of sulphur deposits arose. But there is stronger evidence. Professor H. Thode of Canada showed, in about 1950, that during biological sulphide formation, some separation of the natural sulphur isotopes took place, and that this did not occur during chemical sulphate reduction.

Perhaps, for non-chemists, I should digress for a moment and explain what an isotope is. Nearly all elements, such as hydrogen, oxygen, nitrogen and sulphur, exist in nature as mixtures of atoms, the majority of which have a certain mass but a few of which have a different mass. Sulphur, for example, consists mainly of atoms that are thirty-two times as heavy as a hydrogen atom, but about two per cent of its atoms are heavier: thirty-four times as heavy as a hydrogen atom. These isotopes can be detected and measured readily in a device called a mass spectrometer, and, no matter what form of chemical combination the sulphur occurs in – as sulphide, sulphate, thiosulphate, organic sulphur compounds, for example – the ratio of the isotopes will be similar. Similar, but not identical. Because what Thode observed was that sulphides and sulphates found in meteors or volcanoes, where no possibility of biological action existed, had identical isotope ratios among their sulphur atoms. So did sulphur-bearing minerals taken from geological strata laid down before life originated on this planet. But sulphide formed in cultures of sulphate-reducing bacteria, or in natural environments where sulphate-reducing bacteria were active, was richer in the lightweight isotope, and the residual sulphate was richer in the heavier isotope. For some reason, it seemed, bacterial sulphate reduction separated the natural isotopes of sulphur appreciably. Volcanic sulphur had the 'natural' or 'meteoric' isotope ratio, but the Texas and Louisiana sulphur deposits, as well as those in Sicily and samples sent from Ain-ez-Zauia, had the biological ratio.

Hence isotope experiments provide very good evidence that bacteria were responsible for the conversion of sulphate to sulphide during the formation of the world's major sulphur resources. But they provide no evidence that bacteria were involved in the next step: the oxidation of sulphide to sulphur. Some authorities believe that bacteria had nothing to do with this, that oxidation by air, or a slow chemical reaction between sulphide and sulphate, provide a sufficient explanation of sulphur formation. Russian workers have provided good evidence that 80 per cent of the sulphur found in Carpathian deposits arises through the action of thiobacilli (which we met earlier in Chapter 2: colourless bacteria that can oxidize sulphide in air to sulphur and, usually, further, to form sulphuric acid). As far as what happened geological eras ago, the point will probably never be settled, but the beauty of conceiving the second step as biological is that it explains how the sulphate-reducing bacteria obtained energy for sulphate-reduction. They obtained it from the carbon compounds manufactured from carbon dioxide by the coloured sulphur bacteria or the thiobacilli as the case may be.

I have described sulphur formation as taking place while the sea was receding from what is now Texas, Louisiana and parts of Mexico. I should add that some geologists believe that the evaporation occurred first and that, long after the salt beds were buried in later deposits, bacterial sulphate reduction took place as petroleum, which some authorities believe these bacteria can use as an energy source, seeped into the beds of calcium sulphate. We cannot discuss the pros and cons of these views here; we shall merely note that no one disputes that sulphate-reducing bacteria were involved in the primary step of forming sulphide from sulphate.

The biological nature of sulphur formation has given rise to proposals for manufacturing sulphur industrially using bacteria. We shall discuss these possibilities later in this chapter.

A second important mineral deposit that is formed through bacterial action is soda, sodium carbonate, which is mined in various parts of the world. The sulphate-reducing bacteria are also involved in this process, which takes place when sulphur formation fails to occur on any large scale. If, for some reason, massive bacterial sulphate-reduction takes place in nature, it is usually calcium sulphate that is reduced, because this salt, responsible for permanent hardness in water, is one of the commonest mineral sulphates. Though we have, for brevity, talked so far of the reduction of 'sulphate' to 'sulphide', it is usually calcium sulphate that is reduced to calcium sulphide. In chemical symbolism one can write:

$$CaSO_4 \longrightarrow CaS$$

If carbon dioxide is present, as it always is as a result of the respiration of the microbes, some of this calcium sulphide reacts with it, giving hydrogen sulphide:

$$CaS + CO_2 \xrightarrow{\text{in } H_2O} CaCO_3 + H_2S$$

The hydrogen sulphide has the characteristic bad-egg smell of badly polluted environments. The other product is calcium carbonate or chalk. In certain environments the main sulphate mineral is sodium sulphate – the Wadi Natrun in Egypt is such a place – and in this case the end product is sodium carbonate or soda. Dr Abd-el-Malek in Egypt has studied the Wadi Natrun and produced good evidence that this view of the formation of soda is correct: the numbers of sulphate-reducing bacteria in the environs of the soda deposits increase as the deposits get stronger.

Sulphides are formed wherever sulphate-reducing bacteria become active, but, because these bacteria do not function in air (as we mentioned in Chapter 2, they are strict anaerobes), their activity tends to be rather localized. They need a good supply of organic matter and sulphate to become established, though once established they tend to keep themselves going because sulphide is rather poisonous to other living things, which therefore die and tend, by decomposing, to augment the organic matter available to the sulphate-reducers. As we saw in Chapter 1, other sulphur bacteria may develop and we get the limited ecological system based on the sulphur cycle called the sulfuretum. The world's sulphur deposits were probably formed as parts of gigantic sulfureta; as we have just seen, soda can be formed if a sulfuretum is established in certain environments. Now, most terrestrial waters contain dissolved iron, and some have copper and lead in solution as well. When such waters encounter a sulfuretum an immediate chemical reaction occurs whereby the dissolved metal reacts with the H_2S to form a metal sulphide. This material is deposited as a precipitate. In this manner, it is believed, have many of the world's resources of sulphide minerals been formed. Uranium ores may have become concentrated in this manner; copper and lead occur mainly as sulphide ores, and it has been possible to mimic their formation in the laboratory. But laboratory experiments aimed at imitating nature do not necessarily prove that nature actually ever behaved that way; as far as I know, isotope distribution experiments of the kind that established the biological origin of native sulphur have not been done with copper, lead and other metal sulphide ores, so the theory that they were formed biologically is less well supported.

Except in the case of iron. Iron sulphide is found in many marine sediments and areas where sulfureta have been functioning, and usually the sulphur in such iron sulphide deposits has the 'biological' isotope distribution. An important mineral containing iron is iron pyrites, and this is known to be formed geologically from sedimentary iron sulphide by way of a partly hydrated mineral called hydrotroilite. The precise chemistry of the process need not concern us here; the upshot of the matter is that iron pyrites (which has the chemical formula FeS_2 in contrast to the FeS of iron sulphide) has a biological origin, again largely owing to the sulphate-reducing bacteria. Pyritized fossils – fossils that have been transformed into pyrites while retaining their original form – probably arose because the decaying organism allowed a little sulfuretum to become established and thus a replica of the more rigid parts of the dead creature built up as, atom by atom, dissolved iron seeped into the sulfuretum. But the major importance of iron pyrites is as an alternative to sulphur for manufacturing sulphuric acid. Pyrites can be burned to give iron oxides and gaseous oxides of sulphur, the latter being easy to convert to sulphuric acid on an industrial scale. In 1950 about a sixth of Britain's million-and-a-half tons of sulphuric acid were made from pyrites. The process is not as economical as that using native sulphur, but as sulphur becomes scarcer and more expensive it is being used increasingly.

The sulphate-reducing bacteria, then, are extremely important in the genesis of several of the world's mineral resources, but they are not the only microbes so involved. There is a specially pure kind of iron ore, known as 'bog iron' and found on the edges of marshy areas, which is formed through the action of iron bacteria, of which we spoke briefly in Chapter 2. These bacteria have the property of oxidizing dissolved ferrous iron to ferric iron which, being less soluble in water, precipitates out as a deposit resembling rust. In chemical terms this can be formalized as:

$$FeX_2 + O_2 \xrightarrow{\text{in } H_2O} Fe(OH)_3 + 2HX$$

where X is a monovalent anion such as an organic derivative. (Non-chemists may recall that in Chapter 1 we saw that, when dissolved in water as a chemical derivative, iron exists in two forms, one of which is formed by the action of oxygen on the other, and is less soluble.) The seepage waters from a peat bog, for example, are relatively rich in dissolved ferrous iron and are rather acid. Where such waters flow, say, into a chalky area and become neutralized, iron bacteria grow in great numbers and, in due time, can form massive deposits of ore. As we saw in Chapter 2, it is not clear why the bacteria do this: the idea that the oxidation of ferrous iron enables them to grow autotrophically seems to be mistaken. However, the product is a very pure ore, and was, because of its ready availability and purity, probably the first metal ore to be used by mankind. *Sphaerotilus*, *Leptothrix* and other iron bacteria provided mankind with the means of transition from the stone age to the iron age.

Nowadays, of course, other types of iron ore are mainly used industrially, because there is just not enough bog iron left. But the process of bog iron formation can often be seen on a small scale where peaty and iron-rich waters flow out of springs and bogs, forming a brown rusty deposit on stones and rocks. It is probable that some deposits of manganese oxides were formed in a similar way.

A complicated process due to bacteria occurs in the natural leaching of pyrites. We shall see in Chapter 7 how coal and gold mines contain strata of iron pyrites, and how certain sulphur bacteria (*Thiobacillus ferro-oxidans*) oxidize this to form, among other things, sulphuric acid, which corrodes piping and damages mining machinery. In dumps of pyrites, outside mines, these organisms grow and turn the environment acid. More of the pyrites dissolves – because acid helps to decompose pyrites – and one of the products of this reaction is free sulphur. This, too, is oxidized by bacteria such as *Thiobacillus thio-oxidans*, forming yet more sulphuric acid. Thus one gets an interesting set-up in which rainwater permeates the dump and, with the aid of bacteria, washes out dissolved iron and sulphuric acid. The effluent waters are brown and rusty-looking. Now, all pyrites deposits contain copper in small amounts, which is valuable, and this washes out as copper sulphate. A minor industry has developed for extracting the copper by running the 'leached' water over scrap iron, when the iron dissolves and copper is precipitated. Expressed chemically:

$$Fe + CuSO_4 \longrightarrow FeSO_4 + Cu$$

a reaction known to every schoolboy. Iron bacteria later convert the ferrous sulphate to ferric oxides, which settles as the deposit called 'ochre', which is used in the paint industry. Though the production of ochre by this process far exceeds demand, the copper found is sufficiently valuable to make the process worth while. Reports in the American literature indicate that molybdenum, titanium, chromium and zinc may be concentrated from pyritic strata by the action of *Thiobacillus ferro-oxidans*; of particular importance for the future of atomic energy is the fact that uranium may be leached out of low grade sulphide ores in a similar manner. A rather remarkable claim was made in France in 1964 to the effect that an aerobic sporulating bacterium had been isolated from tropical soils that released gold from combination in soils called laterites – but before the reader invests his savings in a microbiological gold rush, I should mention that the amounts of gold made soluble were very small.

To return to our opening theme – that the most important economic activities of microbes took place geological eras ago – we may consider the case of coal, the basic fuel of the Industrial Revolution. The genesis of coal is pretty well understood nowadays: huge forests of plants, mainly related to present-day mosses and ferns but gigantic in size, flourished about 300,000,000 years ago in a geological period called the carboniferous era. The environment was warm and humid, with swamps and bogs abounding, and as the vegetation died and decayed it formed a sort of vast compost heap in which any oxygen that penetrated was immediately consumed by putrefactive bacteria. Thus an anaerobic fermentation took place and methane – marsh gas – was formed while the plant debris became converted to materials of rather indeterminate chemical composition called humic acids. This process still occurs today: the product of such decay in bogs, when it dries out, is peat, itself a valuable fuel. The will o' the wisp, a flame of burning methane dancing over a peat bog, is an important element of Irish folk lore which has the unusual status of being a genuine natural phenomenon, if a rare one. Humic acids are distantly related, in a chemical sense, to phenols, the disinfectants we met in Chapter 3, and they have preservative properties in that, though formed by microbial action on plant material, they tend to prevent further bacterial action. This is why metals, wooden objects and even corpses, when recovered from peat bogs, often show remarkably little decay.

Peat, then, is an early stage in the formation of coal. From the chemical viewpoint it is plant material, which consists mainly of carbon, hydrogen and oxygen, though depleted in oxygen and enriched in carbon and hydrogen, so that, when dry, it burns readily in air. During the carboniferous era, as millennium succeeded millennium, the peat deposits became overlaid by sand and rocks and thus compressed. As the pressure increased, the peat turned into coal, first becoming brown coal or lignite, which is structurally rather like peat, later forming the familiar 'bituminous' coal widely (and extravagantly) used by the domestic British. (To pollute, if readers will forgive a petulant aside, their atmosphere by sucking warmed air up chimneys, in the belief that they are warming their houses.) Under very high pressures the very pure coal called anthracite was formed. During the compression process a one-foot stratum of peat yielded about an inch of coal, and the mineral underwent further chemical change, becoming enriched in carbon and depleted in hydrogen, so much so that anthracite is almost pure carbon. Quite why pressure should have this effect on peat is not at all clear; it is fairly certain that, in the early stages, residual action by bacteria resistant to the disinfectant action of peat assisted the removal of hydrogen. Anyway, the important point from the economic point of view is that the primary process leading to coal formation was the putrefaction of plant material by methane bacteria which, as the reader will recall from Chapter 2, are strongly anaerobic bacteria: they do not grow in air.

Methane is marsh gas. If you find a pond that has had regular seasonal deposits of leaves and other vegetation in it and poke a stick into the bottom mud, bubbles of marsh gas will emerge. This is formed by methane bacteria; it can be caught in a jam-jar and burnt. If it ignites spontaneously, it forms the will o' the wisp mentioned earlier. Methane must have been formed in enormous quantities during coal formation and it is the main component of natural gas, which is becoming an increasingly important source of power. At the time of writing, the North Sea is revealing reserves of subterranean methane that may well exceed in energy value the whole coal reserves of Britain. (A most satisfactory prospect, if I may digress once more, since both coal mining and coal burning are hazardous to health, and the burning of coal wastes valuable coal tar products.) Natural gas is a relatively clean fuel and an increasingly useful one – the U.S.A. consumed over 10,000 *million* cubic feet in 1965. Methane is normally found in coal mines – it is the hazardous 'fire damp', the cause of many tragic explosions in mines – and it is tempting to assume that the vast reserves of subterranean gas that are only now being tapped resulted from the action of the methane bacteria over geological eras. Indeed, this must be true, but at least some of it may have been there since the earth originated because methane is one of the few interplanetary gases (Jupiter consists largely of methane together with ammonia) and the primitive atmosphere of the earth, before life originated, undoubtedly contained methane. Much of this could have been entrapped as the earth cooled and settled down. A partial origin of this kind could account for the presence of such gases as ethane and propane, which are found in small amounts in natural gas but which are not formed by any known microbes.

Man's third main fossil fuel is oil and the distillation products of oil collectively called petroleum. The question whether oil originated as a product of microbial action is still not settled, largely because no one has successfully caused bacteria to form oil in laboratory conditions – at least in important amounts. Oil hydrocarbons could have been formed chemically by the action of water on metal carbides during the infancy of this planet, but oil deposits have the characteristics that make a biological origin highly probable. First, they are rich in anaerobic bacteria, particularly the by now familiar sulphate-reducing bacteria, and they are associated with sulphur deposits which are known to have a biological origin. Moreover, when scientists have succeeded in detecting oil-like compounds in microbial cultures, they have been formed in mixed populations that included sulphate-reducing bacteria. Secondly, in crude oil one can detect compounds called porphyrins, which are chemicals derived from the respiratory enzymes of living organisms and which are not known to occur away from living things. Thirdly, certain of the hydrocarbons of petroleum are optically active, which means, in non-chemical terms, that their molecules have a special kind of configuration that is only known to result from the action of biological systems. (I shall explain the type of configuration more precisely later in this chapter.) None of these points is conclusive: all could have resulted, for example, from the action of microbes on oil *after* it was formed, an action which is quite familiar to microbiologists as we shall see in Chapter 7. But the chances are that oil was formed by microbial processes analogous to those that led to the sulphur, coal and natural gas reserves of this planet.

If the responsibility of bacteria for oil formation is not proved, there is little doubt about their role in the coalescence of oil deposits. Much oil in deposits is absorbed on rock – called 'oil shale' – and this usually consists largely of calcium sulphate. Professor ZoBell of California has shown very clearly that our old friends the sulphate-reducing bacteria, when grown in the presence of oil shale, cause the absorbed oil to be released from the rock and to coalesce as droplets. The bacteria do this by a variety of mechanisms, one of which is to reduce the rock chemically to sulphide, thus changing its configuration and releasing the absorbed material, another of which is to form a detergent-like substance which 'cleans off' the oil. Other anaerobic bacteria contribute to the effect, and the great oil deposits of Texas and California, which are enormous subterranean pools of oil released from shale, are believed to have formed as a result of bacterial action on the shale. Spent oil wells, wells that have ceased gushing because the pressure under which they existed before they were tapped has been released, still have much useful oil in them, and some of this can be displaced by injecting brine or sea water under the oil stratum and 'floating' the oil out. (This process is called 'secondary recovery' in oil technologists' jargon.) But much oil remains absorbed on the associated shale and, in Czechoslovakia, secondary recovery of oil has successfully been enhanced by pumping nutrients for sulphate-reducing bacteria into the well. Unfortunately, as might be expected if one is persuading bacteria to do something in weeks that they hitherto did over centuries, the improvement is but modest and transient in most cases.

Microbes in Industry

We have discussed the importance of microbes in the formation of the resources of industry. The last paragraph brings us to the question of the deliberate use of microbes in industry. Can any of these processes be made use of today, or do they take so long as to be worthless?

The broad answer is that, at present, there are sufficient coal, oil, methane and sulphur reserves on this planet to last mankind for some time to come and, if a global shortage of any of these basic materials did occur, it would be most logical to prepare them by some industrial chemical process using atomic or hydro-electric energy, rather than to mimic their natural origin. But mankind, in the mass, is not logical. Because of what seems to be a natural-born parochialism, he is incapable of utilizing his planetary resources on a global scale. Local shortages of raw materials are a chronic disease of our only partly civilized planet, and a classic example of this kind occurred in the world sulphur shortage of the early 1950s. At that time British industry, typical of most West-European industry, was geared to using native sulphur imported from the U.S.A. By 1950 the rate at which existing sulphur domes were being exhausted had exceeded the rate at which new ones were being discovered, the price of American sulphur went up and, starved of dollars as a result of the war, Britain and most of Western Europe found its industrial recovery drastically hampered by a world sulphur shortage. The shortage stimulated further prospecting, and many new deposits were discovered, but the sulphur crisis was only pushed ahead for a decade or so. By the mid-1950s the shortage had eased, but in 1963 output exceeded the discovery of new resources once more and a new sulphur shortage is developing – though it will be less drastic because several major industries transferred to pyrites and other minerals as their sources of sulphuric acid during the 1950s. As a result of the earlier crisis, a process was developed in a British government research laboratory for making sulphuric acid by a process using microbes, based on the way sulphate-reducing bacteria function in nature. The late K. R. Butlin and his colleagues, with the present writer interfering at times, showed that one could ferment sewage using sulphate-reducing bacteria and, at least in theory, obtain up to a fifth of Britain's requirement of

133

sulphur by a process that might be called 'composting' sewage sludge with gypsum (calcium sulphate). Actually, the product was not sulphur but hydrogen sulphide, but this was equally useful because it could be converted to sulphur or sulphuric acid as desired by established industrial chemical processes. The sewage sludge, after treatment, had certain advantages as a disposal product (its settling properties were improved, so less water had to be handled to get rid of it) and a London sewage works developed it to a pilot plant scale. However, by a regrettable decision that we shall allude to again in Chapter 8, the work was discontinued and the prospects of Britain becoming even partly self-sufficient in regard to sulphur receded accordingly. But, generally speaking, a microbiological process for producing sulphur from sewage could be useful for countries having a low degree of industrialization and limited resources of foreign currency; a comparable process using industrial wastes has been used in Czechoslovakia. Similarly, devices for producing methane by bacterial fermentation of farm waste and sewage could be used to supply power to poorly industrialized areas in Asia and Africa. 'Sulphur farming' has been proposed as a possible 'cottage industry' in parts of India such as Masulipatam; installations for running refrigerators on methane generated by bacteria from farm wastes have been devised for use in tropical areas. Methane is, in fact, the normal product of one stage of conventional sewage treatment and, in highly industrialized countries, the more sophisticated sewage works use the methane formed in sewage digestion to run their machinery and even, in some instances, to run lorries. In recent years the Gas Council's objections to adding methane to town gas have been overcome and some sewage works supply methane to their county's gas grid. We shall discuss methane production in connection with sewage disposal in Chapter 8.

When the product is a simple chemical such as sulphur or methane, an industrial process based on microbes needs a cheap waste product to work on if it is to be economic. Industrial alcohol, for example, used to be obtained by the fermentation of molasses (a waste product of the sugar industry) by yeasts. Acetone and butanol, both important industrial solvents, have been made by the fermentation of molasses by *Clostridium acetobutylicum*. Glycerol can be produced industrially by conducting the alcoholic fermentation in the presence of sulphite. Acetic acid has been produced industrially by the traditional vinegar fermentation. All these products, however, can now be made as easily by purely chemical processes as by-products of the petroleum industry and though, since the equipment is there, some industries use fermentation processes to make these simple chemicals, it is fair to say that, as industrial fermentations, they are obsolescent. Microbes always form their products in fairly dilute solution, which means that the industrially expensive process of concentrating them has to be undertaken. This, and the fact that their raw material has to remain cheap despite the ever-increasing demands of industry for the product itself, makes the use of microbes for 'heavy' chemicals – those much in demand – a generally uneconomic prospect.

The future of microbes in industry lies mainly in the preparation of substances that are for one reason or another difficult for the chemist to prepare on an industrial scale. Citric acid, much used in the soft drinks industry and mentioned in Chapter 5, happens to be an awkward chemical to synthesize, though its chemical structure is simple. Hence it is still made microbiologically on an industrial scale and will probably continue to be. Fumaric acid and itaconic acid are even simpler chemicals than citric acid but are also not easily made chemically; they have uses in the plastics and synthetic lacquer industries and are produced from sugar by fermentation with moulds of the *Rhizopus* and *Aspergillus* groups respectively. Gluconic acid, a derivative of glucose, has uses in pharmacy as a means of administering calcium to patients (calcium gluconate can be injected safely) and is prepared industrially by the action of the bacterium *Acetobacter suboxydans* (which we met in Chapter 5 making vitamin C) on glucose.

A general class of 'awkward' compounds are those that are optically active. This means that they have a particular kind of distorting effect on polarized light which can be detected with appropriate optical instruments. We shall not bother with details

135

of what this effect is here, but its significance is of some importance because it indicates a subtlety of their molecular structure. For the benefit of non-chemists I shall describe the simplest possible case of an optically active molecule. Consider a carbon compound whose chemical formula is Cwxyz. C is the carbon atom and joined to it are four different atoms w, x, y and z. If you could actually see a molecule of that compound in 3-D, as it were, it would look like this:

(a)

where x and w lie in the plane of the paper, z sticks out above and y below it. (Geometrically, w, x, y and z lie at the points of a tetrahedron, with C at its centre.) This molecule is unsymmetrical: if you held up a mirror to it its reflection would look like this:

(b)

The original molecule and its reflection are different because, however you twist *b* around you could never super-impose it on *a*. It follows that any chemical compound which contains a carbon (or other) atom linked to four *different* atoms (or groups of atoms) can exist in two forms corresponding in structure to these mirror images. But in all their gross chemical properties the two forms behave similarly; they only differ in certain fine details such as their effect on light. When a chemist synthesizes such an asymmetric compound in the laboratory he normally obtains a mixture of the two forms in equal proportions. But when bio-

136

logical systems make or utilize asymmetric compounds, they usually make or utilize exclusively one of the two forms. Indeed, most biological molecules are unsymmetrical, and almost all belong to what is known as the left-handed class of molecular configurations. Microbes are used for the preparation of optically active compounds for two reasons: the first is that some microbes will use the left-handed form preferentially, thus enabling the chemist to achieve a separation of the two forms because the microbe leaves one behind; the second is that, if they form a product that is asymmetrical, they usually form only one of the two forms (usually the left-handed form). Pharmaceutical activity often depends on getting the right configuration of molecules that may have not one but several asymmetric centres, and in these circumstances biological, and particularly microbial, methods are the only practical procedures.

Optically active compounds may be needed in pharmacy and research, but they are not the sort of chemicals required by the heavy industries of a nation. They represent a class of fine chemicals for which biological processes will probably always be necessary, but they are far from the sole province of microbes: alkaloids, hormones and the many other natural products of the Pharmaceutical Codex are obtained from plants and animals as much as from microbes.

The classical instance of microbes being used to produce something that could not be made otherwise is, of course, in the antibiotic industry. Antibiotics are substances produced by one species of microbe that either kill other microbes or prevent them growing. Sometimes they are extraordinarily active: penicillin is still one of the most powerful drugs known against sensitive bacteria. It is formed by a filamentous mould, rather like that which grows on blue cheese, called *Penicillium* (there is a variety of species that produce substances of this kind but *P. chrysogenum* is the one used industrially) and, in the pioneer work, the amounts produced were minute. The story of penicillin, the first of the antibiotics, is so well documented that we shall not go into it here, though we gave an indication of it in Chapter 3. For our purposes, limiting ourselves to the industrial importance of microbes, we

137

shall only note that penicillin is a highly awkward compound to synthesize chemically and that, despite the existence of resistant bacteria and allergic patients (see Chapters 3 and 5), it has revolutionized medicine and is still one of the most valuable drugs we have. It will continue to be made microbiologically, simply because it is so difficult to prepare chemically. One point of interest to us is that the strains of mould now used to make penicillin produce at least three hundred times as much as did Fleming's original strain, and the reason for this illustrates an important point concerning the flexibility of industrial micro-biology. We mentioned in Chapters 2 and 4 how microbes show great adaptability or, in other words, can adjust themselves to new environments. The process of adjustment involves a process called mutation (which we shall discuss in Chapter 10), and just as we can obtain mutants resistant to drugs or able to grow at the expense of unfamiliar materials, so we can obtain mutants that will produce more (or less) of by-products such as penicillin. Maltreatment of strains with substances such as mustard gas, or with ultra-violet radiation, γ- or X-rays, increases mutation among those individuals that are not killed, and in these ways mutants of *P. chrysogenum* have been obtained which have the enhanced penicillin productivity just mentioned. All strains used industrially are mutants, and their productivities are closely guarded commercial secrets.

Penicillin itself – or rather the three or four penicillins that are formed by various strains in various conditions – are normally produced by batch culture fermentations (see Chapter 4). Continuous culture has not so far been of much use. But in recent years Beecham Research Laboratories in Britain have developed a half-microbiological, half-chemical procedure for manufacturing all kinds of laboratory variations on the penicillin molecule, and some of these promise to be exceptionally useful. The penicillin molecules have this formula:

$$R-NH-CH-CH \overset{S}{\diagdown} C(CH_3)_2$$
$$\underset{\underset{O}{\overset{\|}{C}}}{C} - N \underline{\hspace{2cm}} CH.COOH$$

where 'R' signifies a group of atoms whose precise composition determines which of the penicillins it is. It is possible, using special mutant strains and cultural conditions, to make the mould form penicillanic acid, which has the formula:

$$NH_2-CH-CH \overset{S}{\diagdown} C(CH_3)_2$$
$$\underset{\underset{O}{\overset{\|}{C}}}{C} - N \underline{\hspace{2cm}} CH.COOH$$

(Notice that it is the same as a penicillin but with an 'H' where an 'R' should be.) This substance is not an antibiotic, but it becomes one if, by chemical manipulation, one of the groups 'R' is attached to it. Now, by attaching groups in the position 'R' that would never have turned up in nature one can make an enormous variety of 'unnatural' penicillins. This has been done by the Beecham's group and a measure of their success is that some of them are active against bacteria that have become resistant to the natural penicillins.

In this instance, a combination of microbiological and chemical processes has been used industrially. One of the antibiotics to be discovered soon after the emergence of penicillin was chloramphenicol, formed by the actinomycete *Streptomyces venezuelae* and active against bacteria (such as the typhoid organism) that penicillin hardly touched. This material has a relatively simple chemical structure, is not difficult to make chemically, and is now made industrially without the aid of microbes. All the other antibiotics are, however, made by fermentation processes, and though hundreds have been reported in the scientific literature

139

(fifty-nine new ones were reported in 1963), surprisingly few have proved to be of any real value in pharmacy. It is possible, however, to classify their types and this we shall do to obtain a synoptic view of those antibiotics that have proved to be of some medical use.

Penicillins: The first, least poisonous and most useful antibiotics to be discovered. Formed by moulds of the genus *Penicillium* and by some species of *Aspergillus*. More than half a million pounds of penicillin are produced each year in the U.S.A. Though penicillin is extremely effective when it does work, its anti-bacterial spectrum – which means the range of bacterial species against which it is active – is rather narrow. Cephalosporins are antibiotics related to penicillin which have a rather wide range of action and which often attack bacteria which are resistant to ordinary penicillin; they are formed by fungi of the genus *Cephalosporium*.

Polypeptide antibiotics: These are protein fragments, of rather unusual structure, produced by bacteria of the *Bacillus* group and active against other bacteria. They act rather like detergents, damaging the cell wall, and though they are too toxic for internal use in medicine, they have been used to treat external wounds. Examples are gramicidin, polymyxin and bacitracin.

Tetracycline antibiotics: These are broad-spectrum antibiotics which, though they are rather rough on the normal bacteria that live in association with us, are proving popular with doctors for controlling the secondary bacterial infections that often accompany virus diseases. They have a peculiar chemical structure consisting of four joined-up rings of carbon atoms. Aureomycin (chlortetracycline) and terramycin (oxytetracycline) are widely used in general medicine; they are produced by the actinomycetes *Streptomyces aureofaciens* and *S. rimorus* respectively and are produced today in amounts comparable to the output of penicillin.

Glycoside antibiotics: Streptomycin, the next antibiotic to be discovered after penicillin, is produced by the actinomycete *Streptomyces griseus*. It is rather more toxic than penicillin and the tetracyclines, but still of great medical value, notably in the treatment of tuberculosis. It attacks a variety of organisms that are insensitive to penicillin and is chemically distinguished by including modified sugar molecules in its structure. Neomycin is related to it and is formed by *Streptomyces fradiae;* it is too toxic for internal use but valuable for skin infections. Novobiocin belongs to this group and, more distantly related in a chemical sense, is erythromycin, which has been used to control penicillin-resistant infections. These substances are all produced by species of streptomyces and, in the case of streptomycin, high-yielding mutant strains have been developed for use by industry.

Polyene antibiotics: Some streptomycetes produce compounds distantly related to vitamin A which are active against fungi. They have been used to treat fungal infections and include mystatin, which is the one most widely used in medicine.

Unclassified: Between 1938 and 1963 over 1,100 antibiotics were reported, of which fifty-four got as far as being produced commercially. It is impossible to mention them all here, but we have touched on the major ones. A group of some special interest is the anti-tumour agents, which cause regression of some kinds of cancer. Actinomycin, the first to be discovered, is intrinsically very poisonous and not of much practical value, but research on less toxic ones such as mithromycin (from the U.S.A.) and olivomycin (from the U.S.S.R.) has led to some clinical successes. They are all formed by strains of actinomycetes, and they act by interfering with the function of ribonucleic acid ('RNA'), a component of living cells which controls growth. Other antibiotics that deserve special mention are chloramphenicol, a broad-spectrum antibiotic which, as mentioned earlier, is the only one to be produced chemically. Cycloserine, another *Streptomyces* product, is useful in the treatment of tuberculosis. Griseofulvin should be mentioned because it is produced by the same fungus that makes streptomycin (*S. griseus*) and is active against plant pathogens, particularly fungi such as mildews and rusts. It promises to be of considerable value in agriculture. Nisin, produced by the bacterium *Streptococcus lactis*, is in fact an enzyme and has been used in food preservation.

The last two examples show that antibiotics, though normally regarded as wonder-drugs for use on people, also have applications in agriculture and food preservation. They have also been used as additives to animal fodder, a matter discussed in Chapter 5. They are certainly the mainstay of industrial microbiology today, in the sense that they are reliable, saleable items which industry can only produce using microbes. Consequently an enormous amount of money has been spent by industry in the search for antibiotics and in their development; it is really rather remarkable that less than a dozen are in fact well suited to use in general medicine and that the best of all should have been the first to be discovered: penicillin. It is also surprising what a variety of antibiotics is produced by the actinomycetes, notably the genus *Streptomyces*, and it has been suggested that, since these are slow-growing soil microbes that exist in competition with soil bacteria, production of antibiotics may be of selective advantage to them in their natural soil environment. The flaw in this argument is that, in nature, they never seem to produce anything like enough antibiotic to influence their neighbouring bacteria.

Microbes, when used by industry for the production of material such as antibiotics, or the vitamins discussed in Chapter 5, are used by the industrialist as a special kind of chemical reagent. The industrialist uses microbes to convert one kind of substance into something more useful, and it is a small step from this kind of activity to that of using both microbes and chemicals in a sequence of chemical syntheses. We have met examples of this already: the formation of vitamin C using *Acetobacter* on a chemically produced reagent (see Chapter 5), or the 'artificial' penicillins produced by doing some chemistry on penicillanic acid. One of the most impressive instances of the use of microbes as reagents in a sequence of chemical syntheses occurs in the industrial production of steroids. These are hormones, and materials related to hormones, which are of importance in pharmacy. The earliest examples were the ergot alkaloids which can have actions resembling certain sex hormones and which are formed naturally by a fungus called *Claviceps*. This fungus attacks wheat and has occasionally got into bread by accident, causing hallucinations and a variety of other disorders in people who eat it. Ergosterol, one of this group of alkaloids, also occurs in yeast and could, as we saw in Chapter 5, be extracted and made into vitamin D. But most spectacular has been the recent use of moulds of the *Rhizopus* groups to alter the chemical structure of plant steroids and to convert them to pharmacologically active hormones. Most people have heard of cortisone, a hormone of the adrenal cortex which has proved dramatically effective as a palliative in rheumatoid arthritis. It can be obtained in minutely small quantities from the natural glands of, for example, cattle, and, in 1949, the only other method of preparing it was to conduct thirty-seven separate chemical operations on one of the bile acids. No wonder it cost something like $500 a gramme! In 1952 research workers at the Upjohn Company in the U.S.A. discovered that *Rhizopus* would act on a fairly readily available sex hormone called progesterone to make a product that could be converted to cortisone in only six chemical steps. (Progesterone, originally obtained only from the gonads of animals, could be made from a steroid called diosgenin, found in an African plant called 'elephant's foot'.) Since then a vast literature has developed on the use of moulds, mainly *Rhizopus* and *Neurospora*, for the transformation of steroids from one chemical configuration to another. In principle the procedure is quite simple: the mould is grown with, say, some glucose and an extract of corn as nutriment, in a medium containing an emulsion of the steroid. (Steroids are inclined not to dissolve in water and must therefore usually be emulsified.) After a suitable time the culture is killed, the steroid material extracted and, in favourable cases, up to 95 per cent of it has been transformed into a new steroid. As well as being useful in rheumatic and arthritic diseases, steroids can be useful in preventing premature abortion, and in dealing with disorders of the menstrual cycle; they show promise as oral contraceptives. This is a rapidly expanding field of applied microbiology.

Antibiotics, steroids and the vitamins discussed in Chapter 5 might be called the money-spinners of present-day industrial microbiology, at least as far as the pharmaceutical industries are concerned. There are, however, many more workaday industrial processes in use in which microbes are used. Dextrans are starch-like materials formed from sugar which are valuable because they can be used as substitutes for plasma in blood transfusions. They are prepared industrially by letting the bacterium *Leuconostoc mesenteroides* act on ordinary sugar; sometimes the bacterium is killed and the enzyme responsible for the conversion of sugar is extracted from it, because this gives a rather more controllable process. Anti-sera (see Chapter 3), which are used to protect people who have been exposed to risks of diseases such as tetanus, are prepared by injecting live bacteria into animals and obtaining preparations of the anti-bodies they form. Vaccines, likewise, are prepared by culturing pathogenic microbes in 'safe' hosts or cultures and rendering them harmless by heating or killing with a disinfectant. They may then be safely injected into patients.

Clearly many industrial products made using microbes are of medical use, and some are of gastronomic use, but we should mention one or two products that have value outside these fields.

Enzymes, the biological catalysts that cause biochemical reactions to take place, can be extracted from all kinds of living tissue, and microbial tissue is often industrially the most convenient. Amylases, for example, are enzymes that break down starch, and are used in laundering and in the paper industry (they dissolve starchy dressings from fabrics which are to be pulped for paper manufacture). They are prepared industrially from the mould *Aspergillus oryzae* among other aspergilli, or from bacteria of the genus *Bacillus*. (A cellulase, the enzyme that breaks down the cellulose of plant material to sugars, ought to be useful for making otherwise useless raw materials into fermentable products but, though wood-rotting fungi such as *Myrothrecium* possess such enzymes, they have not yet been widely used industrially.) Pectin, the gelatinous component of fruit that causes jam to set, can be broken down by enzymes called pectinases which are formed by many bacteria, and enzymes prepared from these are used in stabilizing fruit juices. The 'retting' of flax, steeping it to remove pectins and leave the plant fibre, is a traditional procedure that is fundamentally an exposure of the plant to bacterial pectinases; as far as I know, neither pure cultures of bacteria nor preparations of pectinases are used industrially, the traditional retting being preferred. Proteinases, enzymes that break down proteins, are used to clarify beer, for removing protein stains in laundering, for conditioning dough in baking, for removing extraneous 'meat' and hair from hides prior to tanning and for removing gelatin from spent film emulsions; they have even been claimed to accelerate the clearing of blood clots and bruises such as black eyes. They are prepared from plants or various microbes including fungi of the genus *Aspergillus*. Invertase is an enzyme that converts cane sugar into glucose and fructose; it is prepared from yeasts. It has been used for making artificial honey but its most curious use is in making soft-centred chocolates. In this process, a hard sugar fondant containing the enzyme is rapidly coated with chocolate. When it has set and been allowed to stand, the invertase in the fondant breaks down the sugar to the 'invert sugars' with the result that the fondant becomes partly liquified.

Once again, it seems, our survey of industrial microbiology has returned us to thoughts of food. It is certainly true that the major deliberate uses made of microbes by man are those that further the interests of his stomach and health, but are these not the primary interests of the average specimen of mankind? Certainly industry has no illusions about where the money lies in economic microbiology – as we shall have cause to regret in the next chapter. Some industrial microbiologists, indeed, regard production of materials by microbes as encompassing the whole subject of industrial microbiology and, indeed, whose textbooks purporting to cover industrial microbiology have been written which dealt with little more than the subjects raised in the second half of the present chapter. Scientists are no more immune to the smell of profits than anyone else!

CHAPTER 7

Deterioration, Decay and Pollution

I am the proud father of a young family. One of the more un-expected results of this worthy estate, and it will be familiar to readers who find themselves in a comparable position, is the amount of junk that accumulates in the house. (I hasten to add, lest one of my children should read this, that I know it is not junk to them: that every celluloid duck, plastic brick, nursery-rhyme record, fluffy rabbit, Ludo board and paint box is known per-sonally to each child, complete with history and ownership.) When *I* was young, toys had a finite, almost predictable lifetime: a clockwork train, for example, would break, be repaired a couple of times, then find its way to a dustbin – within weeks if one was unlucky, in months on an average, in years if one was careful or the toy was particularly good. Today, it seems, toys are indestruc-tible. Bouncer, my fourteen-year-old daughter's brushed nylon washable cuddly-dog (made in the U.S.A.) is two years younger than its proprietor, having survived unscathed for three average lifetimes of the pre-war teddy bear, and looks set to accompany my daughter far into adult life. Well, as far as Bouncer and my daughter are concerned, I am happy for both of them; it is the great number of objects of uncertain function, usually fashioned from some kind of plastic, that leave me with the impression that, in another decade, whole rooms of my house will be given over to the storage of beloved toys belonging to beloved offspring. . . .

What has this to do with microbes, you ask? Ah! I see you have taken the point. But I shall spell it out for my own satisfaction, anyway. Just as a small family collects a sort of sediment of indestructible matter, so civilized man, on this planet, accumu-lates a mass of artefacts, many of remarkable durability, made of wood, iron, stone, concrete, brick, plastics, tin, glass, pottery, and so on. Moreover, he discards clothes, remains of food, husks and residues of vegetation, the bodies of his fellows, corpses of pets and domestic animals, excreta, paper, hair and nail parings on to the biosphere of this planet. What prevents us from being knee-deep in our own detritus?

Microbes, you reply. Quite so. Micro-organisms in soil, water, sewerage systems and refuse dumps transform the detritus of human society, converting them to materials that can be re-used, or that are at least innocuous. It is here that microbes provide their most valuable function for mankind, for picture what the world would be like if wood did not rot, corpses did not decay, excrement and vegetation lay where it fell and so on. An impossible situation, of course, because the biological cycles of the elements would have come to a standstill millennia ago, but one which is instructive for considering the economic value of microbes. Microbes return materials that man has withdrawn from the biological cycles (discussed in Chapter 1) that keep life going on this planet. Though mankind contributes something when he burns combustible detritus (he returns CO_2 and water vapour to the atmosphere, trace elements in the ash to soil or water), such activities play a trivial part in the turnover of biological matter. Decay, deterioration and destruction are the reverse of growth, synthesis and production, but are quite as important for the terrestrial economy. Regrettably, however, they are not obviously important to the economy of industrialists, so we shall find, as we survey these processes here, that there are gaps in our knowledge of the microbiology of these processes. They arise from the relatively moderate research effort that has been put into understanding them, which, in its turn, has been determined by the availability of funds and laboratories for basic research in economic microbiology. But let us not grind an axe just now; let us look at what microbes actually do on the 'return' side of this planet's economy.

Deterioration, decay and disposal are three names for what, microbiologically, are similar processes. We use the name 'deterioration' for something we wish did not occur; 'decay' is on the whole neutral; 'disposal' is to be encouraged. We shall discuss disposal processes in the next chapter; in this one we shall look upon the worst side of the picture and note the corrosive, destructive and generally obstructive parts microbes can play in our dealings with the inanimate world.

As usual, we shall think of our stomachs first, and consider the spoilage of food. As everyone knows, food goes bad if it is kept around too long, unless it is pickled, sterilized, dried or deep frozen. The process of going bad occurs when microbes grow on or in the food, altering its consistency, taste and smell; the processes used to preserve foods are those that delay or prevent microbial growth.

It will be reasonably clear to anyone who has read Chapters 3 and 4 that almost any form of food is a good medium for bacterial growth. A meat stew, left open in a warm kitchen for a day or two, will collect all the airborne microbes that happen to fall into it, plus those coughed or sneezed about the place by passing humans and pets, those scattered by the wings of insects, those falling off the hair and clothes of the cook. Let us imagine that the ingredients have been prepared, put together but not yet cooked, so that, in addition, they are liberally infected with organisms from the cook's hands, and have a modest infection of miscellaneous mouth and other contaminants on the cooking vessel, left over from when it was dried with a contaminated cloth last time it was washed up. A depressing prospect, it may sound; but in fact the preparation at this stage is perfectly wholesome. The microbes are mainly dormant, few if any are multiplying and most of them are harmless – though if the cook has a cut finger that is going septic, a few potentially nasty pathogens may be present. Even so, the mixture is harmless, because of the small number of microbes present. The meat and vegetable tissue is largely intact, as it was in the living animal or vegetable, the water is pure enough and the salt and flavourings are not much use as nutrients for the microbes. If it were to stand in a warm place for a few hours, the meat and vegetable tissues would begin to break down, partly by the action of the microbes, partly by intrinsic chemical processes, and more nutrient would become available for the microbes to multiply. But for the while the mixture is quite safe. Then the cook boils it for some hours, either in a casserole or a saucepan, and all the microbes are killed. Unless she is very unlucky, all the spores are killed, too. Let us assume the cook is preparing a casserole stew: if she were to remove it from the oven at the end of three hours and serve it hot, a nourishing and, one trusts, delicious food would be provided to which the microbes we talked about made an undetectably small contribution. Let us now assume there is some left over. It has cooled, so that air-borne and hair-borne microbes start to fall in it again, and now, because it has been cooked, all the most nutrient juices and substrates have been extracted from the ingredients. The microbes find a perfect, warm culture medium, like those we discussed in Chapter 4, and they start to multiply.

Supposing, as an illustration, ten staphylococci got into it from someone's thumb as it was carried out at 8 p.m. after dinner. It is covered up, put on one side and forgotten. The kitchen is warm – there is a boiler at the other side of the room – so the staphylococci start to multiply. By 9 p.m. there are twenty, by 10 p.m. there are forty, by midnight one hundred and sixty. If we assume that the organisms divide every hour – and in a really warm place they can divide four times as fast as this – then by next day at noon there will be something like 600,000 staphylococci in that stew. It will be beginning to smell a bit, but it will look all right still (the population of microbes has to reach about 100 million in each thimble-full to *look* bad) but some rather depressing chemistry will be taking place in it. Amino-acids, components of the meat and vegetable proteins, are being transformed into substances called ptomaines and rather toxic products of the growth of the microbes are being formed. Suppose the cook does not notice, but warms it up in the oven for lunch. The microbes will be killed, but the ptomaines will remain, with one of three consequences. Whoever eats it will have an upset tummy; but it will probably be over quite soon. Or he may just find it tastes a bit 'off' but does no further harm. Or he may not notice. Which of these things happens depends really on how warm it was when it was stored: by a stove it could become quite toxic overnight, in a cool larder it might last a day quite safely. In a refrigerator the staphylococci would not have grown at all. However, psychrophilic bacteria (see Chapter 2) could grow slowly and cause additional ptomaine formation, but this would take several days.

Now just imagine what would have happened if it had been not a reheated stew, but a pie that had been intended to be eaten cold. Whoever ate it would have ingested a jolly good dose of live bacteria, and if those had happened to be pathogenic, he could have got a nasty infection of the mouth and intestines. This is how most cases of food poisoning happen: pre-cooked food has been stored in too warm a place and has not only gone bad faster than it ought to have done, but has grown pathogenic bacteria picked up from someone who handled it during preparation. This is why preservatives are put into prepared foods: they are in fact disinfectants that have a negligible effect on man but keep the microbes at bay. Personally, I should often prefer to do without the foods than bear with some of the preservatives that are in common use, but that is a matter of taste.

Though chemical preservatives are widely used and unavoidable, there are many traditional processes available for preserving food from microbes. Pickling, which is steeping the food in acetic acid (vinegar), preserves food by making it too acid for bacteria to grow. Sugaring also preserves, as in jams and syrups, because few bacteria can grow in strong sugar solutions. Yeasts and moulds can grow in sugar preserves, but they usually do no harm or else become so obvious that no one would think of eating the food. Salting is a method of preserving meats and fish that depends on the fact that most putrefactive bacteria cannot grow in a strong brine. If the brine contains potassium nitrate (saltpetre) or sodium nitrate, the microbe called *Micrococcus denitrificans* grows and converts the nitrate into a preservative substance called nitrite. This forms a red compound with meat protein which is much less susceptible to ordinary microbial attack, and the meat is called 'cured'. Bacon is red because of this curing process; it is not really necessary to grow the microbes to cure meat (the chemical sodium nitrite will have a similar effect) but as it is slightly poisonous its use is controlled by law in most countries. (But, often, one can use as much nitrate and *M. denitrificans* as one likes!) This is why one so often sees 'sodium nitrite' as one of the ingredients of canned meats: it is a preservative and curing agent.

Deterioration of canned and bottled foods can occur if they are inefficiently sterilized: *Desulfotomaculum nigrificans* forms spores that resist prolonged heating and can grow at a high temperature in strong sugar solutions. Being an anaerobe, it positively welcomes being canned; being a sulphate-reducing bacterium (see Chapter 2), it produces the evil-smelling gas hydrogen sulphide. It is obvious why this kind of spoilage of canned foods (such as canned corn) is called 'sulphur stinker' spoilage. Molasses, which is unrefined treacle, is heated to quite a high temperature when it is processed so that it will flow easily, and it is then hot enough to kill most bacteria. But *D. nigrificans*, being thermophilic, grows quite well in this environment and is a source of constant nuisance to the sugar industry. Another anaerobe, *Clostridium thermosaccharolyticum*, can generate gas in canned foods and cause explosive effects when the can is opened; but one of the most dangerous is *Clostridium botulinum*, which appears occasionally in canned or potted meats. We met it first in Chapter 3. Though it is not itself pathogenic, the toxin it forms is one of the most poisonous substances known. (It has been proposed as an agent for biological warfare.) Botulism, usually a fatal condition, results from eating food made poisonous by this organism.

Moulds spoil foods such as bread, cheese and so on, and are usually obvious and fairly harmless. But there are more drastic effects. Moulds of the group *Aspergillus* can spoil grain that has been stored insufficiently dry, and the solution to this particular problem is to damp-store the grain in hermetically sealed chambers, when the grain produces so much carbon dioxide by its own respiration that the mould is prevented from growing. *Aspergillus fumigatus* is a mould that is pathogenic to poultry; it grows through the shells of eggs, forming spores on the inside, and the chicks develop a lung infection when they hatch. Pigeon-pluckers in France have developed a pseudo-tuberculosis from plucking infected birds. One of the most spectacular cases of spoilage by moulds emerged in connection with groundnut (peanut) production in the 1950s. *Aspergillus flavus*, another mould, may contaminate harvested nuts, and when it does so, it forms within the nuts poisonous materials called 'aflatoxins'. These were first detected when poultry, fed on groundnuts, developed liver damage; alarm increased considerably when aflatoxins were found capable of producing cancer in people and animals, and to be present in some batches of food intended for human consumption – peanut butter, for example. Though the situation is now under control, there was a period when the possibility of carcinogenic matter in peanut preparations was a cause for anxiety.

Spoilage of foods by microbes is familiar to everyone. It could be said that the whole distributive and catering trade in civilized communities is based on procedures, traditional or modern as the case may be, designed to delay or arrest microbial deterioration of the product being purveyed. Think of the problems in the distribution of fish, for example, and the manners in which they have been overcome. A whole technology of food microbiology has grown up concerned with the understanding and control of deteriorative, infective and protective processes in the food industry; the examples given so far in this chapter and in Chapter 5 have been illustrative rather than comprehensive because, as with almost every chapter in the book, a proper survey of the field would require a book on its own. For our synoptic view of microbes and men, it is more interesting now to turn to the destructive action of microbes on materials that are not foods.

Have you seen a pair of old shoes, gardening shoes, for instance, that have gone mouldy? Or observed the efflorescence of mildew over the walls and ceiling of a derelict house? These are two examples of microbes attacking and damaging materials that one expects to have a reasonable degree of permanence. In fact, however, I have chosen those two examples rather carefully, because in neither case is the basic material itself being attacked. Leather, even in tropical countries, is remarkably resistant to microbial attack, and insects and worms are its most serious destructive agents. But the dressings and conditioning agents used to polish or improve leather can be attacked by microbes. It is generally these that the moulds use as food when they grow on leather, but having grown, they form pigments, erode the surface of the leather and generally make an unsightly mess of it. Similarly the growth of mildew on ceiling plaster or walls is not really because it can use the plaster itself as food, but because fining agents, paper and, often, the paste used to stick on wall and ceiling paper, can be used as substrates for growth. Most decorating materials contain microbicides to prevent growth of moulds, but where a house is excessively damp – being very new, or derelict, for example – the microbicide may leach away and moulds will grow. The 'stain', so infuriating to househoulders, is usually the pigmentation of the spores of the moulds. In the tropics, moulds can cause enormous damage. Lacquers, resins, the insulating layers of electrical equipment all contain materials that can support growth of moulds. *Aspergillus restrictus* and *A. glucus* are notable in that, when they grow, they produce substances that can etch glass, and during the Second World War they damaged lenses of cameras, binoculars and such by growing as a film on the glass.

Wood is a fairly resistant material, but anyone who has encountered dry rot domestically will realize the expense and trouble that fungal attack on wood can cause. In this instance, the wood itself, and not any kind of dressing, is the substrate for growth of the microbe. There exists a wide range of wood-rotting fungi, ranging from the huge 'beef-steak' fungi one sees in woods or on fallen logs – the 'beef-steak' is its fruiting body – to the ubiquitous *Myrothrecium verrucaria*, which is invisible except when it forms spores. Wood conditioners such as creosote protect against wood-rotting fungi for a time, for years even, but the really effective treatment is to keep the wood dry. Even in a country as damp as Britain, roof beams will last for centuries if damp is avoided.

As we saw at the beginning of this chapter, destructive microbes play an important part in the re-cycling of the biological elements, and the wood-rotting fungi are valuable in nature because they bring the carbon of wood back into biological circulation. Paper is also attacked and destroyed by fungi, and in this case bacteria

153

play a part also. Cellulolytic bacteria, as they are called, break down the cellulose of wood, paper and plant material to simple fatty acids which other microbes can use. Since fungi require air to grow, a mound of garden refuse, for example, tends to be broken down more by bacteria than by fungi, and the interior of a compost heap usually consists of a mass of various anaerobic bacteria all living on the products formed by cellulolytic bacteria from cellulose. As we saw in Chapter 6, methane (natural gas) is one end product of this process, and it is probable that vast natural 'compost heaps' of this kind developed during the carboniferous era and ultimately formed coal. On the horticultural scale, of course, the process does not even go to the stage of peat formation because it is interfered with, but even on that small scale the compost can get quite hot (some of the energy generated by the microbe's metabolism is released as heat – just as you and I get hot if we run) and one can then understand why thermophilic bacteria are so widespread on this planet. They come into their own during large-scale natural fermentations.

Microbes can degrade paints and, here again, as with leather and wall plaster, it is the additive rather than the pigment itself that they use. Oleic acid and related materials such as linseed oil are widely used to support the pigments used in paint manufacture and, particularly in tropical areas where the paint may be exposed to warm and humid conditions, bacteria and fungi may attack these materials and destroy paint rapidly. An interesting side-issue to all this, of one may call it such, is that until the 1930s arsenic compounds were used as pigments in some paints and wallpapers. Many of the more primitive moulds, belonging to genera such as *Aspergillus*, *Mucor* or *Penicillium* can, when growing on other materials in the arsenical pigments, convert the arsenic to the gas arsine. This has a garlicky smell and is intensely poisonous; deaths have occurred because people breathed air containing arsine, formed in this manner, over a long period; the last death of this kind in England was recorded in 1931.

Rubber is usually regarded as a fairly stable material, but it is in fact attacked by a particular species of actinomycete. Dr La Rivière of Holland has shown that rubber gaskets and washers, all over the world, act as 'enrichment cultures' for this particular actinomycete, which can be found anywhere. This organism attacks the actual polymer (latex) that constitutes rubber. But there is a second way in which rubber can be 'corroded' by microbes, which depends on the fact that natural rubber, before it is used, must be vulcanized. Vulcanization involves adding sulphur to the rubber; if the rubber is wet, the sulphur-oxidizing bacteria *Thiobacillus thio-oxidans* grow at the expense of this sulphur, converting it to sulphuric acid. This acid attacks the rubber and any fabric associated with it: during the Second World War considerable damage was done to National Fire Service fire hoses for this reason. The remedy was to dry out the hoses adequately, which is why fire drill is so insistent on this seemingly trivial detail. Cases of a similar kind leading to destruction of rubber gaskets sealing bottled fruits and other materials have been described; in all such instances the breakdown of the rubber is associated with the formation of sulphuric acid. This is not the only time that we shall encounter thiobacilli behaving destructively as a result of their ability to form sulphuric acid.

Some synthetic rubbers (the chlorinated rubbers or the silicones) and some plastics (the fluorinated hydrocarbon polymers) are, as far as we know, immune to microbial attack. What is surprising is that polythene, although it did not exist until man made it during the last quarter century, is attacked by soil actinomycetes and bacteria. This fact has only been demonstrated conclusively during the last six or so years; one wonders what will become of the polythene and polypropylene piping that was so gaily laid in soil during the 1950s and 1960s as an escape from underground corrosion of metal piping. . . . It will probably last as long as metal would have done because that, too, is subject to microbial corrosion as we shall see shortly.

Polythene is a man-made hydrocarbon. The reason why some microbes fairly easily adapted themselves to consume it is presumably that many microbes can consume naturally-occurring hydrocarbons. The commonest are the methane-oxidizing bacteria, organisms capable of growing while oxidizing natural gas, but bacteria, moulds and yeasts capable of oxidizing oil hydrocarbon are also known – we met both methane-oxidizing bacteria and yeasts able to utilize oil hydrocarbons in Chapter 5, where they appeared as possible sources of food protein. Hydrocarbon-oxidizing microbes occur naturally in oil deposits and their presence around seepage areas has been used in oil prospecting. It is when they get involved in stored petroleum products that they become a nuisance, because they can spoil the fuel. Petroleum and kerosene are stored in huge tanks at the bottom of which is usually a layer of water. This 'water bottom' is normally unavoidable. If the storage tank is by the sea, the fuel has usually been pumped into the tank from an oil tanker, and the pipe along which it was pumped started full of sea water. Inland tanks do not get wet in this way, but petroleum dissolves an appreciable amount of water, and releases it on cooling, so that, even inland, water tends to accumulate as a layer in the bottom of the tank. In this water, mainly at its interface with the petroleum, hydrocarbon oxidizing microbes grow. It is important to emphasize that they grow in the water, not in the oil, petrol or kerosene as the case may be. (I have seen quite learned accounts of microbes in oil technology in which this point is not clear, so perhaps I should be more emphatic: microbes crop up in many aspects of oil technology, including the case of spoilage that we are now discussing. In none of these do they grow in anything but water.) Growth of microbes in water beneath stored fuels always occurs and, generally, it does little harm. A moderate sludge of microbes appears in the water layer and an infinitesimal amount of the fuel is consumed, but little damage is done. However, if the sludge gets too thick and the turnover of fuel is slow, the water can become anaerobic (because the microbes consume all the dissolved oxygen) and this is when trouble starts. The sulfuretum, discussed in Chapter 1, gets established because sulphate-reducing bacteria grow, reducing sulphate dissolved in the water by means of organic matter made available by the hydrocarbon-oxidizing bacteria. (Some authorities believe that sulphate-reducing bacteria can oxidize hydrocarbons themselves, using sulphates, but the evidence for this is a little shaky.) Hydrogen sulphide is formed and contaminates the fuel, becoming at least in part converted to free sulphur, and rendering it corrosive to certain parts of the fuel injection system of aircraft. This problem occurs particularly in tropical and sub-tropical areas: in 1952 and again in 1956 portions of the R.A.F. were grounded at politically awkward moments because of bacterial spoilage of fuel in storage tanks. The symptom is an increase in the 'copper strip' test, a test based on measuring the speed with which sulphide in the fuel blackens a strip of bright copper. Once spoiled, there is no remedy but to use the fuel in less sensitive engines such as motor cars (to 'down-grade' it); prevention is mainly a matter of cleaning out the bottom waters regularly, though certain chemicals active against sulphate-reducing bacteria are also effective.

The usual consequence of microbial spoilage of petroleum is a simple financial one: the fuel becomes less saleable than it would have been, and its owner loses money. But instances of more serious damage are known. The iron sulphide, formed as a result of bacterial sulphate reduction, becomes oxidized on exposure to air and, on rare occasions, it may become hot enough to ignite petroleum vapour when the tank is being cleaned. Two serious explosions of petroleum tanks occurred in Britain in the 1930s for this reason.

Petroleum is just one of many hydrocarbons of economic importance. Asphalt and bitumen are mixtures of carbon and hydrocarbons and both are used in road surfacing. In wet and warm climates, both can be decomposed by soil bacteria and, in the Southern States of the U.S.A., this process causes appreciable damage to roadways. It probably happens elsewhere, but this particular cause of deterioration has only been established recently and is still not widely recognized. Bitumen coatings have been used to protect buried pipelines and, again, soil bacteria limit the lives of such coatings by 'feeding' on them. An extreme case of microbial attack on hydrocarbons may occur in the spontaneous ignition of coal heaps: even in temperate climates stacks of coal may become mysteriously warm and sometimes catch fire spontaneously. One possible explanation is that bacteria oxidize the coal, or components of the coal, and, as in a compost heap, some of the energy is released as heat so that, in special conditions in which the heat is not readily dispersed, a cycle of oxidation leading to ignition can take place. It must be admitted, however, that the existence of bacteria able to do this have never been convincingly demonstrated, nor does it seem likely that bacteria could generate enough heat to reach the flash point of coal. But we have will o' the wisp as a precedent and there is no better explanation at present.

We mentioned decay of polythene piping brought about by microbes: one might expect iron or steel pipes to be immune to microbial attack, but this is in fact not so. Iron pipes – and all other iron structures that are not protected in some way – rust in damp air. This fact is familiar to most people, and the fact that both water and air are necessary for rusting is also well known. If one immerses an iron nail, for example, in pure, air-free water, and seals it against access of air, it will remain shiny and bright for years. Admit air, and it rusts rapidly. Iron pipes, buried in soil, are pretty well protected from air, particularly if the soil is water-logged and there are plenty of microbes around to consume any air that penetrates to the pipe. Yet, in these circumstances, iron pipes can corrode faster than they would in air, and the cause of this corrosion is now known to be those bacteria we have met so often before, the sulphate-reducing bacteria. Underground corrosion of iron pipes was estimated to cause a loss of between $200 million and $600 million to the U.S.A. in 1948; it is a serious and expensive process, so we shall respectfully devote a little space to studying its subtleties.

If you took a lump of pure, un-rusted iron and put it in water, it would react, splitting the water molecules so as to form hydrogen and iron hydroxide. In chemical terms:

$$Fe + 2H_2O \longrightarrow Fe(OH)_2 + H_2$$

Normally, if nothing but water were present, the reaction would no sooner start than it stopped, because the hydrogen sticks to the surface of the iron and stops any further reaction taking place. If, however, air is present, oxygen from it reacts with the hydrogen, turning it back to water, so the process can go on indefinitely until the iron has rusted away. (Readers with some knowledge of chemistry will remark that rust is not $Fe(OH)_2$. No matter. The process I have described is the first step in rusting and, though all sorts of further reactions take place, iron would not rust if this first step did not happen.) The sulphate-reducing bacteria, as we saw in Chapter 2, do not use air for respiration, they reduce sulphates instead; to save turning back, I shall write the reaction again, using calcium sulphate as an example:

$$CaSO_4 + food \longrightarrow CaS + oxidized\ food.$$

They make calcium sulphate into calcium sulphide while oxidizing whatever material is available as food. They also have the property of being able to use hydrogen for this reaction:

$$4H_2 + CaSO_4 \longrightarrow CaS + 4H_2O$$

and though the hydrogen is not strictly speaking a food (it contains no carbon), the reaction provides the bacteria with energy and enables them to use such carbon-containing food as is available more economically. Confronted with an iron pipe, with its protective film of hydrogen, they tend to use this hydrogen for sulphate reduction, converting it to water. So the iron corrodes. As a further reaction, the sulphide reacts with some of the iron to form iron sulphide, so one can always recognize underground corrosion of this kind because the corrosion product contains iron sulphide. It is black instead of brown and often rather smelly.

Underground corrosion of iron pipes, as I have indicated, is one of the most expensive kinds of microbial corrosion, and a fair amount is known about how it happens and how it may be prevented. It attacks water and gas mains, drainage pipes and, because sulphate-reducing bacteria thrive in sea water, it destroys marine installations and damages the hulls of ships. But there is no easy cure, and the basic principle remains: do not bury iron pipes unless there is nothing else you can do, and if you *do* bury them, either see that air has free access to them, or coat them with so thick a cover that bacteria cannot penetrate to the metal. (Remember that cloth, bitumen, wax, many paints and plastics are decomposed by soil bacteria .... remember that, when you have found a suitably impenetrable coating, it needs only one careless workman with a pickaxe accidentally to make it penetrable again. . . . There are electrochemical methods of protection that are expensive but probably worth it in the long run.) Even hot-water systems are not immune to corrosion of this kind, because some strains of sulphate-reducing bacteria (*Desulfotomaculum nigrificans* whom we met in food spoilage) are thermophilic; in these circumstances they can even corrode copper piping in domestic hot water systems because they grow in the cooler parts of the circulation system and the sulphide they form diffuses throughout the pipes, attacking the copper by converting it to copper sulphide. In the U.S.A. I have taken hot showers which smelled like the spa at Bath and, therefore, noted sadly that my host's domestic water system was due for breakdown in a year or two. A curious case of 'Should a Doctor tell?'; I have only once had the courage to do so, and my host was so upset to be told that his hot water smelled of bad eggs (it had developed so slowly that he and his family had grown accustomed to it) that it would almost have been kinder to leave him in ignorance. (Happily, he was a microbiologist and recovered his morale quickly. His solution? He sold his house and bought another. . . . What, you may ask, is the difference between a scientist and a second-hand car dealer? Forgive me if I duck the question.)

One can fairly ask this question. If sulphate-reduction by sulphate-reducing bacteria is the basic process that causes underground corrosion, why not get rid of the sulphate, when the whole process should stop? Indeed it would, but it is in practice impossible to remove the sulphate. The hardness of ordinary tap water is due mainly to calcium sulphate; all soil waters contain sulphates; plaster and other building materials contain lots of calcium sulphate. Thus three inescapable materials of everyday life, water, mud and dust, are sources of sulphate for these microbes and there is almost nowhere on this planet that remains wholly deficient in sulphate for long. The bacteria, after all, require very little sulphate and they are in no hurry: the fastest recorded corrosion of a water main took about three years. Even the sulphate-deficient soils we shall mention in chapter 11 probably contain enough sulphate for those bacteria to grow on; it is with plant crops, which need much more sulphate, that the soil deficiency shows.

Underground corrosion is not the sole manner in which microbes attack metals, but it is the most important one. (I should, for completeness, mention that corrosion *can* occur underground without the intervention of bacteria, but the reasons are usually rather special. 'Underground corrosion' is something of a misnomer, though widely used, and a better term is 'bacterial corrosion'.) Ordinary microbes growing in films of water on metals can accelerate the normal corrosion process by altering the electrochemical character of the metal surface in ways that we cannot discuss here (specialists may like to be told that they form 'differential aeration cells'). Acid-forming bacteria, such as the thiobacilli, can generate enough acid to destroy metals and machinery. Moulds, as we have seen, can attack the coatings of cables and wires, and, where they do so, some of the products they form from the coating materials attack the metal; both lead and zinc can be corroded in this way. In these instances it is a product of the microbe's action that is corrosive.

Perhaps the classical example of corrosion by a microbial product is the case of stone and concrete 'disease'. The temple of Angkor Wat, in Cambodia, is apparently a glorious relic of early Malayan architecture, ante-dating most European buildings (I have only seen pictures of it). It is now slowly decomposing, overgrown in the jungle. The reason for its breakdown, according to Dr Pochon and his colleagues at the Pasteur Institute in Paris, is that sulphide soaks up the stone from the relatively polluted tropical soil on which it is built. This sulphide, the reader will by now hardly need telling, is formed by sulphate-reducing bacteria. At the surface of the stone, the sulphide becomes oxidized to sulphur and sulphuric acid, largely through the agency of thiobacilli, and it is this acid that is destroying the stone. Angkor Wat is a particularly tragic case of microbial corrosion of stone, but many similar instances are known, nearer home, as it were. Stone statues in Paris have been found to corrode in a similar way. Sewer pipes are often made of concrete and may corrode rapidly for analogous reasons: in this instance the sulphide comes from the sewage itself, diffuses as hydrogen sulphide to the roof of the pipe, and here the thiobacilli convert it to sulphuric acid. A characteristic of this type of corrosion is that the roof of the pipe caves in. Many industrial effluents contain sulphide, so cooling towers, concrete pipes and concrete manhole covers have been known to corrode for similar reasons. It should not be assumed, however, that all corrosion of buildings is bacterial: sulphur oxides are major components of atmospheric pollution and in big towns these chemicals can have quite as big an effect as microbes. Westminster Abbey, for example, is being corroded as a result of a process that includes sulphuric acid formation, but thiobacilli play little if any part and the main source of corrosive acid is London's polluted atmosphere.

We could go on looking at microbial deterioration indefinitely. I have said nothing of the damage moulds, cellulolytic bacteria and sulphate-reducing bacteria can cause in the paper industry, of how cutting emulsions in the machine tools industry can be destroyed by microbes and even rendered capable of spreading disease; of how oil wells can become clogged by sulphate-reducing and associated bacteria, of how iron bacteria and algae can obstruct water supplies and filters causing what water engineers refer to rather charmingly as 'water calamity'.

But we ought to say something about the question of water pollution, because anyone who has bathed in the seas and rivers of this island knows something of the damage pollution causes. If any organic matter – leaves, paper, food and so on – gets deposited in water, microbes grow and the water becomes polluted. The sea, or a fresh running river, can take a fair amount of pollution, because there is plenty of air available and the microbes can oxidize the organic matter to carbon dioxide and products such as lignin and humins, which are pretty well immune to microbial attack and merely settle harmlessly as sediment. Serious pollution occurs, however, when the water is so stagnant that the microbes use up all the air available. Not only do anaerobic bacteria start growing, and producing putrescent smells, but fish and plants die, making the pollution worse. Sooner or later the sulphate-reducing bacteria start growing, too, and since the hydrogen sulphide they form, as well as smelling particularly nasty, is toxic to most living things, they augment the pollution even further. Hence microbial water pollution is self-perpetuating: it is far more difficult to stop once started than to prevent.

Natural lakes and ponds usually have polluted zones near the bottom where free sulphide is present. Normally, just above this layer, there is a zone of sulphide-oxidizing bacteria making use of this sulphide; since, as we saw in Chapter 2, many sulphide-oxidizing bacteria are photo-autotrophs (i.e. they need light to grow), the depth of this layer depends on how clear the water is and how far into it light penetrates. Above this layer, fish, algae and plankton grow and the whole lake is a stable system with the sulphur cycle progressing quietly in its lower reaches. Lakes, canals, even seas (such as the Black Sea) are like this; the drawing illustrates a typical system:

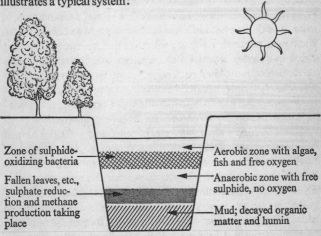

Zone of sulphide-oxidizing bacteria

Fallen leaves, etc., sulphate reduction and methane production taking place

Aerobic zone with algae, fish and free oxygen

Anaerobic zone with free sulphide, no oxygen

Mud; decayed organic matter and humin

Artificial pollution with, for example, sewage or industrial wastes can have a catastrophic effect on the natural balance, causing the anaerobic zone to spread to comprise the whole water system. Sometimes a sort of transient condition occurs when a whole lake or stream turns red owing to the growth of coloured sulphur bacteria – I once encountered an ornamental lake in Middlesex which looked as if it consisted of red paint – but this situation depends on a rather fine sulphide concentration being maintained and rarely lasts long. Nevertheless, do you remember '. . . and all the waters that were in the river were turned to blood. And all the fish that was in the river died; and the river stank, and the Egyptians could not drink of the water of the river; . . .' (Exodus 7, vii, 20, 21)? Moses may well have been aided by coloured sulphide-oxidizing bacteria of the genus *Chromatium*, because the Wadi Natrun in Egypt, which is rich in these microbes, is traditionally associated with the First Plague. Many coloured waters are due to sulphur bacteria, and characteristically they smell of hydrogen sulphide. Blooms of brown algae and green algae, as well as small aquatic plants, can also cause such colours.

The lower reaches of the Thames are a good example of a moderately polluted river, too toxic for fish, with a fair level of dissolved sulphide in most circumstances. Ships' hulls corrode in it, paintwork darkens and there is generally a nasty smell around the place. Industrial waters are often like this, despite government action intended to control such pollution, and though industries were often responsible for initiating it, the larger manufacturing concerns are now usually reasonably responsible about not polluting inland waterways. It is the small producer, the house-boat or the drain that everyone has forgotten, that tends now to keep the trouble simmering gently. Sewage is only discharged into rivers after highly controlled treatment and is usually innocuous; its discharge into the sea is less carefully regulated and, as we observed in Chapter 3, we are fortunate that most sewage microbes are killed by the salinity of sea water. Estuarine waters are often very polluted: the black sand, familiar at estuarine resorts, is black because sulphide, formed by sulphate-reducing bacteria, reacts with iron salts in the sand, forming black iron sulphide. On exposure to air the sand turns brown again because the sulphide oxidizes back to brown iron oxides. In warm weather, particularly in tropical climates, such polluted sand and water can develop blooms of luminous bacteria, so that, at night, each footprint or swirl of water glows with light.

The bacteria usually responsible, *Achromobacter fisherii*, glow when oxygen reaches them, stirred into the environment by the pressure of a foot or the turbulence of an oar. In nature, the effect can be both dramatic and romantic; it is a pity that the smell is usually less conducive to romance.

(We have not encountered the luminous bacteria before in this book. They are a small group of bacteria whose metabolism causes the emission of light by a biochemical process similar to that found in fireflies, for which they need air. They may be found free-living in the sea or in the luminous organs of deep-sea fish.)

Venice, one of the most beautiful cities of the Western world, is a haven of pollutant microbes. My colleague, the late K. R. Butlin, answered the question why the gondolas of Venice are black. He pointed out that, owing to pollution of the canals with hydrogen sulphide, they would turn black soon enough whatever colour they started out. Where does the sulphide come from? Why, from our old friends the sulphate-reducing bacteria. Water pollution of this kind can occur on a dramatic scale in nature without the intervention of mankind. Walvis Bay, an area off the south-west coast of Africa, suffers from periodic eruptions of hydrogen sulphide from the sea bed which kill fish for many square miles. The sea breezes then carry so much sulphide that they tarnish metalwork and paint in the in-shore town of Swakopmund and blot out the face of the town-clock, and, in the evocative words of a local reporter, 'Sharks come gasping to the surface on the evening tide.' I have seen pictures of the beach near Swakopmund nearly three feet deep in dead fish as a result of one such 'disturbance' in 1954: the smell of rotting fish apparently added piquancy to the general sulphurous smell as putrefaction set in. This is a most dramatic consequence of the actions of the sulphate-reducing bacteria, and one that is quite uncontrollable.

We could, as I said earlier, continue indefinitely on this theme, but the examples I have given should be sufficient to illustrate the extraordinary ramifications of microbes in what one might call the negative side of mankind's economy. Before we look at the reverse side, at how we can make use of these proclivities, is there any moral we can draw? I think there is. If we compare the amount of research being put into steroid transformations and antibiotics with the amount of effort expended on, say, sulphate-reducing bacteria and water microbiology, we reach a melancholy conclusion. Research that produces pounds sterling or dollars for a company can be sure of support; research that shows prospects of profit nowadays stands a good chance, because most industrialists are fairly 'science-minded'. But research that promises only economies, or furthers only the general public good, with no obvious reward to any particular person or group, attracts no one. Generally speaking, it only gets done because things get out of hand, so that someone darned well has to have a go at it. As a result, not to put too fine a point on it, some thoroughly bad work is performed and published and, what is really more serious, particularly good research is wasted because one man with a half share in an assistant is plodding on with some fragment of the field, in some backwater of the main stream of scientific advance. The problem is essentially an administrative one, for there is no scientific reason for this neglect. The questions raised by the curious microbes concerned in the destructive processes we have discussed are of enormous intrinsic scientific interest because they represent the chemical fringes of living things: the extremes, as it were, of terrestrial biochemistry.

CHAPTER 8

Disposal

In the last chapter we looked at the destructive effects that microbes can have on materials. We noted at the start, however, that these destructive effects represented an important function that microbes perform in the natural economy of this planet: that of removing the detritus generated by higher plants and animals so as to re-circulate the biologically important elements contained in it. Deterioration, corrosion and pollution, when brought about by microbes, are simply special cases of this general function, and so are disposal processes, in which microbes are deliberately used to get rid of unwanted matter.

The most important example of a microbiological disposal process is sewage treatment and, since it is fundamental to the health of all civilized societies, as well as being intellectually a most satisfying form of applied microbiology, we shall spend a little time discussing it.

When the population of the world was small, sewage disposal presented few problems. The Greeks and Romans had hygienic systems, often building their baths and lavatories over or near running water, and these sewerage systems are often all that remain in excavated Roman communities. Standards then fell, and descriptions of life in the Middle Ages and during the Renaissance tell us that human habitations must sometimes have resembled pig-sties: steps and odd corners were used as lavatories, refuse was thrown into streets, chamber pots were emptied into the streets, and people rarely bathed. The widespread use of scents and nosegays becomes understandable. By the mid nineteenth century, with the populations of towns increasing as a result of the industrial revolution, it became obvious that it was dangerous, as well as disagreeable, to behave in this manner.

Diseases such as typhoid and cholera were widespread, and the River Thames, by 1860, had become a vast open sewer, with the rain-washed refuse of London flowing into it. Civic action in sewage collection and treatment was initiated in Britain by the Public Health Act of 1876 and a Royal Commission of 1898. By the early twentieth century sewage was collected and piped in most urban centres, though often the sole treatment it received amounted to discharging it onto municipal land (which was cropped for produce such as tomatoes – the origin of the term 'sewage farm'). The water usually became purified as it percolated through soil strata, and the soil became incidentally fertilized, but it soon became evident that the purification was a haphazard process and that, without detailed knowledge of subterranean water flow, there was a serious risk of polluted water reaching drinking wells. Though a few sewage farms still exist (and in too many coastal areas raw sewage is still discharged directly into the sea), on the whole, sewage technology has made enormous strides in the last half century and, in a modern sewage works, sewage treatment is a highly automated and efficient process.

Some idea of the magnitude of the problem can be obtained by quoting a few figures. In West Middlesex the population uses about 50 gallons of water a day per head, all of which washes detritus to the local sewage works. An installation serving one and a half million people must handle more than seventy-five million gallons of raw sewage a day, which it collects through a local network of pipes running from drains, sinks, baths, lavatories and industrial effluent conduits (the sewerage system). This sewage represents something like five thousand tons of organic matter; something has to be done with it before it gets into the rivers and seas, or it would cause unimaginable pollution as aquatic microbes recycled its carbon, nitrogen, sulphur, phosphorus and so on. In effect, what a sewage works does is to allow these processes to carry on in controlled conditions, so that the water which carried the sewage is purified and the solid components of sewage are rendered innocuous. This is easily done by modern sewage techniques: the processed solids reach a state in which they can be sold as soil conditioners or fertilizers and the treated water is so pure that, at the Mogden works in Middlesex, for example, the staff will demonstrate the purity of their effluent water by drinking a glass for visitors. (The visitors are unaware that they do something of the sort themselves daily: the water economy of this country is such that quite a lot of purified water finds its way back into the drinking reservoirs. I sometimes wonder how often an average glass of water has been drunk by someone else before I consume it.... I can find no calculations of this figure.)

Sewage from a typical city, as we have seen, consists mainly of the rinsings from sinks, lavatories, bathrooms, mixed with some industrial effluents and a certain amount of natural drainage water. A little thought makes it obvious that its main component is human excreta, supplemented with hair, paper, food debris and detergents. It is a suspension of solid matter, rich in bacteria, in a rather strong solution of organic substances; it is an extremely satisfactory medium for the growth of bacteria. The way in which it is treated can be best described by considering an imaginary sewage works, into which we shall introduce the main sewage treatment processes used today.

The sewage, then, flows into settling tanks, in which the solid matter settles as a sludge to the bottom. The settled material is called 'settled sludge', and we shall describe what is done with it shortly. The liquid part flows into special ponds where it is stirred and aerated vigorously, so that aerobic bacteria grow in it and oxidize much of the organic matter away to carbon dioxide. This escapes to the atmosphere, and one step of the purification process has thus occurred. However, more bacteria have grown, so the sewage needs to settle once more, to yield a sludge of bacteria. This second kind of sludge is called 'activated sludge', and some of it is collected and added back to the aerated ponds to accelerate the original formation of CO_2: the whole process is a sort of aerated continuous culture in which some of the microbes produced are returned to the original culture vessel (represented by the aerated pond). The rest of the activated sludge is either added to the settled sludge, or packaged and sold as fertilizer. This whole process is called the 'activated sludge process', and after such treatment the water is considerably purified. It is then sprayed over beds of a porous material such as coke, often by the rotating sprays that one sees in the grounds of sewage works, and allowed to trickle through several feet of this. Here films of moulds, streptomycetes and bacteria grow on the coke, removing the last traces of organic matter and yielding an effluent of almost 'sweet' water. Sometimes particles are removed by filtering through sand, but the water is usually pure enough to be discharged forthwith into a river or the sea.

The settled sludge presents a rather more difficult problem. Though it has 'settled', it is still more than 90 per cent water, so it can be pumped into huge vats called 'digesters'. These are continuous cultures of a different kind: they are not aerated, so that mainly anaerobic bacteria grow. Sulphate-reducing bacteria produce hydrogen sulphide from the sulphates dissolved in the water, cellulose bacteria destroy paper and similar materials, but the main microbes to grow are the methane bacteria. These, aided by the other anaerobes, break down the organic matter, mainly to CO_2 and methane, both of which are gases. Now, this methane is the same gas as marsh gas or natural gas: it is a valuable source of power, and though some old-fashioned sewage works still burn it away, most modern ones collect it and use it to drive their machinery. Sludge digesters need to be stirred slowly, and the methane is used to drive the stirrers and pumps; it may also be compressed into cylinders and used to drive lorries; sometimes it is sold. The methane fermentation of settled sludge is therefore a useful source of power to a modern sewage works.

A digester may have a capacity of as much as 20,000 gallons of sludge. Every day between five and ten per cent of the treated sludge is added, so the digester is an anaerobic continuous culture whose contents are replaced every ten to twenty days. The fermentation is usually so active that the fermentors have to be cooled. The 'digested sludge' still consists largely of water, and is again held for a while in tanks so that the bacteria and 'recalcitrant' solids (those attacked only slowly or not at all by microbes) will settle out. Usually this process – called 'dewatering' – is rather inefficient because some residual methane production continues and prevents the solid from settling well; settling agents that inhibit methane production can be added at this stage. After settlement, the water is run off into activated sludge plants, thus ultimately finding its way into a river or the sea. The settled, digested sludge has to be carted away and disposed of somehow; it is fairly innocuous and can be spread on soil as a soil conditioner – it has some value as a fertilizer though most of the useful soluble elements (nitrogen, sulphur, phosphorus) have been extracted from it. For this purpose it must usually be dried and, despite the ready availability of methane to heat it with, this process is rarely economic. In Britain it is often carried out to sea in barges and dumped: by law it must be carried some 20 miles offshore and so it contributes negligibly to the pollution of coastal areas.

A small sewage works may use only some of these processes, but most modern installations use them all; yet one must record dismally that, in 1966, there were still 119 local authorities around Britain's coasts who discharged untreated sewage into the sea.

Trouble comes when the in-flowing sewage contains materials that overload the plant or poison the microbes. Abbatoir effluents and dairy wastes, for example, are examples of waste fluids that are so rich in organic matter that they must be diluted with great quantities of water before the average works can handle them. Industries dealing with such materials on a large scale are often obliged to set up their own plant for dealing with their wastes: 'biological effluent treatment', the process is called. Chemical industries and the gas industry have comparable problems because their effluents are poisonous to ordinary sewage microbes. But, as we saw in Chapter 2, there exist bacteria that can metabolize a wide variety of curious chemicals, and it is possible to set up biological disposal plants using them. The Monsanto Chemical Works at Ruabon, Flintshire, produces effluents containing various phenols, most of which act as antiseptics towards normal microbes; by establishing populations of phenol-oxidizing microbes in activated sludge plants and trickling filter systems they can so purify their effluents that the water can be released

171

into the River Dee without further treatment. The gas industry produces effluents that contain phenols, cyanides and other poisonous substances, and biological effluent plants have been devised to treat these. The paper industry produces effluents rich in organic matter, extracted from wood, and containing sulphites, which are used in pulp preparation. This effluent is a particularly noxious brew, because, though the sulphite is toxic to many microbes, it is received with delight by sulphate-reducing bacteria (it is as good as sulphate for their metabolism); so, given careless handling, it causes the worst kind of pollution at once. Again, it must be extensively diluted before it can be accepted by a normal sewage works, or a special population of microbes must be developed to deal with it in a special plant. Methods have been developed for using sulphate-reducing bacteria to remove the sulphite in a special kind of trickling filter, but they have not, to my knowledge, been adopted by the industry.

Another effluent that causes considerable public nuisance, though it does not occur in sewage, is 'sea oil', the oily, tarry material that accumulates on beaches as a result of the discharge of oil by ships at sea. Despite international legislation, accidental and partly accidental contamination of the sea regularly takes place, and normally the oil is oxidized away by marine bacteria of the kind we encountered in Chapter 7 contaminating the bottom waters of petroleum tanks. Unfortunately, the sticky, tarry components of crude oil are oxidized only slowly, and the tarry material that today contaminates one's clothes and children on most European beaches is the residue of such pollution, still undergoing microbial decay.

The nuisance occurs because more oil is discharged on the sea than the natural microbes can dispose of before it is washed up on the beaches. A spectacular disaster of this kind occurred in the spring of 1967 when a huge oil tanker, the *Torrey Canyon*, was wrecked off the south-west coast of England and thousands of tons of oil were released to contaminate the beaches of England and France. Unfortunately, detergents were used to clear the beaches as an emergency measure and, from a long-term point of view, this was unwise because most detergents are disinfectants and delay the action of microbes. As well as causing public nuisance, such pollution kills thousands of sea birds and does enormous damage to the shellfish and crustacean industry; it should be possible to derive a microbiological method of combatting small-scale pollution of this kind – a *Torrey Canyon* disaster, of course, demands crisis measures for which microbes would be far too slow – but to my knowledge little research on this problem is taking place.

Oil is not the only contaminant of the natural environment that could be treated with microbes. We mentioned in Chapter 2 the field in Smarden, Kent, which became contaminated with fluoracetamide, a powerful poison used as a pesticide; emergency measures were taken to remove and dispose of the contaminated soil and only later did it become obvious that bacteria exist able to decompose fluoracetamide to harmless products. It is probable that treatment of the soil with microbes adapted to decompose fluoracetamide would have provided a quick and effective remedy. Selective herbicides, insecticides and such materials disappear from soil as a result of microbial action; there are impressive possibilities for the deliberate use of microbes to remove unwanted toxic materials from the natural environment, but they remain largely unexploited at present.

An important problem in sewage practice is how to deal with materials that are not attacked by microbes at all. Wastes from chromium-plating industries, for example, contain the chromate ion which can upset the microbial population of a sewage plant and thus put the whole process awry. Since the industries producing such effluents are generally known, their discharge into the sewers can usually be regulated sufficiently to avoid trouble. What is more troublesome is the domestic use of recalcitrant materials. Some of the detergents now in use interfere with sewage treatment, and this can happen in two ways. In the first, the microbes may be capable of handling the detergent chemically, but it produces such a froth in the activated sludge plant that the access of air to the sewage is restricted and the whole purification process slowed up. I recall the director of a local sewage works in the early 1950s telling me that he could tell when a detergent firm was having a sales campaign in his area: his activated sludge plants disappeared under the mound of froth. Expensive use of anti-foaming agents was then necessary. Such treatment is not always successful, and detergent foam can pass right through a sewage works and contaminate rivers – I have seen rivers a-froth with foam both in London and in the Midlands, and this problem is still with us.

A more insidious problem occurs with certain non-foaming detergents, which are used in the catering industry and in domestic washing-up machines. Some of these are recalcitrant: no microbes are known that attack them at all rapidly, with the result that they may come through the sewage process quite unaffected and, in fact, get into our drinking water supplies. I write 'may come through': by 1960 it was known that minute traces of these substances had reached several reservoirs of drinking water and, though they caused no obvious harm, the amounts were obviously going to increase and could become harmful. Though some success has been obtained in developing strains of microbe that attack them, the solution has lain more in the direction of altering the chemical character of the detergents so as to make them susceptible to microbial attack: 'bio-degradable', as the Americans call them. Legislation regarding the marketing of non-degradable detergents has been proposed, here and in the U.S.A., but I believe that, at present, the detergent industries are abandoning 'hard' detergents voluntarily.

Modern sewage treatment is usually high automated: flow, settlement, charging of digesters and so on are generally directed from a central control area by push-button mechanisms of which sewage engineers are justly proud. The unsavoury nature of physically handling sewage has contributed in part to this high degree of automation, but in addition an important factor has often been the fact that sewage works can be self-sufficient as regards power. The methane produced by anaerobic sludge digestion, as we saw earlier, is usually more than sufficient to power the pumps and machinery used in sewage processing, and several sewage works have been able to sell excess methane to the national gas grid. Small sewage plants for making methane from domestic and farm residues have been devised to power refrigerators and domestic machinery in tropical countries such as India.

The productive nature of waste treatment has caused scientists to consider what useful products other than methane might be obtained from sewage, and a number of interesting projects has arisen. Sulphur, as we saw in Chapter 6, is an element which is becoming scarce, at least in its reduced form. If, instead of methane, one digested sludge with a population of bacteria that formed sulphur from sulphates, for example, one could produce a product intrinsically more valuable than methane. No microbe is known that produces sulphur directly from sulphate, but the sulphate-reducing bacteria produce sulphides from sulphate and these, as hydrogen sulphide, are easily converted to sulphur or sulphuric acid by standard industrial chemical processes. A method of making sulphur in this manner from sewage sludge was developed during the 1950s by the late K. R. Butlin and his colleagues: sewage sludge was composted semi-continuously with gypsum (calcium sulphate) and the bacteria converted this to calcium sulphide. Sewage gas (methane plus carbon dioxide) was used to scrub out the sulphide by converting the calcium sulphide to carbonate and releasing the sulphide as H_2S. A net purification of the sewage took place, with release of H_2S, while the gypsum became converted to calcium carbonate. Butlin calculated that a North London sewage works which processed about one million gallons of sludge per day could be adapted to produce 5,000 tons of sulphur per day – but it would then have no methane. In practice a balance between sulphide and methane fermentation would have to be reached, not only because the methane is useful to carry off the H_2S, but also because the CO_2 that accompanies it is needed to displace the H_2S. The process was developed successfully to a pilot plant stage, and proved to have an additional virtue from the sewage engineer's point of view: the sulphide-digested sludge settled more efficiently than conventional methane digested sludge; disposal of the digested product was thus a much more economical process because less water needed to be transported with it.

In circumstances that achieved some notoriety in the late 1950s, the British research on sulphur production was closed down by the Department of Scientific and Industrial Research, the government department that was sponsoring it. It could have made an appreciable contribution to Britain's sulphur supplies – though it could never have produced enough to replace imported sulphur entirely – and, at the time of writing, the process is being mentioned anew in the technical press as another world sulphur shortage gets under way. Comparable processes have been developed in India, in the U.S.A., and in Czechoslovakia; in the latter country sulphur fermentation has been used successfully to pre-treat strong wastes – effluents from yeast and citric acid manufacture – that are too rich to be handled by conventional sewage processes: a preliminary sulphate fermentation downgrades the effluent sufficiently to make it acceptable to a normal sewage works and yields sulphur as a bonus. We mentioned earlier the particularly noxious character of wastes from the paper industry which contain sulphite and organic matter. Sulphate-reducing bacteria can be used to pre-treat these also, but the yields of sulphur are, according to Russian workers, too small to be economically worth collecting. American workers have used paper wastes to grow yeasts which could then be used as animal fodder, and a project was developed to grow mushroom spawn on paper and woody wastes, to make packaged mushroom soups. I believe the flavour did not come up to standard. Sewage sludge itself is a useful source of vitamin B_{12}, though at the present time I am not aware of any commercial exploitation of this source. It also contains a number of rare trace elements such as zirconium, germanium, gallium and selenium, largely originating in industrial effluents; projects for their extraction have not, to my knowledge, got beyond the planning stage.

One of the most awkward effluents, which has only arisen in the past decade or two, is that which arises from industries and laboratories making use of radio-active products. Microbes can contribute little to the disposal of such effluents, and indeed have the inconvenient property of concentrating them. Moulds, algae and bacteria, as well as plants, may concentrate radio-active isotopes and there seems to be no particular rhyme or reason in whether or not a given species will concentrate a given substance. For these reasons such effluents must be segregated carefully and are not normally accepted by ordinary sewage works; the use of microbes and plants deliberately to extract useful isotopes from such effluents has been proposed.

The main bulk products available from sewage treatment are methane and sulphur (or rather, hydrogen sulphide). The other product (besides water) is the digested sludge, and, though this can be used as a fertilizer and soil conditioner, it is often rather unsuitable because of its high content of trace elements referred to already. Besides the rare metals mentioned there are usually quite large amounts of copper, zinc and lead salts present which are not good for plants. One disappointing aspect of conventional sewage procedures is that they lead to loss of inorganic constituents that would be useful to agriculture. Potassium, phosphates, sulphates and nitrates tend to be removed from sewage during the treatment, becoming diluted in the purified water and eventually finding their way to the sea. Quite a lot of nitrate is lost by bacterial denitrification to nitrogen gas during the activated sludge process and subsequent settling. Thus there is a net loss of useful agricultural elements from the land to the sea. One of the long-term problems of civilized communities is that of returning these elements to the land: in the old days, when sewage could be spread on land and sewage farms could be operated, this drainage of intrinsic fertility did not occur. Today the deficit must be made up with chemical fertilizers and careful husbandry.

Sewage treatment deals with a waste material that is fluid: it can be pumped around a sewage works and handled like a bulk liquid, despite its content of solid matter. But a lot of urban, agricultural and domestic waste is solid or semi-solid. While much of this can be burned, there is much that cannot be, and to dispose of this many local authorities use processes that are basically similar to the gardener's composting. Urban refuse has a high content of vegetable matter, from paper and food residues, and, after removing useful items such as tin cans (the tin can be recovered and sold), many municipal refuse works bulldoze refuse into huge compost heaps, where microbial degradation sets in.

177

The interior gets so hot that thermophilic bacteria grow and cause very rapid breakdown of the organic matter. Development of insects and multiplication of rodents at the surface of such refuse dumps has to be controlled, but in a surprisingly short time quite fertile soil may so be formed.

Some ingredients of urban refuse, as we saw, can be burned, but it is not always desirable to do this. Plastics of the chlorinated hydrocarbon kind (polyvinyl chloride, for instance) are widely used and disposed of today, and if these are burned, hydrochloric acid is released and damages the furnace and flues as well as producing noxious fumes. There exist bacteria which can degrade these materials, and composting processes for disposing of them, developed at the National Physical Laboratory, seem to be more useful than burning in practice.

An interesting adaptation of the problem of disposal of town wastes has been made in the reclamation of waste land. The area round West Middlesex, on the outskirts of London, is scarred with old gravel pits; great man-made ponds which are now useless because most of the exploitable gravel has been removed, and the pits abandoned and allowed to become waterlogged. Because of the intense demand for building land, efforts have been made to reclaim them by filling them in with urban refuse. Yet to tip raw refuse into a waterlogged pit is to court disaster: a most glorious pollution will develop within weeks and the local authorities will be deluged with complaints, injunctions and legal actions caused by the resulting smells and damage to paint and metal-work. Mr A. S. Knolles, Borough Engineer of Twickenham, developed an ingenious procedure for containing such pollution and yet reclaiming land: the clinker from the combustible part of urban refuse was used to divide the pit into lagoons, each of which was filled with raw refuse rapidly before pollution could get established. Provided the lagoon walls could be built ahead of the influx of raw refuse, whole lagoons could be filled in and recovered for building without nuisance. The clinker contained sulphate, the refuse contained organic matter, so the ingredients for massive pollution by bacterial sulphate reduction existed, with the consequent risk of the most noxious kind of nuisance. However, provided the process was conducted rapidly, with an understanding of the processes involved, the pits could be filled and the land recovered with nothing but benefit to all concerned.

From the point of view of disposal, then, microbes are essential to the social organization of civilized communities and, as we pointed out at the beginning of this chapter, if it were not for their activities we should be up to our necks in an appalling morass of the detritus of human activity. The character that makes microbes so valuable in this context is their extraordinary chemical versatility, which we noted in Chapter 2: there seem to exist microbes capable of destroying and degrading almost any material mankind can produce. We understand but little of the biochemistry of these processes, and, indeed, we have only a vague knowledge of the microbes involved. This ignorance arises because, as with the corrosion and deterioration processes discussed in Chapter 7, fundamental research has lagged behind practical experience in these areas of knowledge. The fragments of knowledge we have concerning the roles of methane bacteria, sulphate-reducing bacteria, detergent- and plastic-degrading bacteria make it clear how rewarding a sustained and basic scientific investigation of microbiological disposal processes could be; the problem is, who will pay for it?

We have, in the last three chapters, seen how basic to our economy the microbes are and have, I hope, noticed how unbalanced is research on economic microbiology and how fragmented is our knowledge of the processes underlying the economic effects of microbes. This situation arises from the cock-eyed way in which research on microbiology is organized and financed, particularly in Britain. Let us, briefly, step aside from our main theme and look at these matters. It will be a melancholy spectacle, but it will not take long.

CHAPTER 9

Second Interlude: How to Handle Microbiologists

In the last few chapters I have occasionally alluded to areas of neglect and maladministration in microbiological research. In a book concerned with microbes and men it would be wrong to neglect entirely the men who study the microbes, yet just to mention the Great Names, the pioneers of the field and those who made its most fruitful discoveries, would be to give a false impression of the nature of microbiology today; for research, as I pointed out in Chapter 4, is largely a matter of day-to-day plodding: the day of the devoted scientist in his ill-equipped basement laboratory – the backroom boy making spectacular advances on a shoe-string – is long past. Now scientists need highly specialized apparatus and equipment: they need to travel and to talk with colleagues; they need technical assistants trained to a high degree of expertness, and comprehensive and highly efficient library services. And, if they do not get all this, they go and work elsewhere; which, in Britain today, generally means they 'brain-drain' to the U.S.A.

Microbiology has suffered as much as any science from the rather knotted-up situation that bedevils British science today and has brought the 'brain-drain' into the newspaper headlines. Because I have had to allude to areas of neglect, to progress being made despite, and not because of, scientific administration, it is only fair that I should say something of what I think the situation ought to be like. Destructive criticism, after all, is easy; constructive criticism at least indicates concern with the situation. Therefore, I have decided to deal with these matters in a separate chapter, which the uninterested reader may skip if he should so wish. I have also resolved to keep it short – because nothing is more tedious than long-winded axe-grinding on behalf of a 'cause', scientific or otherwise. Finally, I must admit that the state of microbiology in Britain is probably no different from that of other branches of biology, biochemistry, pure chemistry, physics or mathematics; I merely happen to know the position of microbiology most intimately myself.

It is really quite simple. At the basic or fundamental level – in that part of research that is concerned with scientific knowledge for its own sake – Britain has so far had quite a creditable record. The contributions of our bacteriologists and microbiologists to basic problems, particularly in the thirties and forties of this century, have been in the same class as those of Americans, Frenchmen and the Dutch (who can, with admittedly a certain injustice to other nationalities, be said to have led the world). This situation is no longer true; if we look upon international microbiological research as a sort of race, it is obvious that, since the war, Britain and France have flagged; that countries such as Sweden, Czechoslovakia, Japan, Australia, Canada have entered the first division; that the U.S.A. has forged ahead.

It is important to get this matter in perspective. It is entirely proper and admirable that the U.S.A. should forge ahead, and that other competitors should enter the field. National prestige, in basic research, is absolutely trivial. A rich and highly educated population such as that of the U.S.A. ought to produce more topflight scientists, microbiologists and others, than any other country in the world, and if it did not do so it would be no credit to the British, nor to anyone else: it would be simply a reflection on the state of U.S. science. Moreover, in basic research, scientific information is international, so we cannot even claim that the information obtained from such research is denied us. What should concern us is that Britain has flagged.

Britain has been remarkably poor at making use of basic scientific knowledge. The case of penicillin, which we encountered briefly in Chapter 3, is a classic of its kind because we ended up having to pay royalties to the U.S. for licences to produce a material discovered in Britain. Generally speaking, our failures have been of a less spectacular kind, but they have similar patterns: we have not been at all good at following up the practical ramifications of basic discoveries. Even in basic research, we now tend to make some original initial observation and find the subject followed up by well-staffed and well-equipped research teams in the U.S. Why?

This question has occupied politicians, civil servants, scientists, and various committees for many years, and the answer has been inconclusive. Yet for the special case of microbiology the answer seems fairly self-evident, because microbiology is a 'cheap' science. By this I mean that the equipment and installations needed by microbiologists are much cheaper than those needed by space scientists, nuclear physicists, and the like. The cost of a single experimental aircraft, for example, would finance a 200-strong microbiology laboratory for a decade, so we cannot argue that costs are, in themselves, inhibiting research in the field. It is in fact a case of mental attitude. The only good, well-organized laboratory engaged in exclusively microbiological research in Britain today is devoted to biological warfare, and this, if one stands back and views the situation dispassionately, is a ridiculous state of affairs. Elsewhere microbiology is left in the hands of tiny research groups in technological research laboratories, industrial laboratories or university departments. None of these is capable of advancing the main corpus of microbiological knowledge on the sort of scale that is needed in these days of rapid scientific progress, even if they may make rapid and impressive progress in limited research areas for a short time. Let us consider why.

Technological research organizations are government-sponsored laboratories, or research units at universities, founded to work on specific problems. Water pollution, deterioration of materials, food science and so on are examples. This they may do very well, but they do it by applying existing knowledge to practical problems. You may say this is just what we need – as it is – but it is not enough. We also need to acquire new knowledge. Since these organizations deal with existing knowledge, they are rarely able to develop the new information on a broad front. When they advance knowledge, they generally do so within the confines of their technological interest. If, as a hypothetical example, a worker on water pollution comes across information of critical importance to energy transfer in respiration, he is quite likely not to notice it and, if he does, he can rarely do more than publish it and hope that someone interested in energy transfer will pick it up. In order to make progress in a technological field the scientist voluntarily narrows his sights and, being human, he rarely remains in touch with the forefront of academic progress in his subject. For this reason technological research teams tend to have a limited productive life: they do a decade or so of valuable work and then, almost invariably, they become stale.

Of research in industrial laboratories we need say little. If a research field is obviously going to be profitable, it will be worked over, 'wrapped up' and finished efficiently and rapidly. If it has some prospect of profit, it will have some prospect of support. But, as soon as the market declines, as it has done every few years in Britain over the last two decades, economies must be made and research is first candidate for the financial chopper. It is fair to say that nearly all the major British industries that use microbes have pruned out all but their most applied research in the last decade.

University departments are the last resort of basic research at present, and they are, by British standards, reasonably well supported. Unfortunately, they get this support because an absurd myth has grown up to the effect that research and teaching are in some mystical way inseparable. In fact, good teachers are rarely good research workers, and, conversely, good research workers are often bad teachers. (There are, in our country as in others, gratifying exceptions to this generalization, but in the main it is so.) University research may occasionally be brilliant, but generally speaking it is a slow, inefficient process conducted, often rather amateurishly, by scientists in the spare time left over from teaching. In many ways this is as it should be. In these days, when attempts are at last being made to meet the demand for higher education, people who are paid to teach should teach. And, if they need to do research to keep themselves in touch with their subjects (and to train their students), it is vitally important that they should be enabled to do so. But to leave the advance of present-day science in such preoccupied hands is absurd. It is also uneconomical, because it usually means that expensive instrumentation remains idle while its proprietor grapples with his lectures and tuition. (Lest I annoy university colleagues with these strictures, let me say at once that I realize the case is oversimplified. I know well that the more research-minded university employees often unload their teaching duties on more pedagogically inclined colleagues and get on with what is, to them, the real business. Fair enough. And what do their less-favoured colleagues say about them?)

The need, in this country, is for professional research of a basic character with the economic value of such research in mind, not its profitability or its use for training post-graduates. Anyone who has noticed how often the sulphate-reducing bacteria have cropped up in various parts of this book will realize how much more efficiently research on these beasts would be conducted if it were centralized, along with the study of other economically important microbes, in some Institute of Economic Microbiology, not distributed among laboratories concerned with the various technologies in which the microbes turn up. At the end of Chapter 2, I described the subject of economic microbiology, pointing out that it is taught at no university. There is no need for it to be taught as a degree subject; indeed it is preferable that scientists should come to it with good academic groundings in microbiology, biochemistry and chemistry. But what is exasperatingly obvious is that the training of such people is, today, largely wasted as far as Britain is concerned. It is as if we trained experts in computer cybernetics and then offered them the choice, as employment, of teaching or servicing cash registers. (My mathematical friends tell me that we do something horribly like that anyway – but let them fight their own battles.) I assert once more that this country needs at least one large, central research institute (comparable to the National Institute for Medical Research or the National Physical Laboratory), where the ramifications of chemical microbiology as they affect the community in general could be followed up in a professional fashion.

Yet, if I may now grind the last spark from my axe, the only institution remotely qualified to fill this gap, and it is quite a small institution, is devoted to biological warfare. An odd nation, the British!

*

So, back to our main theme. In the early chapters of this book, as I pointed out at the end of Chapter 5, we looked at microbes from the point of view of an individual, even if that individual seemed over-preoccupied with his health and food. Then for a few chapters we studied microbes from the point of view of society and its economic structure. Now we shall study the relevance of microbes to man as a biological species; look at the part they played in his evolution, and in the evolution of other living things. Then, finally, we shall be able to say something of microbes and men in the space age and even make predictions, not all absurd, of what the future may have in store for us.

CHAPTER 10

Microbes in Evolution

So far, in this book, we have interested ourselves in the contemporary importance of microbes for mankind, even when, as in the example of the formation of sulphur deposits, that importance derives from microbial activities which took place millions of years before men appeared on this planet. In this chapter we shall consider the place of microbes in the evolutionary sequence of living things and attempt to assess what importance they had in influencing the directions which biological evolution has taken. Since we shall be dealing with questions that are usually incapable of experimental verification – for we shall be mainly concerned with events that took place in the darkest recesses of pre-history, even before recognizable fossils were formed – I must recall to readers the warning I gave about scientific fact early in Chapter 4. Even in everyday matters, laboratory science contains elements of uncertainty, particularly in interpretation of experimental findings. When one is concerned with retrospective deduction from today's knowledge about the state of our planet during its juvenile millennia, interpretation is so uncertain a process that it amounts to informed speculation. The surprising thing, really, is that we can say anything at all about the biology of those distant eras. Yet, as the reader will see, if we accept geologists' views about the broad outlines of this planet's geological history, we can put together a coherent and reasonably plausible account of how the earliest living things developed. Whether it bears any relation to the truth is another matter – but it is a form of speculation that widens our understanding of life and its potentialities, as well as exercising the imagination. So let us, for this chapter, subdue our scientific puritanism and see what sort of theoretical picture can be built up about the infancy of terrestrial life and the way in which today's microbes arose.

The 'accepted' age of this planet, by which I mean the period for which geologists and cosmologists believe it has existed as an independent celestial body, has doubled during my lifetime. It is deduced by such scientists from the distribution of naturally radio-active materials, whose half-lives are known very precisely, and is now taken to be in the region of 5,000,000,000 years: five thousand million years. This is an unimaginable figure, and could well be out by several hundreds of millions, but we can take it that it is unlikely to be doubled (or halved) yet again. If we accept that the earth was hot at the time of its formation – not all scientists do, but we shall follow the majority – there followed an immensely long period of cooling, involving intense volcanic activity, during which time the 'land' remained too hot for liquid water to exist. Such free H_2O as there was took the form of steam. Various chemical fractionations took place in this period; these we shall disregard and we shall only begin to show interest when, around three thousand million years ago, the earth had cooled sufficiently for liquid water to exist permanently on the earth's surface. At this time it seems fairly certain that the atmosphere contained no oxygen – this fact is not only likely from cosmo-chemical considerations, but can be deduced from the chemical composition of rock formations that were exposed at this time – and the atmosphere consisted mainly of methane, hydrogen and ammonia, probably with small amounts of carbon dioxide, hydrogen sulphide, nitrogen and the rare gases (helium, neon, argon, krypton and xenon). There would have been almost constant thunderstorms, with consequent lightning and electrical disturbances; moreover, there was no ozone layer, which today protects the surface of the earth from much of the ultra-violet radiation emitted by the sun, so the type of radiation received from the sun would have been quite different from today's.

A most suggestive set of experiments, performed by Dr S. L. Miller in Professor H. C. Urey's laboratory in the early 1950s and abundantly confirmed in other laboratories, showed that a wet mixture of methane, hydrogen and ammonia, exposed to an electrical discharge for a while, formed traces of organic compounds including organic acids and amino-acids hitherto regarded as exclusive products of living things. Subsequent experiments, adding traces of hydrogen cyanide, hydrogen sulphide, phosphates and so on have shown that all sorts of organic chemicals turn up in these conditions, many of them, such as the purines, being particularly characteristic of living things. Moreover, ultra-violet radiation is also a potent agent for causing the formation of organic matter from gas mixtures of the kind likely to have existed in the primitive atmosphere. It follows that, before life originated here, the seas of this planet were probably dilute 'soups' of organic matter formed by electrochemical and photochemical reactions of this kind. The seas became the sort of environment in which many present-day anaerobic bacteria, for instance, would flourish. But there were no such bacteria, nor any other living things, so those materials accumulated, interacted to form new compounds, became absorbed onto rocks and washed off again to react anew. The seas, in fact, must have been a turmoil of photochemical reactions with all sorts of organic compounds forming, interacting and breaking down. Lest the term 'soup' give the wrong impression, however, I must emphasize that the concentration of these materials was probably very low. The seas, believed to be about a third as salty as they are today, contained vastly more inorganic matter, salts and so on, than amino-acids and other organic chemicals. The only places where the concentration of organic matter would be high would be at the edge of drying pools, or adsorbed on the surfaces of materials such as clay, which have a particular affinity for organic matter.

In Chapter 4, I was very emphatic about spontaneous generation being an event of astronomical improbability today. Three thousand million years ago, with the electrochemical and photochemical turmoil that I have described taking place, it may have been less improbable. Bernal, Oparin, Haldane, Pirie and others have discussed how organic matter, concentrated by adsorption at rock or clay surfaces, might easily take on complexities analogous to present-day biochemical molecules; that a sort of chemical evolution could take place, with molecules forming and breaking down in all sorts of ways, until one emerged with the capacity to facilitate the synthesis of others like it. This property might never have been an attribute of one molecule – a fortuitous conjunction of molecules might have led to reproduction of the whole set. Such a molecule or molecular complex would have one of the basic properties of living things: self-reproduction. No doubt many such systems were formed and fizzled out before one became established, but once one *did* get established, it would tend to prevent the emergence of others by using up the available organic matter to form more of its own type.

These mechanistic views of the origin of life, which I have sketched very superficially, are popular today among scientists who consider these questions, though they differ about the details. Some place emphasis on local volcanic heating as against radiation as the source of chemical 'turmoil' that allowed the evolution of pseudo-living molecules. Others insist on the importance of forming co-acervates: droplets of organic matter which form under special conditions in water and which divide in two when they exceed a certain size, rather like a living microbe. Yet others prefer to postulate the intervention of a Divine agency. And the view that terrestrial living things were seeded by dormant living matter from elsewhere in space is not excluded though it is at present unfashionable; it displaces, but does not answer, the question of how life originated. For our purposes, in this chapter, we shall accept that living creatures appeared somehow, in a slightly salty, watery environment containing all sorts of dissolved organic materials, some of which would become concentrated at the surfaces of solids such as rocks, clay or sand particles. The atmosphere contained little or no oxygen and the primitive organisms, though we have no idea what they looked like, behaved like microbes as far as their chemistry was concerned, in that they formed more of themselves from available organic matter. In particular they performed the first step of an evolutionary process: they used up the available material and thus made the emergence of competitive organisms less probable.

What kinds of microbes did they most closely resemble? If we refer back to Chapter 2 it becomes obvious that the anaerobic bacteria have properties in common with these primitive creatures. They can grow in the absence of air by breaking down organic materials and obtaining energy for growth from these reactions. Present-day anaerobes have quite complex structures – for microbes – and it is most unlikely that they include any representatives of the earliest living things, but we can say that several species of present-day anaerobes would have managed quite well in what we imagine the pre-biotic environment to have been like.

One important difference would be that these primitive microbes probably had very limited synthetic abilities – they themselves probably consisted of a relatively small number of complex molecules, and they made themselves from precursors that were almost as complex, available in the 'soup' around them. They needed to conduct very few chemical reactions to duplicate themselves. Yet they did not resemble viruses, as some people have been inclined to believe, because viruses need a complete living system to grow on: as we saw in Chapter 2, they 'programme' another organism's enzymes to make more virus instead of normal products; viruses depend on the existence of quite a complex biochemical system.

Our primitive microbes had no such systems to work on, but they had a splendid reserve of food, at least to start with. Moreover, they were subject to constant ultra-violet irradiation, and ultra-violet light causes chemical transformations in a variety of molecules, even those composing our primitive microbes. Many such transformations probably killed the microbes: put a stop to their ability to multiply. But it is probable that, over millions upon millions of years, a few altered their chemistry appreciably without impairing their ability to reproduce themselves. Thus a new organism, inherently different from its predecessor, could be created, able to reproduce itself in the new form. This process is a crude example of what we know as a mutation: a change in the inheritable structure of a living thing brought about by some accident, which leads to the formation of progeny having a different character from the parent. As every reader knows, mutation is the basis of evolution; if a mutation confers an advantage on a mutant, that strain tends in the long run to outgrow and replace its predecessor and in this way, by the process called natural selection, the slow transformation of living species we call evolution has taken place, over the millennia, on this planet.

We shall say more about mutation later in this chapter, for we know a lot about how and why mutations occur in present-day organisms. For present purposes, however, we need only note that one of the most effective inducers of mutation is ultra-violet light. Therefore, if our primitive microbes bore any relationship to present-day organisms, their mutation rate was probably very high.

Since the emergence of living things in the primordial soup would lead to the removal of complex organic molecules from that soup, and their incorporation into primitive organisms, it follows that any mutation that enabled the organism to make do with less complex organic matter would give that mutant an enormous advantage over its neighbours. Thus there would be a strong selective pressure in favour of development of increased synthetic ability: biological evolution would take place in the direction of simpler and simpler nutritional requirements until, ultimately, the first autotrophs appeared. (To save flipping to the glossary, I shall remind readers that autotrophs are microbes that can use wholly inorganic materials for growth: sulphur, CO_2 and oxygen, for example, or sunlight, CO_2 and water.)

The idea that autotrophs developed after heterotrophs arises naturally from this picture of evolution, though this point has not always been accepted. Thirty years ago most microbiologists were inclined to regard the autotrophs as the most primitive of living things, simply because the majority of present-day microbes are heterotrophs and it is possible to plot plausible evolutionary pathways among existing microbes in the direction of heterotrophy. In this latter point they were quite correct, as we shall see later, but it is difficult to regard autotrophs as representatives of the *most* primitive living things, simply because of the enormous number of separate enzymes they need to possess to be able to make up their bodies from inorganic matter. There is no doubt that autotrophs appeared pretty early in evolution, but it is most logical to consider that they developed from even more primitive creatures that were heterotrophs.

What kinds of autotrophs do we know today that might resemble the earliest kinds of autotrophs? They would need to be anaerobes, so the coloured sulphur bacteria, which oxidize sulphides to sulphur and sulphate with the aid of sunlight, are candidates; there are certain blue-green algae that can grow anaerobically, if sulphide is present, and also reduce CO_2 with sunlight; there are bacteria that can reduce carbonates to methane or acetic acid using hydrogen; one strain of bacterium has been reported that can reduce nitrates while oxidizing ferrous iron to ferric; another can oxidize sulphur with nitrates; another can oxidize hydrogen with nitrates. Yet the choice among anaerobic autotrophs is not very wide: some of those we have mentioned are not very likely candidates because, though there was probably plenty of sulphur and sulphide around, there was not, in the chemical conditions then obtaining, likely to be much nitrate.

One answer to this question arises from the discovery, in 1960, of a nutritional group of microbes that seems half-way between autotrophs and heterotrophs. *Desulfovibrio*, a group of sulphate-reducing bacteria, can, for example, oxidize hydrogen with sulphate forming water and sulphide:

$$CaSO_4 + 4H_2 \longrightarrow CaS + 4H_2O$$

and use the energy of this reaction to assimilate organic materials. There exists also a species of the sulphur bacteria *Thiobacillus*, called *T. intermedius*, which can couple the oxidation of sulphur to the assimilation of organic matter; there is evidence that hydrogen-oxidizing bacteria of the genus *Hydrogenomonas* couple hydrogen oxidation to assimilations and the writer has seen at least one publication indicating that methane-oxidizing bacteria perform similar processes when oxidizing methane. Some of the photosynthetic sulphur bacteria certainly assimilate acetate as a result of photosynthesis, and, as we saw a moment ago, photosynthetic sulphur bacteria are among the best candidates for primitive status among present-day microbes.

Thus it seems likely that true autotrophy, though it probably developed at an early stage in evolution, was preceded by what has been called 'chemotrophic assimilation': the coupling of an inorganic reaction that yields energy to the assimilation of simple organic matter into the cell, and its use to form cell material. It is but a short evolutionary step from such assimilations to true autotrophy, the assimilation of CO_2, and among microbes there is an overlap between the two types of nutrition. Within the same groups of bacteria, as in the thiobacilli, one can today find types that conduct either or both processes. But the emergence of autotrophy was a vital step in evolution because it provided the first reliable alternative to a primeval photochemical turmoil for the accumulation of organic matter on this planet. Though the 'partial' autotrophs we have described might utilize the components of the primeval 'soup' much more efficiently than their primitive predecessors, they still depended on it absolutely for their existence. They could grow no faster, and no more abundantly, than photochemical formation of organic matter permitted. The true autotrophs were the first creatures to become independent of spontaneous organic synthesis, and it is most likely that the most effective ones were those that used solar radiation to do this: that is, the anaerobic precursors of green plants.

One problem arises if one assumes autotrophs had such an importance in the primitive economy of this planet: where did they get the CO_2 to fix, when the atmosphere consisted largely of methane, ammonia and hydrogen? The probable answer is that oxygen would be formed continuously by a photochemical reaction of ultra-violet light on water but, because of the character of the atmosphere, it would react rapidly with methane to give CO_2, with ammonia to give N_2 and with hydrogen to re-form water. Thus a steady conversion of methane to CO_2 and of ammonia to nitrogen would have been taking place on earth, leading to the formation of carbonate rocks on the one hand and, on the other hand, the free nitrogen prevalent in our atmosphere today.

Let us pause at this stage and see if we can rustle up some facts bearing on this picture. We envisage a world with permanent seas which, though they were once rather weak, had probably become quite saline as storms and rains washed soluble salts out of the rocks, hills and mountains. No oxygen was present in its atmosphere, but there was plenty of sunshine with a strong component of ultra-violet light. A fair amount of free H_2S was present in the seas, formed partly by microbial action, partly remaining from the primitive atmosphere, and a population of primitive microbes existed, conducting the sulphur cycle (reducing sulphates to sulphides; oxidizing these via sulphur to sulphate) and assimilating photochemically produced organic matter together with any organic matter produced by the emergent autotrophs. Though iron- and hydrogen-oxidizing microbes may have been present, we are prejudiced against them because their present-day representatives generally need oxygen or nitrates and these were probably rare. Thiobacilli were probably rare for a similar reason, but methane-producing microbes, though they are not autotrophic, were probably abundant, reducing CO_2 to methane while oxidizing any available organic matter. Likewise, organisms capable of reducing CO_2 to acetate could well have been plentiful and would have provided, in acetate, one of the best-known substrates for the chemotrophic assimilations we described.

Facts, you remind me? Well, there is one set of experiments that has considerable bearing on this question. The sulphate-reducing bacteria, as we saw in Chapter 6, fractionate the isotopes of sulphur during sulphate reduction, a point that is of considerable importance in establishing the microbial origin of sulphur deposits. By examining the distribution of sulphur isotopes in minerals laid down during known geological eras, one can tell whether they have been subject to microbial action, and this has been done exhaustively by various American geologists. There is clear evidence of microbial action by sulphur bacteria as far back as 800,000,000 years ago, and some samples dating back as far as 2,000,000,000 years ago show positive fractionations. Moreover in some pre-Cambrian rocks dating back further than 2,000,000,000 years ago, (called the 'Gunflint chert', lying north of Lake Superior in Canada) Dr Barghoorn has found microscopic formations that look very like traces of blue-green algae – and the blue-green algae are today most closely related to the photosynthetic sulphur bacteria.

(Perhaps I should add here that the Gunflint chert formations also look like the thermophilic flexibacteria we met briefly in

Chapter 2. There is a certain logic in the view that the most primitive microbes were thermophilic, because the first liquid waters of this planet would be hot. But for present purposes we must leave that thought as just one of many speculations that are possible about the state of primitive life.)

Microscopic traces in old rocks are perhaps rather dangerous pieces of evidence to support an evolutionary scheme, but isotope fractionation seems pretty reliable and provides us with our first cogent fact. We can assert that, between 2,000,000,000 and 800,000,000 years ago, abundant microbial sulphur metabolism was taking place. (Let us note in passing, to get our time scale into perspective, that the first definite fossils appear in rocks of about 500,000,000 years old.) During all this time this planet's atmosphere was anaerobic; the dominant living things were the distant ancestors of our present-day sulphur bacteria, and the main biochemical process on Earth was the sulphur cycle. Or so it seems.

What happened between 800,000,000 years ago, when there was no oxygen, and 500,000,000 years ago, when there was some, if not as much as today?

The coloured sulphur bacteria today contain chlorophyll, the green pigment of plants that is essential for photosynthesis. One can represent the chemistry of their photosynthesis very crudely this way:

$$2H_2S + CO_2 \xrightarrow[\text{chlorophyll}]{\text{sunlight}} 2S + [CH_2O] + H_2O$$

where $[CH_2O]$ represents carbohydrate. (For non-chemists this means they make carbohydrate from carbon dioxide, with the aid of sunlight, while splitting hydrogen sulphide to sulphur and water.)

Today there exists a group of coloured non-sulphur bacteria which conduct a photosynthesis using organic matter in place of H_2S (we met them briefly in Chapter 2). They are still anaerobes (at least when they photosynthesize) and they can be regarded as removing hydrogen from organic matter and using it to reduce

195

CO_2. If we write 'H_2A' as a formula for an organic molecule from which the bacteria can remove hydrogen, then their photosynthesis can be represented so:

$$2H_2A + CO_2 \xrightarrow[\text{chlorophyll}]{\text{Sunlight}} [CH_2O] + O_2$$

very like the mechanism in the sulphur bacteria.

By the wisdom of hindsight we can see that it was only a matter of time before sufficient mutations took place to enable organisms to do the whole exercise without H_2S or 'H_2A', using only water:

$$H_2O + CO_2 \xrightarrow[\text{chlorophyll}]{\text{sunlight}} [CH_2O] + O_2$$

splitting water to release oxygen.

This reaction, if it became at all widespread, would have had an interesting effect on the whole planetary ecology, because H_2S and O_2 (hydrogen sulphide and oxygen) react with each other. They do so only slowly, but they cannot co-exist for long: they form sulphur and water. Thus, the emergence of microbes able to make oxygen from water would have a catastrophic effect on the sulphur cycle. It would remove H_2S, deplete the sulphide by oxidation and tend to put a stop to the whole process – and if the process stopped, it meant that the organisms responsible for it would cease to flourish; most of them would die and the survivors would persist only in limited environments, in the sulfureta described in Chapter 1, for example, where special local conditions kept oxygen away.

In this way we can see a logical process leading to the emergence of photosynthetic autotrophs that generated oxygen from water while converting CO_2 to organic matter. Slowly, because of the chemical reactivity of oxygen, gases such as ammonia and hydrogen sulphide would be removed from the atmosphere. Hydrogen would escape continuously into space – it is too light to be retained for long by a planet having the mass of the earth. So the atmosphere would tend to consist of oxygen, nitrogen and CO_2; possibly residual methane as well, but most of the residual ammonia would be dissolved in the seas. Our primitive anaerobic microbes would be finding conditions highly unsatisfactory in general: the environment would favour creatures able to develop some way of making biological use of the oxygen. The oxygen in the atmosphere would form ozone at the outer fringes of the atmosphere, as it does today, and this would screen out much of the ultra-violet light responsible for the early photochemical turmoil. Thus spontaneous generation would become an even less probable event, and the average mutation rate of organisms would decrease. But this situation would favour the living things that were already established, for mutations would still occur, though less often. Heredity, like the environment, would become a more stable quality and species of a given type would persist for longer periods unchanged. We know that oxygen-breathing creatures did develop; can we say anything about how?

Among the enzymes that present-day air-breathing organisms possess are a group called cytochromes. These are chemically related to the red haemoglobin of blood: in addition to the usual amino-acids they contain iron atoms bound in a special chemical grouping called a porphyrin. The porphyrin group, as classicists will guess, gives the molecule a red or purple colour. Cytochromes are concerned in the final reactions with oxygen that take place during respiration; they undergo reversible oxidations and reductions (the iron atom switching back and forth from the ferrous to the ferric state) and, by some process not yet wholly understood, all air-breathing organisms, from men to microbes, obtain much energy for their biological processes from these changes.

Fermentative anaerobes do not possess cytochromes. They have brown iron-containing enzymes called ferredoxins which undergo reversible oxidations and reductions, but, as far as we know, these have no energy-providing function. To make efficient use of oxygen, it seems probable that our evolving microbes would need to develop the iron-porphyrin system and integrate it with an energy-generating process. We know, of course, they did; but how? One suggestive point is the fact that, almost uniquely among the anaerobes, the sulphate-reducing bacteria contain cytochromes. And, generally, they have just one cytochrome, being in this respect simpler than aerobes, which usually have two or three different kinds in one organism. There are other anaerobic bacteria that possess cytochromes – the photosynthetic sulphur bacteria – but their cytochromes seem to be concerned in photosynthesis and not in respiration. (Photosynthesis in green plants also involves cytochromes.) Thus the sulphate-reducing bacteria contain today a representative of the cytochromes universally encountered in aerobic organisms; if their primitive ancestors also contained such enzymes, then it was probably a fairly simple evolutionary step for organisms to develop the capability of reducing oxygen from the capability of reducing sulphates. Simple, that is to say, compared with the evolution of the complex synthetic abilities involved in autotrophy.

Once an organism arose able to reduce oxygen to water instead of sulphate to sulphide, assuming evolution did proceed in this way, it would find a new world awaiting it. All those areas of the planet which the presence of free oxygen now rendered unsuitable for the anaerobes would be available to it and its progeny. It is likely, in fact, that air-breathing organisms evolved from several groups of primitive anaerobes besides the sulphate-reducing bacteria, and a second promising ancestor might well have been found among the photosynthetic bacteria which, as I just mentioned, also contain cytochromes. We mentioned in Chapter 2 that there is a link between some of the photosynthetic bacteria and some particularly primitive algae called the blue-green algae. These organisms have a number of characteristics in common, and there exist borderline species that seem to span the bridge between photosynthetic bacteria that are anaerobes and those blue-green algae that are aerobes. Some blue-green algae are both: they can grow with air or metabolize sulphides. At the other extreme there are organisms on the borders of blue-green algae and ordinary green algae, so we can see that, if the types we recognize today are representatives of creatures that evolved at the time that the atmosphere of this planet changed from a reducing to an oxidizing type, then there is a clear-cut evolutionary sequence through the photosynthetic bacteria and blue-green algae to the green algae and, hence, to the whole plant kingdom of today.

We cannot pursue this story into the realms of multicellular organisms – indeed, for reasons of space we are forced to gloss over and disregard many details of the probable evolution of our special subjects, the microbes. But since we have alluded to the evolution of higher plants, we might as well digress long enough to set the animals on their evolutionary path also. . . .

The protozoon *Euglena*, which we met in Chapter 2, is a single-celled animalcule which lies half-way between plants and animals. It contains a body called a chloroplast, which possesses chlorophyll and enables it to grow photosynthetically just like a plant. But it can also assimilate pre-formed food like an animal. If it is cultured in the dark it tends to lose its chloroplast, and after several generations its progeny lose their chloroplasts completely and become wholly animal-like. They come to resemble another species called *Astasia*, whom we also met in Chapter 2. This seems a very reasonable model for the evolution of animals : motile algae might, by virtue of their ability to move around, find it more efficient to seek pre-formed organic matter and assimilate it, thus losing their autotrophic abilities and becoming 'parasitic' on the products of those types that had remained autotrophic. Some would lose their chloroplasts and thus they would become protozoa. Various varieties would develop and, with successive adaptations and variations, multiple aggregrates of cells – 'metazoa' – would emerge and the evolution of the animal kingdom would be under way.

Once again we must break off the story at the microbe stage, but the point that protozoa developed from algae by *loss* of autotrophic function is one of more general significance in the further evolution of other microbes. Fungi, for example, are often filamentous and branched, like the more complex algae, and it is very likely that they developed as 'degenerate' forms of such algae : organisms that found it an evolutionary advantage to assimilate the detritus of algae and other autotrophs, rather than continue to fix CO_2 themselves. Most of the bacteria handled in laboratories today are not autotrophic and, in some groups, one can find examples that have increasingly complex nutritional needs. In our discussion of culture media in Chapter 4 we saw how some bacteria will grow with a few simple chemicals whereas others require the most complex of brews and some, indeed, have not been cultured away from living tissue. One of the early contributions to bacteriology of the distinguished French scientist, Professor A. Lwoff, was the recognition that the trend of evolution among microbes, once micro-organisms were well established on Earth, has been in the direction of *loss* of self-sufficiency. Microbes, particularly the pathogenic ones, have become more and more dependent on organic materials accumulated by plants, animals and more versatile microbes for their existence. Higher organisms or their detritus replaced the primeval 'soup' as the habitat of most microbes; autotrophy, or even highly developed synthetic abilities, conferred no evolutionary advantage, so that microbial evolution tended to go in the direction of loss of biochemical versatility.

Perhaps the extreme case of such physiological degeneracy occurs among the viruses. These are almost structureless creatures which have lost all their enzymes and live wholly as parasites on other organisms. Again we can find models for an evolutionary process by considering intermediate types to be found today. There exist in the soil tiny bacterium-like creatures called *Bdellovibrio* which grow on organic matter and which, given the opportunity, infect true bacteria and parasitize them. There exist tiny organisms, mycoplasms, which are almost certainly like bacteria (though, because they contain sterols, a relationship to protozoa or fungi is also possible) but which lack their structural rigidity, and there exist large viruses which contain quite complex protein structures but no metabolic enzymes. These creatures form a sequence of increasingly refined parasites until one reaches the small viruses, which seem to consist of only two or three huge molecules capable of perverting the metabolism of more complex organisms to synthesize themselves, but unable to do anything whatever with non-living substrates. Though, *a priori*, one's instinct is to think of creatures so chemically simple as the small viruses as extremely primitive, it is in fact most likely that they are elaborately degenerate descendents of organisms that were at least as complex as bacteria.

Viruses are, in fact, almost perfect parasites: they do nothing for themselves until a host appears, whereupon they cause the host to form more virus. Even more refined parasitism is shown by the 'temperate bacteriophages', viruses which are parasitic on bacteria but which do them no apparent harm unless some stress affects the host. We shall discuss them later in this chapter.

Thus, despite the lack of concrete data, we can produce an analogical account of how the most primitive blobs of life might have evolved into present-day microbes, and initiated the evolution of the two great groups of terrestrial living things. Circumstantial evidence makes us attribute crucial importance to the sulphur bacteria, particularly the sulphate-reducing bacteria, but this may be so only because the one fact we have to go on which applies retrospectively is the fractionation of sulphur isotopes. But even if we regard the apparent preponderance of sulphur bacteria as fortuitous, it is still true that the atmosphere of this planet was transformed, about 500,000,000 years ago, through the activities of microbes, and the stage was set for the development of the air-breathing creatures we know and are today. Air-breathers inherited the earth – but not without resistance. Even today, the catastrophic instances of natural pollution that occur, for example, in Walvis Bay (see Chapter 7) can be seen as a sort of mindless take-over bid by the sulphur bacteria. Happily these outbursts are transient, and the surprising thing is that the bacteria responsible survive so successfully in what is, for them, a hostile environment. The persistence of sulphate-reducing bacteria, for example, throughout geological aeons of time undoubtedly depended on the fact that they grow best in an environment that is lethal to most present-day creatures. Successful evolutionary types not only develop characters that suit them to their environment, they also modify the environment to suit themselves.

The reader may care to reflect that this is as true of men as of microbes. Does man count as a successful species?

We have spoken of the variability and adaptability of microbes often in this book, and even mentioned mutation. The time has come to say something of how these variations come about.

There can be few readers of popular science who are unaware of the crucial importance of 'DNA' in heredity. DNA is the technical abbreviation for deoxyribonucleic acid, a chemical found in all living things that acts as a sort of blueprint of what the organism will be like. (It is absent from certain bacterial viruses (called the RNA viruses); it seems also to be absent from sub-viral particles such as the scrapie agent mentioned in Chapter 2, but the status of these agents as living things is still uncertain.) Its precise molecular composition and configuration are now known in considerable detail – it is an array of molecules called purines and pyrimidines, of which four kinds exist in DNA, 'tied' together with molecules of a sugar (called deoxyribose) and phosphate groups. Its composition and arrangement differ from species to species, so that there are as many different DNAs as there are species, some widely different, some only slightly so. DNA molecules are very long arrays of this small variety of components, rather in the form of a spring (technically known as a helix), and the differences lie not in the nature of the components but in their arrangement. The molecule is rather like a sort of coded tape, with four symbols (represented by the purines or pyrimidines), which spell out what enzymes and structural components, and roughly how much of them, the organism will consist of. Every species has its special tape which determines what it will be like; indeed, in multicellular organisms every cell carries this tape, and in all but the generative cells the tape is present in duplicate.

The nature of DNA, the way in which it is reproduced and the way in which it influences the nature of living organisms has occupied, indeed sometimes obsessed, biologists for the last two decades. About twenty-five years ago DNA was recognized as the chemical form of conceptual elements called genes, which conveyed the hereditary characteristics of living creatures from generation to generation. Men had pursued the study of heredity – known as genetics – ever since the work of Mendel in the nineteenth century, but in the early 1940s it received an enormous impetus from American experiments on the genetics of a microbe, the bread mould called *Neurospora*. By treatment with ultra-violet light, X-rays and certain chemicals, mutants of *Neurospora* were obtained that had lost certain biochemical abilities – they became, for example, unable to synthesize certain vitamins – and by a systematic study of the progeny of such mutants, duly crossed sexually, the concept emerged that one gene was responsible for the ability to make one enzyme. The discovery that bacteria formed mutants of a similar kind in comparable conditions initiated an extremely rewarding period of research in microbial genetics, as a result of which the chemical pathways were elucidated by which all sorts of components of microbial cells were made. If the biochemistry of the two pre-war decades had been concerned largely with the breakdown of natural products, the war-time and first post-war decades were concerned with their synthesis, and microbes – bacteria and moulds – were the major research material for such studies. As metabolic pathways became clear, or reasonably clear, one after another, interest began to shift in the direction of how these syntheses were controlled: what precise mechanism 'told' the cell what to synthesize, and how much. By now the basic importance of DNA in these processes was clear. DNA was the 'tape' bearing all the hereditary information available to the cell; some form of message was transferred from the DNA tape to those centres of the cell ('ribosomes') actually capable of synthesizing cell material. Much of the information on the tape remained masked; it passed out no message, until some stimulus of a chemical character removed the mask, permitted release of the appropriate message and initiated synthesis of something new. The procedure by which the message was transmitted, and read, involved a material called ribonucleic acid ('RNA'), similar in its general chemical pattern to DNA but differing in important details. Internal 'feedback' processes have been recognized in the synthetic pathways, whereby products of a certain sequence of reactions slow down and even stop the earlier steps and, in such a manner, ensure that the organism does not make too much of any particular component. In the last decade our understanding of these processes has developed even further: it is possible in some degree to relate the precise chemical

203

structure of DNA to the precise chemicals used in synthesis. Proteins are built up of amino-acids, and the 'code' structures in DNA corresponding to almost all of the amino-acids are now known. In a crude way the basic alphabet of heredity is now understood.

It is impossible to go into the details of these advances here – it would occupy a whole book. Readers with even a nodding acquaintance with the field will have noticed how deliberately general my account has been. Microbial genetics has proved to be the clue to the understanding of the genetics of most living organisms and, in the last twenty years, it has led to advances in biology corresponding to the flowering of atomic chemistry in the early years of this century. Just as Dalton's conceptual atoms were shown to have a physical reality in those early days, so Mendel's genes have been recognized as chemical entities and their structure and function understood to a remarkable degree. Small wonder, then, that enthusiastic biologists have dignified biochemical genetics with the name 'Molecular Biology' (there is nothing like a new science for attracting research grants) and tended to accept that what is true of *Escherichia coli* is true of all living things. Scientists have their fads and fashions, and if ever one justified itself it is the current passion of biologists for molecular biology. Yet for our purposes there still exist problems remote from the genetic code.

We have become deflected from the evolution of microbes to the evolution of microbiologists, and must sternly pull ourselves back to our track. Mutation, which was the question we started out to discuss, arises simply as a chemical change in the DNA of an organism. If a microbe, for example, is exposed to X-rays, ultra-violet light or certain chemicals, its DNA is damaged. It may be able to repair this damage, in which case it will be able to multiply unchanged. It may not, in which case part of the code on the DNA 'tape' will become nonsense. If it is drastic nonsense the microbe will be unable to multiply and will die; but if it is modest damage the organism may be able to multiply, but with changed hereditary characteristics. It will have undergone a mutation, and its progeny will be mutants. The value of microbes, to scientists, has been the enormous variety of mutants one can detect in microbes and the relative ease with which they can be studied.

Mutations represent one way in which microbes can change and so adjust themselves to a changed environment. The 'switching-on' of masked information on their DNA 'tapes' is another mechanism of variation. A third process, which arose from the study of mutants, is known as recombination. If mutants of an organism requiring a vitamin (X) are made to mutate twice more, one can get a strain needing, say, X, Y and Z. If one takes a different mutant of the same organism requiring different vita-mins (A, B, C) and grows them together in the same culture, some of the progeny are found to require X and B, X and A, Y and C and so on. Obviously some transfer of genetic material has taken place between individuals of the ABC type and those of the XYZ type. This process, called recombination, is now known to result from the conjugation of individuals in the populations; it has been observed in electron micrographs. Con-jugation is pretty rare in most bacteria but some strains of intestinal bacteria have a high frequency of such recombinations (the so-called 'hfr' strains). The process seems to be a very primitive kind of sexuality. It might well be an evolutionary precursor of the sexual reproduction of higher organisms, but bacterial sexuality has several peculiarities, not least of which is the fact that the act of conjugation confers the property of 'maleness' on the 'female' or recipient cell. The hereditary factor responsible for 'maleness' seems to be distinct, except in the 'hfr' strains, from the rest of the genetic material, yet it con-sists of DNA. It has, in fact, many properties in common with a temperate bacteriophage (discussed further below). The 'hfr' strains, which are sexually the most active, have such a factor but it is incorporated with the rest of the genetic material in the chromosome. These facts lead us to an interesting speculation on the evolution of sexuality: if bacterial sexuality originated as a mechanism for the transfer of a bacterial virus, has sexuality in higher creatures a similar origin? Is it a degenerate mechanism for transferring what was once, in an evolutionary sense, a parasite?

Another mode of microbial variation is called transformation: if the DNA from one type of bacterium (P) is added to a culture of another (Q), a proportion of those in the Q culture can absorb some of the P-type DNA and take on P-like characteristics. This process is of more than just academic interest: there is evidence that drug resistance can be passed on in this way in nature, possibly because some microbes die, disintegrate and release their DNA in the neighbourhood of receptive individuals, possibly by conjugation of the kind we have just discussed, but leading to the transfer of factors concerned with drug resistance. A particularly alarming practical instance is antibiotic resistance among *Salmonella*-type bacteria in cattle. If calves are infected with a few drug-resistant organisms, this resistance can be passed on to some of their native microbes without their ever having encountered the antibiotic in question.

Finally, there is a process called transduction that can lead to variation among microbes, and it involves participation of bacterial viruses or 'bacteriophage'. Many bacteriophages kill their hosts, but some, called temperate 'phages, do not. They appear to live peacefully within their hosts and only multiply and damage them under the influence of some external stimulus (ultra-violet light is an example). They can then re-infect new hosts and, when they do so, they may carry some of the hereditary characteristics of their previous host into the new one.

Temperate 'phages, as we just mentioned, are highly refined parasites that live undetected in normal, healthy hosts and, since they may introduce new hereditary characteristics into a host, they may have been of considerable importance in evolution. Their ability to transduct hereditary properties suggests that evolution could well have been an accretory process: that association of two distinct creatures could develop to such an extent that the 'pair' became a single, new species with genetic characteristics derived from both of its progenitors. Some authorities suspect that the photosynthetic apparatus of certain protozoa, called their chloroplast, is a vestige of what was once a symbiotic alga; there is little doubt that the protozoon *Crithidia oncopelti* (which we met in Chapter 5) contains symbiotic bacteria in its protoplasm that aid in its nutrition. It is a small logical step from such symbioses among microbes to combinations in which one symbiont has become part of the genetic apparatus of its colleague. It is interesting to speculate what proportion of the complex chromosomal apparatus of higher plants and animals arose from total assimilations of this kind, and the concept opens vistas for the future modification of genetic material, even that of humans, by deliberate manipulation. Already transformable bacteria have been used successfully as hosts for animal viruses.

Microbes, having the mutability we have just discussed, can adjust themselves to the wide variety of physical conditions we discussed in Chapter 2 – which is one reason why they have persisted so successfully throughout geological time. They provide us with an indication of the intrinsic versatility of living things. Though the larger denizens of this planet are oxygen-breathing creatures living in a temperate environment, this is just a freak of evolution. The existence of anaerobic bacteria, sulphate- and nitrate-reducing bacteria, makes it clear that oxygen is a prerequisite neither of life nor of evolution. The waters of this planet are about neutral, neither particularly acid nor particularly alkaline, but the existence of *Thiobacilli* and their associated acid-tolerant flora tells us that life could have developed and evolved on a much more acid planet. Water is sufficiently abundant here to be fresh or only weakly saline, but the existence of halophiles shows us that, had water been much more restricted and, therefore, had the few seas and lakes been highly saline, living things would nevertheless have managed. Barophiles tell us that high pressure would have been no obstacle; psychrophiles indicate that a temperature constantly near freezing would have been acceptable. Spore formation shows that life could have adjusted to periods of considerable heat and desiccation – as have some desert plants; thermophiles tell us that life could have developed at temperatures of up to 90 degrees C. Even here we must make the proviso that this limit is set by the boiling point of water in Yellowstone Park, U.S.A. Under high pressure water boils at much higher temperatures and microbes have been grown in such conditions; there seems to be no upper limit to the temperature of terrestrial-type life provided liquid water persists.

The earth's ordinary flora and fauna, then, today represent only a limited aspect of the biochemistry of which terrestrial life is inherently capable: our communal biochemistry became dominant about five hundred thousand millennia ago and only among microbes do we find representatives of what might have been. But it makes one think. How might carbon-based life have fared elsewhere in the universe? Shall we find halophilic psychrophiles on the arid, cold wastes of Mars? Or CO_2-fixing thermophiles on Venus? If inter-stellar travel is for ever closed to mankind, as relativists would seem to have us believe, may we nevertheless hope one day to receive television pictures of the sulphate-reducing equivalent of *Homo sapiens* from his anaerobic home in a distant solar system? I opened this chapter with a warning that much of what I should write would be of a speculative character; perhaps I should now separate off the really wild speculation by opening a new chapter.

CHAPTER 11

Microbes in the Future

One statement can be made with as great certainty as any other in this book: short of some cosmic catastrophe, such as the sun becoming a nova, microbes on this planet have a future. This is more than can be said for many animals and even for mankind. We know, for example, that the days of the sperm whale are numbered. Though attempts are regularly made to keep whaling within bounds, it is unlikely that they will succeed while whole populations hunger for whale oil products. Likewise the rhinoceros, the pangolin, the osprey and at least a hundred and fifty other animals and birds are destined to disappear from this planet unless they are successfully preserved in zoos or game reserves. Plants suffer too: the domestic goat converted the North African coast into a desert after it was introduced by the Muslims in the twelfth century; previously it had been a fertile, wine- and olive-producing agrarian zone.

Even mankind's future is in doubt. In this decade of this century it is obvious to most civilized people that atomic armoury has powers of universal destruction that even writers of science fiction had not imagined thirty years ago. Militarists have to consider quite seriously devastation and radio-activity spread over hundreds of square miles, such that no visible living thing survives. It is not beyond the powers of a war-based technology deliberately to sterilize this planet of plant and animal life; it is fairly easy to calculate the number of nuclear weapons that would need to be exploded to do this and the figures have been published.

In these circumstances, microbes would still survive. *Micrococcus radiodurans*, for example, is a remarkably radiation-resistant organism, that tolerates some hundreds of times the γ-radiation of ordinary cells, and other microbes are known that tolerate considerable amounts of radio-activity. They appear to be able to repair the damage caused by radiation very effectively – a good example of the adaptability of micro-organisms. To produce a level of radiation sufficient to eliminate such microbes from this planet would require an almost inconceivable number of atom bombs.

Of course, in this decade, it is almost inconceivable that mankind would be so stupid. Today even the most megalomaniac and ignorant of political leaders seem to realize that atomic war is to be used as a threat rather than a matter of practical action. Yet one thing must be obvious to people of all political persuasions: if the threat of atomic holocaust has diminished in the last decade, even if temporarily, it is because the standard of living has risen in one of the countries that offered the major threat. Mankind cares more about survival the more it has to lose.

In my opinion – everything in this chapter is my opinion, of course – mankind's control over microbes provides a greater threat to his own future than his control of the atom. And the reason for this is quite unconnected with biological warfare and its possibilities, disgusting as those may be. The reason is simply this. By the control and prevention of disease, civilized communities have prolonged the lives of their own individuals, increased their potential fertility and decreased infant and child mortality. They have also, and quite rightly, introduced such medical benefits to backward and under-developed countries. Therefore we have the 'population explosion'. Professor P. M. Hauser of the University of Chicago has quoted a simple calculation to the effect that, if the population of the world keeps increasing at its present rate, by about the year 2,600 there will be one person for every square foot of the planet's land, poles, deserts and mountains included. This sort of calculation is good for coffee-table conversation but is, of course, meaningless, because it will not happen. But the serious information underlying such calculations is this: today more than half the world's population lives at a level approaching starvation. Even if present birth-control programmes proceed smoothly, the world's population will double by the year 2,000 and double again by 2,040, according to Dr Worthington, Director of the International Biological Programme. Though the world's population expands, the world's capacity to feed its people increases much more slowly. So the standard of living drops, people have less to lose, and the probability of atomic holocaust increases. The population must be limited, and if man does not limit his fecundity voluntarily he will do it by war.

These considerations take no account of the minor ancillary disadvantages of over-population: economic crises, raw material shortages, the prevalence of neurotic, irrational and criminal behaviour among people crowded closely together. Such considerations should be familiar to every thinking person; for the purposes of this book we shall regard war as an extreme case of neurotic, irrational and criminal behaviour, and note that it is largely our control of microbes in sickness that keeps the threat with us.

The answer is not, as some might think, a deliberate reintroduction of disease, a sort of controlled biological warfare. Nor, obviously, could anyone of humanity withhold the benefits of medicine from communities simply because they then breed too rapidly. Obviously, – and again every thinking person accepts this, unless some religious or political dogma prohibits the thought – births must be reduced and food and consumer goods must be increased. Which means more contraceptives and less dogmatism, more food and the goodies of civilized life, fewer weapons. All so easy, is it not? Forgive me if I do not here explain how to arrange these things.

If we have taken a gloomy view of the future, we have at least justified to ourselves a preoccupation with the good things of life. What goodies have microbes, or rather, has applied microbiology, in store for us?

It is possible that new and more effective antibiotics will be discovered though, as we saw earlier, penicillin was the first to be discovered and remains the best when it can be used at all. We have already discussed the problems presented by resistant strains; one can be fairly confident that more antibiotic-resistant strains will develop, but that these will be kept in bounds by the discovery of new antibiotics or the deliberate modification of existing ones. It is likely, generally speaking, that new patterns of disease will develop as existing pathogens become eliminated and, indeed, we can see this happening already. The bacterial diseases are of minor importance in civilized communities today and the troublesome diseases are caused by viruses. One class of diseases, classified under the general name of 'cancer', has no obvious microbial origin (except for one or two types which are definitely caused by viruses). Nevertheless, the manner in which the disease develops has much in common with the consequences of certain types of viral infection, and the reasons why the disease sometimes regresses seem to be much involved with the general topic of immunity and antibody formation. Thus a furtherance of our knowledge of virus infection and of the processes involved in immunity, both originally microbiological topics, will probably lead to the most practical of medical advances.

We saw in Chapter 6 that the use of microbes to produce heavy chemicals, such as alcohol and industrial solvents, is obsolescent. Generally speaking, as we noted, microbes can only be used economically to produce chemicals that are too difficult to synthesize chemically on a factory scale. But, on the other hand, their role in the manufacture of such materials will surely increase. Their use in the production of steroids, where the industrial chemist uses them rather as a chemical reagent, turned up in Chapter 6. There is a touch of poetic justice about the thought that the systemic contraceptives are steroids: it is possible that microbes, whose control in medicine made the development of systemic contraceptives a matter of social urgency, may help in their manufacture.

The most complex chemical mixture mankind needs is food. Food, one trusts, will remain outside the province of the synthetic chemist for many centuries. No doubt minor pickling or fermentation processes using microbes will be developed in the future, but the main importance of microbes that one can foresee is as a bulk food themselves. We touched on this question at the end of Chapter 5: a microbial 'crop' such as *Chlorella* would be independent of the weather and require far less space than conventional agriculture. (A culture space 26 yards square would supply the protein needs of a family of five or six people if the productivity of pilot experiments is any guide.) Likewise food yeast, and bacterial food from methane, will probably be made use of and will thus make waste materials palatable and nourishing. A process was recently announced in the U.S.A. for growing mushroom mycelium on meat residues (apparently about three quarters of the material handled by a modern slaughterhouse is thrown away). The product has a meat-like consistency, has all necessary vitamins and proteins, can be minced and made into hamburgers. Above all, it tastes good. The question of taste and palatability is all-important in this kind of discussion, for it is no good producing nourishing foods if they disgust people. In fact, techniques of flavouring and fortifying foods have now developed to such an extent that today the real problem is to ensure that these abilities are used sensibly, to improve the quality and quantity of food, not, as so often in the past, to defraud the customer.

That we shall change our eating habits to match these developments goes without saying. Yeast extract has been part of my daily diet, and of my family's, since I was a boy – it appears daily on the breakfast table with the marmalade and such, and this is true of millions of English families. Thirty years ago eating yeast extract was an eccentric practice of vegetarians and food faddists; at the turn of the century it was unheard of. No doubt chlorella cookies and methano-burgers will one day be a delicious meal that one will take for granted; as one reconstitutes one's dehydrated *Chateau Latour* (esters specially blended to reproduce that greatest of great years, 1937) one may wonder at the barbarian habits of one's ancestors who grew large animals, killed them and actually ate their flesh. . . .

Perhaps the most significant development in pharmacy in recent years, one which society is only just beginning to come to terms with, is the arrival of psychomimetic drugs. These are the tranquillizers, anti-depressants, hallucinogenic drugs that have revolutionized the practice of psychiatry. It has been said that one third of the population of a civilized community is neurotic. This sort of statement depends on how eccentric the speaker allows

213

his neighbours' (but rarely his own) activities to become before he regards them as neurotic, but it has a certain substance. As soon as mankind's existence becomes sufficiently comfortable for him to consider the question, he realizes he is crazy, knotted-up and illogical in a variety of his responses, and that these responses get worse the more complex, stressful and crowded his daily life becomes. (And let us be quite clear, parenthetically, that Noble Savages, carefree nomads, sturdy peasants and such paragons are equally subject to neurosis, anxiety and obsession – it is just that in their way of life it does not show.) These disorders are not new, nor are they particularly a product of modern civilization; they have been part of everyday life for centuries and the major advance made in the last few decades has been to recognize them and treat them. One can laugh at the idea of a San Francisco beatnik, trying peddled lysergic acid derivatives to enhance aesthetic and sensual perception, but in a crude way he is pointing a road mankind will have to take. Mentally, men live with a heritage of reflexes left over from aeons of savagery: aggressiveness, dread and gregariousness, which lead him to wars, race riots, child beating, murder, religious manias and all the rest. Fleetingly he may even recognize the irrationality of these responses, but they are generally outside his individual control. For the first time pharmacy has developed drugs that enable one to stand back from, to reflect upon and even control this mental lumber. At least some of these drugs are of microbial origin, derivatives of fungi. As their constitution and action become better understood it is likely that microbiological processes will be involved in the manufacture of the acceptable varieties. At the simplest level, tranquillizers have already removed burdens of wholly unnecessary misery from the lives of millions of struggling citizens; if men can use like materials, without abuse, to improve the rationality of their social structure and behaviour, then once more microbes will have made a transcendent contribution to the human condition.

Without abuse, I said. Lysergic acid derivatives have been proposed as weapons in chemical warfare, the idea being that the enemy becomes so depressed and introverted that he cannot be bothered to fight. They would work, and so would 'peace drugs', derivatives of tranquillizers that render the enemy too peacefully inclined to struggle. Such weapons would certainly humanize warfare, but one fears for the state of mind of the victors, given such power. Perhaps good, old-fashioned atom bombs are to be preferred? Or a really virulent microbe for biological warfare? I offer no opinion; I merely remark that scientific advance has always been subject to abuse.

Leaving our minds alone now, let us return to the more mundane aspects of this planet's economy. Nitrogen-fixing bacteria bring 50 to 200 lbs of nitrogen to each acre of soil, and today this is not nearly enough. Already one sixth of the world depends on artificial fertilizers for its food, and one could foresee the day when the population became so large that all the world's shipping facilities would have to be devoted to carting fertilizer about – the year 2,000, according to one calculation I have seen. One consequence of this use of artificial fertilizers is that nutrients other than nitrogen are running out in certain types of soil. Sulphur-deficient soils were a rarity ten years ago; the only examples I am aware of were found in East Africa. By late 1965 they had been detected in Australasia, Western Europe, India and Ceylon, both North and South Americas, West as well as East Africa. In other areas cobalt and copper deficiencies have been detected. Soils deficient in phosphates have been known for years. Tropical and sub-tropical soils known as laterites are remarkably lacking in minerals because they are regularly washed by the equatorial rains. As mankind learns to add nitrogen to the soil, other defects in the local soil composition become exposed.

Though these deficiencies can often be remedied by the use of chemicals, particularly in advanced communities, it is not easy to see how this could be done in practice on a global scale. The sub-tropical savannah, for instance, is a zone that is almost totally non-productive in terms of human food, though it is warm, wet and has lots of sunshine. The sheer mechanical problems of making such an area productive by chemical means are dispiriting; the solution is far more likely to arise from an understanding of the microbes involved in the local nitrogen, sulphur and phosphorus cycles. Understanding and control of microbes in

215

agriculture, together with their deliberate use for the disposal and re-cycling of complex products, seem to me to be the obvious large-scale contribution applied microbiology has to make to this planet's economy.

A mundane, plodding field of advance, you may say? Perhaps, but even the most romantic research is mundane and plodding in its day-to-day reality. Let us, however, indulge our romanticism and look outside this planet. What of microbes in the space era?

One consideration arises at once. If men go into space, microbes go too. You cannot produce a germ-free man; moreover, as we saw in Chapter 5, even if you could he would probably die of obscure kinds of malnutrition. Anything mankind handles, indeed, anything that emerges from the biosphere, is contaminated by microbes. For this reason both Russian and American space agencies have so far been at pains to sterilize equipment sent up outside this planet's atmosphere. But a space probe has in fact already crashed accidentally on Venus and the question how efficiently it was sterilized is a matter of considerable concern to microbiologists. It would be a tragedy if the moon and nearer planets became contaminated by terrestrial microbes before a proper evaluation of indigenous biological conditions there could be made. For terrestrial microbes might swamp, and conceivably eliminate, indigenous populations before space travel became sufficiently advanced to permit the detection of alien life. Then one could never be sure that the microbes one found had not arrived with the early moon, Venus or Mars probes. For we can be certain of one thing: the cold airlessness of deep space provides no obstacle to the survival of bacterial spores. Radiation in deep space may be lethal, we do not know; but the average bacterial spore, within the shell of a space vehicle, would have no difficulty in remaining viable through an inter-planetary journey, provided it survived the initial heating-up that occurs as the projectile traverses the earth's atmosphere.

The probability that the earth has been scattering creatures the size of bacteria throughout space during the period since life originated is negligibly small. The earth's gravitational field is so strong that the probability that a particle with the mass of a bacterium could reach escape velocity is infinitesimally small. Even effects of high speed atmospheric winds and volcanic explosions do not significantly increase this probability. Viruses, being one or two orders of magnitude smaller, could reach escape velocity somewhat more readily than bacteria and so, presumably, could the tiny microbial parasites called *Bdellovibrio*. Yet it is unlikely that actual living material has escaped from the earth, except via the space probes of the last few years. Hence any planetary exo-biology that space exploration may encounter can be expected to have developed independently of terrestrial life. The notion that the surface of the moon will be peppered with spores of *Bacillus subtilis* (a common aerial bacterium), though attractive to scientists with a taste for anti-climax, is not likely to be correct.

Can we say anything about what extra-terrestrial organisms might be found? Assuming that extra-terrestrial life bears some relation to terrestrial life, by which I mean that it is based on carbon molecules, conducts its life processes in water and sustains continuity through some such material as DNA, then one can make one or two informed guesses. The first is that the asteroids and the planets farther out from the sun will be too cold for liquid water, and hence for our kind of life, to exist. The second is that the planet Mercury will be too hot on one side and too cold on the other. It also seems, according to the latest space probes, that Venus is too hot – a disappointing piece of information because its atmosphere is rich in CO_2 and its cloud cover suggested a fine environment for anaerobic microbes which might, by now, have evolved into quite interesting higher creatures. On present information, however, we are left with the moon and Mars as the only serious candidates for habitation.

On any inhabited planet it is likely that there will be microbes, since it is unlikely that living things would evolve without a microbial stage and it is equally unlikely that microbes, once evolved, would be eliminated. The moon is a dry body with no atmosphere, subject to meteoric bombardment at the surface and a large temperature gradient between the insolated face that we normally see and its dark rear. Such liquid water as exists

217

there probably rests beneath the surface as saturated salt solution, protected from temperature extremes. As we saw in Chapter 1, life depends on cyclical transformation of biological elements such as in the nitrogen, carbon and phosphorus cycles. Though one could imagine salt-tolerant sulphate-reducing bacteria surviving beneath the surface of the moon in, for example, a saturated magnesium chloride solution, they would require a source of carbon to use. But it is difficult to envisage a carbon cycle, for what microbial process could one envisage that would then return CO_2 to an organic form? An anaerobic oxidation of iron, perhaps? We need to know more about the chemistry of the moon to reach a useful conclusion, but the primary moral is obvious: to seek life on the moon, dig, and look for halophilic, chemotrophic, anaerobic microbes.

Mars is a rather more promising candidate for our kind of life. Though it is cold and has a most tenuous atmosphere, it does seem to have water, and near its equator this is probably liquid for much of the martian year. Its microbes would need to be anaerobes, but several terrestrial types might survive there. The psychrophiles would be tolerant of the low temperature; the water would be pretty briny, there being little of it, so again one would expect halophiles. But they could exist on the surface and be reached by sunlight – so a carbon cycle based on photosynthesis is feasible. Anaerobic iron bacteria might have developed; sulphate-reducing bacteria and sulphide-oxidizing bacteria could be expected; there seems to be reasonable scope on that planet for several combinations of chemotrophy and phototrophy.

As many readers will know, there is slight evidence for seasonal colour changes on Mars, indicating some analogue of terrestrial plant life. If this theory is correct, these creatures will be associated with quite a complex microbial flora. It seems possible, indeed, that Mars is a planet in the terminal stages of habitation: that life once flourished there but, as the atmosphere became increasingly tenuous and water more scarce, only the toughest organisms persisted. If our terrestrial biology is any guide, microbes are the toughest of organisms: at the terminal stages of evolution, as at its commencement, it seems that microbes would predominate. Mars certainly seems to be the planet any dedicated biologist would most wish to visit.

On such a visit, the biologist would have problems with his own microbes. A space ship with a few astronauts taking a year-long trip to Mars would be a physically isolated community, and a peculiar thing happens to the commensal microbes of people in such communities. One type of microbe tends to become dominant, from mouth to anus as it were, and if this germ happens to be pathogenic the situation can be dangerous. Likewise, immunity to infection by ordinary microbes tends to be lost. It seems probable that astronauts will have to keep cultures of the varieties of microbes they started out with, and will need deliberately to re-infect themselves at intervals. On the other hand, astronauts will have considerable disposal problems: getting rid of urine and faeces; removing carbon dioxide exhaled and regenerating oxygen. A most pleasing microbial system has been proposed to help in these processes, which seems quite feasible. A solar cell on the space ship would generate electricity which would be used to electrolyze water. Oxygen and hydrogen would thus be formed, which would be used to grow the bacterium *Hydrogenomonas*, a chemotroph that fixes CO_2 while forming water from hydrogen and oxygen. Thus, with no net waste of water, CO_2 would be removed from the atmosphere. But these creatures require a nitrogen source, for which the urea of urine will do very well. Thus one would grow microbes at the expense of urine and CO_2; these, once a well-trained astronaut got used to the idea, would be a useful protein food. *Chlorella*, the alga, could also be used to form oxygen and yield food since sunlight would be available; a methane fermentation of faeces would dispose of waste and, aided by methane-oxidizing bacteria, produce food. In all, there would be a curious fulfilling of the biblical threat of Rabshakeh (2nd Kings XVIII, 27). To generalize, it will be almost impossible to transport the bulk food, water and disposal requirements of astronauts for long space trips; little microbiological microcosms will have to be set up to re-cycle the chemical environment which the astronauts inhabit, and here an understanding of terrestrial microbial ecology will be critically important.

Can one say anything of life outside the solar system? Some cosmologists believe there must be many thousands of planets suitable to terrestrial life even in our own galaxy, and it is likely, if our views of the origin of life on earth are correct, that life will have developed on them. Dr H. Shapley's estimate of 100,000 habitable planets in our own galaxy, the Milky Way, is often quoted. The prospects of exploring and visiting such planets seem remote indeed; unless our theories of the cosmos are completely awry, journeys lasting not only centuries but millennia would be needed. But communication with such systems by radio is feasible, even if conversation would have its one-sided aspects. (Dr F. D. Drake calculates that planets on which life has evolved to a level of being able (and willing) to communicate across space are likely to be separated, on an average, by a distance of 1,000 light years. When one has to wait several centuries for a reply to one's opening remark, the give-and-take of day-to-day intercourse tends to be lost. Obviously a special breed of women will be needed as communicators. . . .) Though such systems will undoubtedly have representatives of the microbes, communication will necessarily be with creatures of advanced intelligence. Hence, though the sulphate-reducing equivalent of *Homo sapiens* is an interesting entity to speculate on, he would be a macrobe, not a microbe, and thus outside the scope of this book.

This chapter is about microbes and the future. One can predict, as I have done, that benefits will arise from further development of economic microbiology, that there will be advances – and retreats – in medicine, health, social behaviour and, indeed, sanity. One can point to roles for microbes in space exploration, food production; even cite a grandiose scheme to melt the polar ice caps by seeding them with red algae and thus increasing their absorption of solar heat. (An expedient which, I am told, would flood many of the lowlands of Europe.) But when all is said and done the real importance of microbes will prove to be, and this I assert with complete confidence, in the advance of knowledge. We saw in Chapter 10 how modern molecular biology has arisen from microbiology; how microbial genetics kicked biology violently into the twentieth century. Biology is today in something of an ecstatic state: information derived from the bacterium *Escherichia coli* is proving, broadly speaking, of universal validity. For some biologists, indeed, microbiology has already made its contribution: the future, they consider, lies in the application of the principles it has engendered to cells of higher organisms. This view is rather like those of certain chemists in the early forties, who thought the subject of inorganic chemistry was finished because the chemistry of all the elements seemed to be known. In fact, the discovery of transuranic elements and the development of ligand chemistry returned inorganic chemistry to the forefront of scientific advance in the fifties and sixties. So it will be with microbiology; already the understanding that there are other microbes than *E. coli* is penetrating to the less obsessed molecular biologists, and, with such experimentally amenable material available for laboratory use, it is certain that microbes will continue to be used to further our knowledge of living things. The techniques of microbiology are used in tissue culture; microbes can be hybridized and transformed; D N A can be passed from one type of cell to an unrelated one and what amount to wholly new species can be created. In Chapter 10 we discussed briefly the view that certain sub-cellular structures, such as the chloroplasts of certain protozoa and portions of the genetic apparatus of bacteria and, possibly, of higher organisms, are evolutionary relics of symbiotic associations. Microbes, it seems, show a remarkable range of capacity for association: the almost casual commensalism of intestinal bacteria, which is essential to the nutrition of many animals, the more obligatory association of root nodule bacteria with leguminous plants, in which neither partner can fix nitrogen alone; the intimacy of the symbiont of *Crithidia*, which actually lives inside the cell protoplasm and reproduces with it; the complete parasitism of a temperate bacteriophage; finally, the total loss of individuality that must occur, if this view is correct, when the symbiont or parasite becomes an organelle such as a chloroplast. Evolution, as we saw, is not wholly divergent: it seems probable that associations of increasing intimacy have developed during evolutionary time leading to the emergence of new creatures by what amounts to accretion. The evolutionary chart may well be a network rather than a family tree. If such associations occur spontaneously, why cannot we induce them deliberately? For example, would it not be convenient if we could confer nitrogen-fixing properties on wheat and thus bypass the use of chemical fertilizer or the ploughing-in of leguminous crops? And plants are not the only creatures that could be so manipulated; in principle, from a study of microbes, we can now see how to alter our own heredity.

Understanding of microbes has opened new vistas for the future of biology, and will continue to do so. We must learn to live with the possibility that we could re-generate individuals from tissue culture lines; deliberately upgrade the intelligence of animals and alter their characters, deliberately alter the heredity of strains even of mankind, so as to adapt them to space travel or life on in-hospitable planets. In millennia to come, it is conceivable that a creature that once was man could meet an intelligent sulphate-reducing organism on his own ground, having survived several centuries of space travel to be there. To such prospects the study of microbes will have made a major contribution, and herein lies their most profound importance for the future of mankind. But such concepts offer horrifying prospects for abuse – let us hope that man will have escaped from the infantilism so apparent today long before these prospects become a reality. Science, perhaps unfortunately, is morally and ethically neutral; it is also irreversible. Its consequences are what mankind makes of it and this, particularly to a scientist, is its most terrifying – if exciting – aspect.

Bibliographical Note

The subject of microbiology is not well documented as far as textbooks and elementary expositions are concerned. There are many books dealing with branches of the subject: bacteriology (medical and agricultural), industrial microbiology, microbial genetics, microbial biochemistry are examples, but even in these specialized areas of the subject few books combine comprehensiveness, readability and comprehensibility at an elementary level. Thus the list that follows is a personal selection of books I happen to be aware of and that I know are available; the omission of a title familiar to the reader does not mean that it is unworthy.

General microbiology

Few authors have attempted a synoptic account of microbiology as a discipline in its own right. Two creditable attempts, pitched at the sixth-former's or first year undergraduate's level, are:

Hawker, L. S. and others: *An Introduction to the Biology of Micro-organisms*, Edward Arnold, 1960.

Stanier, R. Y, Doudoroff, M and Adelberg, E. A.: *General Microbiology*, Macmillan, 1963.

A useful primer for absolute beginners is:

Vines, A. E. and Rees, N.: *The Microbes*, Pitman's, 1967.

Economic Microbiology

There is no comprehensive work on economic microbiology at any level. The industrial side can be filled in with the aid of several standard works, notably:

Rose, A. H.: *Industrial Microbiology*, Butterworth, 1961 – which does not assume too much basic knowledge.

Medical Microbiology

I am not aware of any 'popular' account of this field; a medical student's 'crib' probably contains information in its most concentrated form. A standard work is:

Cruickshank, R.: *Medical Microbiology*, E. & S. Livingstone, 1965.

Microbial Ecology

The author of the first good book on this subject (published in 1966) had realized by 1967 that it would soon need revision; nevertheless, it is a good start:

Brock, T. D.: *Principles of Microbial Ecology*, Prentice-Hall, New York, 1966.

Microbial Chemistry

Several books exist on this subject; a brisk account for students, with reference to more advanced matters, is:

Rose, A. H.: *Chemical Microbiology*, 2nd Ed., Butterworth, 1968.

Microbial Genetics

A popular account of recent developments in this rapidly changing field is:

Clowes, R.: *The Structure of Life*, Penguin Books, 1967.

Origin of life

An accurate, entertaining and sometimes idiosyncratic account by one of the major contributors to this field is:

Bernal, J. D.: *The Origin of Life*, Weidenfeld & Nicolson, 1967.

BIBLIOGRAPHICAL NOTE

Chemistry

Amplification of the purely chemical matters that I alluded to in Chapters 1 and 6 should be found in any ordinary textbook of chemistry.

A good up-to-date one is:

Buttle, J. W., Daniels, D. J. and Beckett, P. J.: *Chemistry: A Unified Approach*, Butterworth, 1966.

Glossary

Aerobe An organism that respires by consuming the oxygen of air.

Aerosol A suspension of droplets in air so fine that it settles extremely slowly.

Anaerobe An organism that does not use the oxygen of air for its respiration.

Antigen A substance, such as a bacterial toxin (*q.v.*), that provokes the formation of antibodies in the blood or tissues of higher organisms.

Antibodies Proteins, formed in response to foreign, usually infectious, materials entering the bodies of higher organisms, that react with such foreign matter, coagulating it and making it easier for the body to dispose of.

Autotroph An organism capable of growing at the expense of wholly inorganic substrates (*q.v.*) (contrast *Heterotroph*).

Bacteriophage A virus parasitic on bacteria.

Barophile A microbe capable of growing at very high pressures.

Biosphere The 'skin' of the planet inhabited by living creatures.

Chemotherapy The science of curing disease with the aid of chemicals.

Chloroplast An organelle (*q.v.*) in microbes and higher organisms that conducts photosyntheses (*q.v.*).

Commensalism The property of living in harmless but independent association with a second organism (contrast symbiosis).

Continuous culture A culture of microbes that is fed slowly but continuously with medium (*q.v.*) so that the microbes multiply continuously.

DNA Deoxyribonucleic acid: a natural polymer that carries the genetic information determining the character of an organism. (See also *RNA*, *Mutation*.)

Enzyme A protein which, without itself undergoing change, accelerates a biochemical reaction that would otherwise scarcely take place at all.

Halophile A microbe capable of growing in solution containing concentrations of salt (sodium chloride) in excess of about 3 per cent; such concentrations are toxic to fresh-water microbes.

Heterotroph An organism requiring pre-formed organic matter for growth (contrast *Autotroph*).

Medium (pl: media) The environment in which a microbe grows.

Metazoa Multicellular organisms.

Motility (adj: *motile*) The property of being able to move deliberately.

Mutation A chemical change in the DNA (*q.v.*) leading to a change in the genetic character which is inherited unless the mutation is lethal. An organism that has undergone such a change is a *mutant*.

Mycelium The thread-like ramifications of a fungus.

Organelle Sub-cellular structures having functions comparable to the organs of metazoa (*q.v.*).

Pathogenic Capable of causing disease.

Photochemical Pertaining to chemical reactions brought about by light.

Photosynthesis The property of forming organic matter from carbon dioxide using radiant energy from light; the basic growth process of green plants.

Protoplasm The living contents of cells.

Psychrophile A microbe capable of most rapid growth at temperatures below 20°C (contrast *Thermophile* q.v.).

Psychrosphere That zone of the sea below the thermocline (q.v.) where the temperature is low and not subject to seasonal variation (see also *Thermosphere*).

RNA Ribonucleic acid: a natural substance concerned with the transfer and interpretation of genetic information (see also *DNA*).

Rumen The first stomach of a ruminant mammal.

Serum The colourless, fluid component of blood.

Spore A dormant form of a microbe capable of enhanced resistance to heat, drying and disinfection.

Sublime, to To distil from the solid state without melting.

Substrates The components of a medium used by the microbes for growth; also the chemicals used by enzymes for their action.

Sulfuretum A microcosm involving the main bacteria of the sulphur cycle.

Symbiosis An association of two different organisms involving some degree of interdependence (contrast *Commensalism* q.v.). The partners in such an association are *symbionts*.

Thermocline That zone of the sea separating the psychrosphere (q.v.) from the thermosphere (q.v.).

Thermophile A microbe capable of growing at temperatures above the 45 to 50° C lethal to ordinary organisms.

Thermosphere The (upper) zone of the sea subject to seasonal fluctuations of temperature (contrast *Psychrosphere* q.v., see also *Thermocline*).

Toxin A toxic protein, usually of microbial origin.

Vitamin An organic substance essential in small amounts for the growth and health of an organism.

Index

More about Penguins and Pelicans

Penguin Book News, which appears every month, contains details of all the new books issued by Penguins as they are published. From time to time it is supplemented by *Penguins in Print* – a complete list of all our available titles. (There are well over three thousand of these.)

A specimen copy of *Penguin Book News* will be sent to you free on request, and you can become a subscriber for the price of the postage – 4s. for a year's issues (including the complete lists). Just write to Dept EP, Penguin Books Ltd, Harmondsworth, Middlesex, enclosing a cheque or postal order, and your name will be added to the mailing list.

Note: *Penguin Book News* and *Penguins in Print* are not available in the U.S.A. or Canada